Orange County

A DAY HIKER'S GUIDE

For more of John McKinney's
hiking tips and trails, take a hike to
www.thetrailmaster.com

Orange County
A DAY HIKER'S GUIDE

by

JOHN MCKINNEY

THE TRAILMASTER
SANTA BARBARA

Portions of this book appeared in the author's hiking column in the *Los Angeles Times*

Cover illustration by Tim Genet
The Trailmaster Series Editor: Cheri Rae
Maps designed by Hélène Webb
Book Design and typography by Jim Cook

Published by: The Trailmaster Inc
www.TheTrailmaster.com
(805) 965-7200
Visit www.thetrailmaster.com for a complete listing of all
Trailmaster publications, products and services.

ACKNOWLEDGMENTS

For their cooperation, field- and fact-checking, the author wishes to thank the rangers and administrators of Cleveland National Forest, Orange County Harbors, Beaches and Parks, and the California Department of Parks & Recreation. The Nature Conservancy and the Irvine Ranch Land Trust contributed much to my understanding of OC's newest preserves. For their help with this book, thanks also to Joslyn Murphy/Genet Studio; Basia Christ; Jonelle Yamasaki/Orange County Ocean Institute; Jim Serpa/Doheny State Beach; Shelly Meneely/Craig Regional Park; Wida Karim/Orange County Harbors, Beaches & Parks. For their special inspiration and assistance, Mary Fegraus, executive director of the Laguna Canyon Foundation, Debra Clarke of the U.S. Forest Service, Trabuco Ranger District, Ranger Barbara Norton of Laguna Coast Wilderness Park, Will Swaim, editor of the OC Weekly, and consummate OC hosts Bill and Nancy Van der Plas.

PHOTO CREDITS

First American Title Insurance, pp. 12 (top), 67, 201, 218; Michael Salas/Courtesy Orange County Harbors, Beaches & Parks, pp. 12 (bottom), 28, 44, 46, 88, 98, 122, 131, 139; Courtesy Doheny State Park, p. 33; Courtesy Orange County Ocean Institute, pp. 35, 36, 37; Courtesy Basia Christ/Niguel Botanical Preserve, p. 52; Courtesy Friends of Coyote Hills, pp. 109, 110; Courtesy Shelly Meneely/Craig Regional Park, p. 112; Cheri Rae, pp. 50, 54, 58, 78, 79, 81, 82, 175, 182, 183, 184, 188, 196, 248; Courtesy California State Parks, p. 96; Daniel James McKinney, pp. 100, 137; Stephen Francis/Courtesy Orange County Harbors, Beaches & Parks, pp. 60, 63, 102, 114, 135, 155, 157, 160, 164, 171, 219; Courtesy United States Forest Service, Trabuco Ranger District, pp. 187, 191, 193, 194, 203, 205, 207, 212, 216; California State Library 232; Courtesy Orange County Harbors, Beaches & Parks, pp. 169, 172; all other photos by author.

ORANGE COUNTY
A Day Hiker's Guide

A Word from The Trailmaster

I've climbed many a mountain above the SoCal metropolis and contemplated the Southland. Sometimes it's the summit view that inspires, sometimes it's the hike itself or one of the region's lovely parklands I've experienced along the way, but always I return home with a slightly different perspective on Southern California.

Today in our frenzied modern world, often so separated from the natural world, this "hiker's perspective" is more important than ever. I know, hikers know, the benefits of climbing the aerie heights, the freedom of the footpath, the joys of experiencing nature. Hiking helps restore the sense of peace and tranquility that our souls require and our hearts desire.

So hike. Contemplate what makes you happy and what would make you happier still. Hike. Enjoy the company of friends and family or the pleasure of your own company. Hike. Delight in the beauty of this world. Hike. Get fit and lift your spirits. Hike. Think about what you can do to expand your life and what you can do to simplify it. Hike.

See you on the trail,
John McKinney
THE TRAILMASTER

Then and now—one of Orange County's oldest and finest parks.

On Hiking
Orange County

DURING THE MID-1990s, when I was writing a weekly hiking column for the *Los Angeles Times*, editors of the newspaper's Orange County edition summoned me from the field into their offices for a discussion about starting a weekly outdoors page to which I could perhaps contribute an Orange County hike-of-the-week. "Are there enough places to take a hike?" the editors asked me. "You're not going to run out of hikes after six weeks are you? Do Orange County residents really like to go hiking or even outdoors?"

I responded with an impassioned detailing of the many wonderful places to explore, and that I could definitely describe a different hike each week for at least a couple of years. In my view, Orange County residents were as outdoors minded as any other Californians, and likely more so, and certainly liked to take a hike—as well as cycle, kayak and enjoy water sports.

Well, I thought *The Times* editors were receptive, even excited about presenting the wild side of OC, but in the end a special OC outdoors section with a weekly hike never got past the prototype stage.

Not to be dissuaded, I kept on hiking around Orange County and sharing my experiences with *Times* Readers in other sections of the paper and in other publications. After years of hiking and collecting the best hikes OC has to offer, my many OC friends, relatives and colleagues who have so encouraged me to write this book will be pleased that I have finally done so.

I would like to report that everyone I talked to while hiking about, and writing about, Orange County immediately saw the wisdom in what I was doing. "What parks?" and "What trails?" were two of the sarcastic interrogatives I thought I would never have to answer this far into the 21st century.

Stereotypes die hard and the prevailing opinion of far too many around SoCal, and among Orange Countians themselves, is that OC residents are looking for bargains in the mall not bliss in the mountains. (By the way, can't you have both?) Still, there are so many more OC outdoors-goers who know better these days: naturalists, land-use managers, and thousands of hikers of all ages, shapes and sizes.

As a writer and hiking expert, I've worked locally, nationally, and even internationally to address what we in the field call "Nature Deficit Disorder." This disconnect with nature has profound effects on us as individuals and as a society. One prescription to combat NDD is to take a hike. I've suggested more than a hundred cures, er, hikes in this book.

In Orange County, the need to diagnose and treat Nature Deficit Disorder is crucial, more so than in most regions of the country, because so many people live, work, and play in such close proximity to each other, and have relatively small amounts of nature in which to commune.

OC now has 34 cities and unincorporated areas that's rapidly expanded into a mega-city/county of more than 3 million people. By the 2000 census, Orange County had a greater number of residents than 20 of America's 50 states, including New Hampshire that so influences the course of the country's politics by hosting the earliest presidential primary election.

Orange County is the second-most populous county in California, surpassing San Diego some years ago, and trailing only Los Angeles. The county is one of the most densely populated regions in America. OC's population density is estimated to be more than 3,665 persons per square mile. It's not uncommon with rapid population growth for this density to increase two percent over the course of the year.

As the population increases, we must see to it that parklands and pathways also multiply. Both conservationists and real estate developers agree: "They're not making any more land."

HIKING OC

Hiking this land is a good way to shed some stereotypes about Southern California in general, and Orange County in particular. One stereotype, that OC is now and only now, disappears when you take a trail through the county's rich history. While hiking in Modjeska Canyon, visit the home of renowned actress Madame Helena Modjeska. A saunter along Serrano creek in Lake Forest leads to Heritage Hill Historical Park and to a collection of buildings that tell the story of the early days of Saddleback Valley.

Another stereotype—that Orange County is nothing more than a monotonous urban-suburban sprawl—vanishes when you witness firsthand the ecological diversity of the backcountry.

The big buzzword among biologists, land-use planners and conservationists these days is biodiversity. By biodiversity, scientists mean a wide range of plants and wildlife within a region. Not surprisingly, California, with its wide range of climates and topography from redwood forests to High Sierra glaciers to Mojave Desert sand dunes is renowned for it biodiversity.

Surprisingly, so is Orange County. OC is one of California's smallest counties and its most densely populated, and yet it is the state's second most biologically diverse county. The most dominant flora is the coastal sage community that thrives in the region's Mediterranean-style climate.

Another stereotype—that Orange County's history is all Anglo—disappears when you walk into the land's Spanish, Indian, German, Polish and Japanese heritage. The names on the land—from Flores to Modjeska to Anaheim—speak of this rich tapestry of cultures. The special places—and the trails exploring them—protected by the County's parks are priceless assets to the megalopolis.

• MOUNTAINS—Extending the entire length of Orange County's eastern perimeter, the Santa Anas roughly parallel the coast. This coastal range is only about 20 miles inland and the western slopes are often blanketed with fog. The coast has a cooling influence on what is often a very hot range of mountains. Except for the dead of summer, most days offer pleasant hiking.

The Santa Anas are round, brushy, inviting. At first glance, they seem to be inundated by a monotonous sea of chaparral. But the chaparral teems with wildlife, and even the most casual hiker will be amazed at the number of rabbit and quail that hop and flutter from the dense undergrowth. The range is covered with great masses of buckthorn, greasewood, sumac and scrub oak. Alternating with the chaparral are oak woodlands, wide potreros, and boulder-strewn creeks with superb swimming holes.

The range is a granite block, which has been uplifted and depressed below sea level several times. On top of the mountains, marine sediments occur in successive formations. The Santa Anas increase in altitude from north to south, culminating in the twin peaks of Old Saddleback—Mount Modjeska and Mount Santiago.

By following trails charted in this guide, the peak-bagger can conquer Orange County's highest summits, the Fab Four of the Santa Ana Mountains: Santiago Peak (5,687 feet) and Modjeska Peak (5,496 feet), the two comprising revered landmark Old Saddleback; Trabuco Peak (4,684 feet) and Los Piños Peak (4,520 feet).

• HILLS—The Chino Hills top out at about 1,800 feet. But summits short in stature can deliver very long views, particularly on a clear winter day. Stand on summits of such high points as Gilman Peak and San Juan Hill and you can see parts of four counties and a delightful expanse of valleys, canyons, hills and steep slopes.

The Anaheim Hills and Laguna Hills have miles of inviting trails and serve up some great views, too. In this guide, you'll find accounts of many excellent paths that lead to hilltops, bumps on ridges, and knolls (many under the 1,000 foot-mark) that offer great views.

• CREEKS AND RIVERS—We hike past portions of Orange County's creeks, both wild and tame, including San Juan Creek, Trabuco Creek (Arroyo Trabuco), Salt Creek, Aliso Creek and Oso Creek. The Santa Ana River extends more than 100 miles from its headwaters in the San Bernardino Mountains and past Anaheim, Orange, Santa Ana—in fact, all the way across Orange County—to the Pacific at Huntington Beach.

• LAKES—Let's face there aren't many lake shores to saunter, but paths do lead around OC's only natural lakes, the rather redundantly named Laguna Lakes in the Laguna Hills. Fans of hiking around freshwater can ramble along reservoirs such as the one in Peters Canyon and around the man-made lakes that form the centerpieces of Craig, Clark, Yorba and other regional parks.

• BEACHES—What could be more (choose one or more) invigorating, romantic, calming, centering or refreshing than a walk on one of Orange County's beaches? Some of the county's beaches attract visitors from across the U.S. and around the world. If you ever get jaded and think "it's just the beach" look at the happy faces and listen to the voices of visitors who may be experiencing what you're missing.

• SUBURBAN EDGE—Many of the county's newest cities have pathways that extend along the border between the built and natural world. While certain purists (those who insist a hike is only a hike if it is in the remote backcountry) will scoff at trails that might be all or partially paved, and don't get all that far away from it all, I believe in a broader definition of a hike in a place such as Orange County. I say hike into the green scene, even if it's closer to home (and the homes and backyards of others) than you'd prefer.

• INLAND EMPIRE—County borders are often as not created from political gerrymandering as much as by geographical boundaries of rivers and mountain ranges. As does Los Angeles County, Riverside County has some natural features in common with Orange County—the Santa Ana Mountains, the Santa Ana River and the Chino Hills. I've included hikes in my favorite Riverside County parks and preserves.

OC Trails

Orange County first got serious about its trails system with a comprehensive trails plan developed in the mid-1960s. (That document is much older than many OC municipalities!) Orange County's trail plan long called for 350 miles of pathways extending from wilderness parks to the most densely populated urban/suburban areas.

Although the expansion of the county's trail system has in no way kept pace with the expansion of its population, it's grown considerably over the past 20 years. Some trails advocates estimate that the total mileage of all federal, state, county and city trails, including all the multi-use ones, now totals more than a thousand miles.

Reflecting a nationwide trend, Orange County regional governments and municipal governments rarely create parks or build trails unless private landholders develop property and directly or indirectly foot the bill for nearby parks. So with more houses and malls come more parks and trails.

With the county's go-go-development, it's been go-go for trail-building as well during the last decade. Local government and savvy developers know that the public demand for walking paths and hiking trails is huge, and never been higher.

On the grand scheme of things, trails activists seem to be successfully making the case for connectivity—linking one park to another, one community to another by trail. Obviously, if residents of Brea can hike into Fullerton and vice-versa, hikers from both cities benefit from a better and longer time on the trail.

The new Mountains to Sea Trail is a shining example of a pathway that links many parks and municipalities in its descent from the mountains in Irvine Park to the ocean at Newport Beach.

The cost per mile for construction of a dirt hiking trail is very low, but just-plain-dirt hiking paths are rarely built these days. The cost of the land or of an easement is often high, and the maximize its investment, its usually only paved multi-use trails that are built to accommodate bicyclists. By the time a multi-use path is paved, crowned to ensure water run-off, striped with lane lines . . . bridges built . . . the cost can go north of a million dollars a miles.

When new developments are constructed, city and county planners often require developers to provide trails. Rarely does a municipality or county government pursue a right-of-way and build a trail by government initiative. Some local governments such as the City of Fullerton, with more than 30 miles of trail criss-crossing its 23 square miles, have made a civic commitment to trails. In other communities, particularly ones in northern Orange County, the hiker will look in vain for a hiking trail of any kind leading anywhere.

I've included more multi-use paths than I would ordinarily would in this guide because many of the regional park trails were originally designed as multi-use paths.

Most mountain bikers are polite and obey the rules of the road. Several parks are out-and-out mountain bike parks, including Crystal Cove State Park and Limestone-Whiting Ranch Wilderness Park. And a number of trails in the Cleveland National Forest, such as the San Juan Trail are very popular mountain bike routes.

Besides sharing the joy of hiking—as I have for more than 25 years and in a book by the same name—I am also committed to sound a warning about potential hazards that hikers may face. While in a book of more than 100 of my favorite Orange County hikes, I obviously didn't leave out very many hikes of interest to the average hiker, I chose not to include some very long Santa Ana Mountains treks suitable for extreme hikers, some trails that have become mountain bike routes far more than hiking paths to the point of being uncomfortable, even dangerous for hikers, and some difficult, trail-less cross-country routes.

OC Geography 101

The name Orange was first applied to the City of Orange, founded in 1872. The settlement was originally named Richland, but founding fathers learned that the name had already been adopted by a town near Sacramento. So Richland was dropped, though its fun to think of a city and county named Richland. Instead of Orange County, *Richland* County?! Some might think Richland County more appropriate. The county indeed was named for its flourishing citrus industry, when it detached from Los Angeles County in 1889 to form the new Orange County

Orange County shares its coastline and coastal plain with neighboring Los Angeles County, but has a distinct geographical identity. This geography, which in the decades since World War II has been almost unbelievably altered by the hand of man, nevertheless retains much intrigue for the lover of wild places.

The orchards that gave Orange County its name are nearly gone, but the hills and mountains occupying half the county still offer invigorating vistas. This guide seeks out what remains of the pastoral in the county's hills and canyons.

San Mateo Point is the northernmost boundary of San Diego County, the southern boundary of Orange County. When the original counties of Los Angeles and San Diego were set up in 1850, the line that separated them began on the coast at San Mateo Point. When Orange County was formed from southern Los Angeles County in 1889, San Mateo Point was established as the southern point of the new county. The northern boundary is Seal Beach. Riverside County and the Santa Ana Mountains form the eastern boundary.

During the last decade of the 19th century and the first few decades of the 20th, the county was known for its fruited plain watered by the Santa Ana River. (Although the Santa Ana for most of its length is now a cement-lined flood control channel, it was once a substantial river and even today is Southern California's leader in average annual runoff.)

Citrus and other fruits, flowers and vegetables were successfully grown on the fertile coastal plain. Valencia orange groves, protected from the wind by long rows of eucalyptus, stretched across the plain to the foothills.

Today the coastal plain has been almost completely covered by residential and commercial development. Once huge farms and ranches such as Laguna Niguel, Mission Viejo and Irvine are now suburbs.

Protecting the last of Orange County's ecological heritage are city, county, state and federal agencies, with assistance from many nonprofits such as The Nature Conservancy and the Irvine Ranch Trust.

STEWARDS OF THE LAND

Without a doubt, the county's theme parks, not the county's nature parks, are Orange County's claims-to-fame. OC got on the map in the mid-1950s when Walt Disney created his Magic Kingdom among the orange groves. Still, for hikers in the know, the "happiest place on earth" may not be Disneyland, but along one of the happy trails in Orange County's backcountry.

Most of the county's trails and terrain are included within four kinds of parks and preserves: county parks, state parks, the U.S. Forest Service (Cleveland National Forest) and the Irvine Company.

COUNTY PARKS

This book puts a special emphasis on county parks, that is to say the beach parks, regional parks and wilderness parks under the stewardship of the County of Orange Harbors Beaches & Parks. Many county parks attract visitors because of their recreation facilities—basketball courts, baseball diamonds picnic areas and much more. However, some of these recreation-oriented parks also have natural areas that invite a hike.

By definition, regional parks are usually 50 acres or more in size and provide a wide range of amenities. These parks were designed to—and indeed do—attract people from up to 30 miles away. Regional parks offer significant recreational or natural attractions usually not found in local city parks.

The county park system includes more than 35,000 acres of varied landscapes that are laced with trails. This guide describes hikes in more than two dozen Orange County parks. The ratio of developed to undeveloped parkland varies widely from park to park.

Some OC parks, such Mile Square Park, are highly improved for recreational purposes and as a kind of afterthought offer the hiker small "Natural Areas" suitable for short walks. Other parks are more evenly divided between natural and developed land. Irvine Ranch Regional Park, for example, has plenty of facilities (plus a zoo and paddleboats around a lake) and yet also boasts an engaging trail systems in the hills surrounding the developed area of the park. William R. Mason Regional Park offers plenty of lakeside leisure activities, as well as a natural habitat that can only be reached by trail.

Wilderness parks, such as Caspers and Laguna Coast, are mostly wild terrain, offer only the most basic of facilities, and are the domain of hikers, horseback riders and mountain bikers. Alas, the county's five wilderness parks—Aliso & Wood Canyons, Laguna Coast, Limestone-Whiting Ranch, Ronald W. Caspers and General Thomas F. Riley—are not evenly distributed through the county, but located in the southern and far eastern sections of OC. Wilderness parks offer the hiker plenty of room to roam. I've included multiple trail write ups in these parks for hikers of all abilities.

STATE PARKS

The California Department of Parks and Recreation Parks has a major presence along the OC coast; in fact, state parkland comprises about 30 percent of the county's coastline. Huntington and Bolsa Chica state beaches add up to more than seven miles of sand strand and a very long beach-hike. Doheny State Beach and San Clemente State Beach offer camping and Crystal Cove State Park offers the hiker several more miles of beach and bluffs to explore, as well as a large expanse in the coastal hills to wander.

Chino Hills State Park, located in Orange, San Bernardino and Riverside counties, preserves some 13,000 acres of rolling grassland and lovely oak woodland. An excellent trail system offers tranquil and away-from-it-all hiking.

CLEVELAND NATIONAL FOREST

The Santa Ana Mountains came under federal protection in 1893 when the Trabuco Canyon Forest Reserve was formed. The name was changed to the Trabuco National Forest in 1906; the forest later was enlarged and eventually assigned to the Cleveland National Forest in 1908. *Trabuco* (Spanish for "blunderbuss" is a name left behind by the 1769 Portolá Expedition. Today, 136,500 acres of the Santa Ana Mountains are included in the national forest's Trabuco District.

The Ortega Highway, which crosses the Santa Anas from San Juan Capistrano to Lake Elsinore, offers access to many trailheads. Other hikes require travel on rough dirt roads.

Highlight of the range is the San Mateo Canyon Wilderness, set aside by Congress in 1984. The 40,000-acre preserve protects San Mateo Canyon, a relatively untouched land of 200-year-old oaks, potreros and quiet pools.

THE IRVINE COMPANY

Make no mistake, the longtime ranching company builds homes, tens of thousands of them since the 1950s when it began to change its business from ranching and farming. The Irvine Company, which at one point in history owned about one acre of every six in Orange County, and seems to do everything in a big way, has created the 50,000-acre Irvine Ranch Reserve in the heart of the county. At present, access to portions of this remarkable country is by guided tour only. The Irvine Ranch Land Trust was founded in 2005 to "protect, restore and enhance the natural resources" of the Reserve.

GETTING THE MOST FROM HIKING OC

There are two tried and true approaches to selecting a hike. One is by mood and the other by scenery.

First decide on the kind of hike you'd like to enjoy. A walk for the whole family? A long lonely trek where you can be alone to think? An after-work workout? A first-date excursion? A scout or youth group outing?

Decide where you want to hike. More than one hundred hikes are described in this guide so it may be a quite a challenge to select one. The Anaheim Hills? Old Saddleback? Laguna Coast? North County? South County? Pick a walk in your geographical area of interest. Next, turn to the corresponding trail description in the main body of the book.

Want some help narrowing the field? Check out my recommended "Best Hikes."

Unsure of what to expect from the Santa Monica, San Gabriel or Verdugo Mountains? Read the chapter introductions.

Beneath the name of the trail is the distance from the trailhead to various destinations. Mileage, expressed in round trip figures, follows each destination. The hikes in this book range from one to fourteen miles. Gain or loss in elevation follows the mileage.

In matching a hike to your ability, consider both mileage and elevation, as well as the condition of the trail, terrain and season. Hot, exposed chaparral or a trail that roller-coasters steeply up and down can make a short walk seem long.

Use the following guidelines:

• A hike most suitable for beginners and children is under five miles of length and requires an elevation gain less than 700 to 800 feet.

• A moderate hike is one in the five- to eight-mile range, with less than a 2,000-foot elevation gain. You should be reasonably fit for these. Pre-teens often find the going difficult.

• A hike longer than eight miles, particularly one with an elevation gain of 2,000 feet or more, is for experienced hikers in at least average condition. Those hikers in top form will enjoy these more challenging excursions.

Season is the next item to consider. Although Orange County is one of the few regions in the country that offers four-season hiking, some climactic restrictions must be heeded. You can hike some of the trails in this guide all of the time, all of the trails some of the time, but not all of the trails all of the time.

Snow occasionally dusts the upper ramparts of the Santa Ana Mountains, but it's usually not snow but heavy rains that lead authorities close trails to public use. Sometimes heavy rainfall causes the closure of access roads to trailheads such as

Trabuco Creek Road, the dirt/mud road that leads into Holy Jim Canyon. State park rangers and rangers at the county's regional parks often close park trails after a heavy rain in order to protect the pathways from erosion by trail users—hikers and particularly mountain bikers. Even the modest trail system in a regional park not at all known for hiking such as Clark Park, can be closed for a day or two or three after a vigorous rainstorm.

For the hiker venturing out into flatland and mountain parks, heat, not moisture, is a more common challenge. Park authorities rarely close parks or trails in the summer so you won't be prevented from taking a hike; the question is: "Should you hike in the heat?"

Early mornings and late afternoons are the times for warm-weather jaunts in the low-elevation mountains and foothills, as well as in the county's various parks and reserves. Trails in the Santa Ana Mountains and in the Chino Hills are often too hot and dry to offer comfortable summer hiking.

Beneath the name of the hike at the top of the page is the trail name, plus the starting point and one or more destinations. Mileage, expressed in round trip figures, follows each destination. The hikes in this guide range from two to twenty miles, with the majority in the five- to ten-mile range. Gain or loss in elevation follows the mileage. In matching a hike to your ability, you'll want to consider both mileage and elevation as well as condition of the trail, terrain, and season. Hot, exposed chaparral or miles of boulder-hopping can make a short hike seem long.

My introductions to the hikes describe what you'll encounter in the way of plants, animals and panoramic views and outline the natural and human history of the region. I'll also point out the good, the bad and the ugly and tell you straight out what's hot and what's not about a particular trail.

DIRECTIONS TO TRAILHEAD take you from the nearest major highway to trailhead parking. For trails having two desirable trailheads, directions to each are given. A few trails can be hiked one way, with the possibility of a car shuttle. Suggested car shuttle points are noted.

THE HIKE describes the hike. The hike write-ups note important junctions and point out major sights. Options allow you to climb higher or farther or take a different route back to the trailhead. These trail descriptions, in combination with the superb maps created by my longtime collaborator at the *Los Angeles Times*, Hélène Webb, will help you stay oriented and get where you want to go. We haven't described and mapped every single feature, though; we've left it to you to discover the multitude of little things that make a hike an adventure.

BEST HIKES IN ORANGE COUNTY

BEST HIKES FOR VIEWS
Santiago Peak in Santa Ana Mountains
San Juan Hill in Chino Hills
Orange Hills
Emerald Bay Overlook in Crystal Cove State Park

BEST HIKES FOR ROMANCE
Any Beach Hike
Moonlight Hike above Irvine Bowl
Laguna Beach Bluffs
Newport Beach–Balboa Island

BEST HIKES FOR BIRD–WATCHING
Bolsa Chica Ecological Reserve
Upper Newport Bay Ecological Reserve
San Joaquin Wildlife Sanctuary
Tucker Wildlife Sanctuary

BEST WATERFALL HIKES
Holy Jim, Santa Ana Mountains
Tenaja Falls, Santa Ana Mountains
Chiquito Falls, Santa Ana Mountains

BEST BEACH HIKES
San Clemente State Beach
Crystal Cove

BEST HIKES FOR WATCHING WHALES
Salt Creek Beach
Dana Point

BEST HIKES INTO HISTORY
Serrano Creek–Heritage Hill
Dana Point
Holy Jim Canyon

BEST HIKES BY GUIDED TOUR
Limestone Canyon
Fremont Canyon
City of Irvine Open Space

BEST HIKE FOR FALL COLOR
Trabuco Canyon

BEST HIKES FOR SUNSET VIEWING
Huntington Beach (Pier)
Laguna Coast Overlook

BEST GARDEN PATHS
Niguel Botanical Preserve
UCR Botanic Gardens

BEST TRAILHEAD MUSEUMS
(Marine Life) Ocean Institute, Dana Harbor
(Prehistoric OC) Ralph B. Clark Regional Park
(Surfing History) Doheny State Beach

BEST WILDFLOWER HIKES
Limestone Canyon
Santa Rosa Plateau
San Juan Loop Trail, Santa Ana Mountains
Caspers Wilderness Park

BEST HIKES TO TAKE GUESTS FROM OUT-OF-TOWN
Laurel Canyon, Laguna Coast Wilderness Park
Irvine Regional Park
Crystal Cove Beach and Bluffs

BEST INTERPRETED NATURE TRAILS
Edna Spaulding Loop, O' Neill Regional Park
Mile Square Regional Park

BEFORE YOU GO

ADVENTURE PASS

CLEVELAND NATIONAL FOREST: The National Forest Adventure Pass is a parking permit that can be purchased for an annual fee that allows parking in Southern California's four national forests: Angeles National Forest, San Bernardino National Forest, and Cleveland National Forest. The annual pass scurrently costs $30 a year for $5 per day and can be purchased at Forest Service offices, outdoor retailers, and local outlets near or within theboundaries of the national forests.

An Adventure Pass is required for parking at "High Impact Recreational Areas," which covers most locales along the main forest highways and all the most popular trailheads. Many of the trailheads in the Santa Ana Mountains within Cleveland National Forest require an Adventure Pass for parking at a trailhead. For more information, call Cleveland National Forest, (619) 673-6180.

COUNTY PARKS: The vehicle entry fee for the county's regional parks is $3 per entry (usually via an "Iron Ranger") Monday through Friday, and $5 per entry on Saturday and Sunday. Major holidays costs $7 to $10 per entry as posted. Wilderness parks costs $3 per vehicle entry, seven days a week. An annual day use pass for the county's regional parks costs $55 a year. For more information about fees, call (866) OCparks.

STATE PARKS: Day-use entry fees for California State Parks begin at $5 per vehicle. An Annual Day Use Pass is also available and The Trailmaster heartily recommends getting one—a very good deal for state park enthusaists.

PLAN AHEAD

Additional maps: The Automobile Club of Southern California publishes several maps useful to the hiker including: Orange County, Orange County North, Orange County Central and Orange County North. The Club's Riverside-Moreno Valley Area map is useful for the hiker bound for the Riverside area.

Add to these city/county maps: Cleveland National Forest (U.S. Forest Service map). I recommend Franko's Map of Orange County and a second publication that highlights the Santa Ana Mountains.

For an extensive discussion
of hiking techniques, apparel,
trail safety, and much more,
visit my website at

www.thetrailmaster.com

• The 10 essentials
• Hiking equipment
• Footwear and apparel
• Precautions and hazards
• Park contact information
• Nature essays and travel stories
• Lots more hikes from across the nation
and around the world

CHAPTER ONE

Orange County Coast

Orange County's 42-mile-long coastline is splendidly diverse,
with bold bluffs and headlands, secluded coves, bays and
estuaries, miles and miles of golden sand strands,
plus large parks and preserves in the coastal hills.
Laguna Beach, Newport Beach and other beaches attract
visitors from across the Southland and around the world.
From Huntington Beach a.k.a. "Surf City" in the north,
to San Clemente Beach in the south, the hiker can explore
busy beaches and tranquil nature preserves backed
by an array of beach cities, each with its own intriguing
historical, cultural and geographical identity.

SAN CLEMENTE STATE BEACH

TRESTLES TRAIL
From State Beach to San Mateo Point is 3 miles round trip

"Our beach shall always be free from hurdy-gurdies and defilement. We believe beauty to be an asset as well as gold and silver, or cabbage and potatoes." This was the pledge of Norwegian immigrant Ole Hanson, who began the town of San Clemente in 1925. It was quite a promise from a real estate developer, quite a promise in those days of shameless boosterism a half-century before the California Coastal Commission was established.

Thanks in part to Hanson's vision, some of the peaceful ambiance of San Clemente, which he regarded as "a painting 5 miles long and a mile wide" has been preserved. And some of its isolation, too. Most everyone in the real estate community thought Hanson crazy for building in a locale 66 miles from San Diego, 66 miles from Los Angeles, but today this isolation attracts rather than repels. This isolation was one of the reasons President Richard Nixon (1969 to 1974) established his Western White House on the bluffs above San Clemente Beach.

San Clemente State Beach is a great place for a hike. The beach is mercifully walled off from the din of the San Diego Freeway and the confusion of the modern world by a handsome line of tan-colored bluffs. Only the occasional train passing over Santa Fe Railroad tracks, located near the shore interrupt the cry of the gull, the roar of the breakers. The trestles located at the south end of the beach at San Mateo Point give Trestles Beach its name.

Trestles Beach is one of the finest surfing areas on the West Coast. When the surf is up, the waves peel rapidly across San Mateo Point, creating a great ride. Before the area became part of the state beach, it was restricted government property belonging to Camp Pendleton Marine Base. During the 1960s and 1970s, surfers carried on guerrilla warfare with U.S. Marines. Trespassing surfers were chased, arrested and fined, and on many occasions had their boards confiscated.

This walk's destination, San Mateo Point, is the northernmost boundary of San Diego County, the beginning of Orange County. When the original counties of Los Angeles and San Diego were set up in 1850, the line that separated them began on the coast at San Mateo Point. When Orange County was formed from southern Los Angeles County in 1889, San Mateo Point was established as the southern point of the new county.

The enthusiastic, with the time and inclination, can easily extend this beach-walk several miles south to San Onofre State Beach. Another option worth considering is to take the train to San Clemente and walk south from the Amtrak station.

Rest a moment in the underpass before hitting the beach.

DIRECTIONS TO TRAILHEAD: From the San Diego Freeway (5) in San Clemente, exit on Avenida Calafia and head west 0.5 mile to Calafia Beach Park, where there is metered parking. You can also park (for a fee) at San Clemente State Beach. A limited amount of free parking is available in the residential area near the state beach.

North-bound motorists on I-5 will exit at Cristianitos Road, turn left and go over the freeway onto Ave. Del Presidente and drive a mile north to Calafia Beach Park.

THE HIKE: From Calafia Beach Park, cross the railroad tracks, make your way down an embankment and head south. As you'll soon see, San Clemente

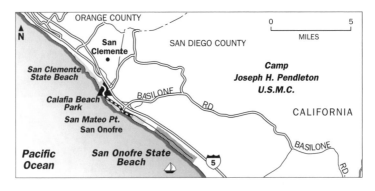

State Beach is frequented by plenty of shorebirds, as well as plenty of surfers, body surfers, and swimmers.

At distinct San Mateo Point, which marks the border of Orange and San Diego counties, you'll find San Mateo Creek. The headwaters of the creek rise way up in the Santa Ana Mountains above Camp Pendleton. A portion of the creek is protected by the Cleveland National Forest's San Mateo Canyon Wilderness. Rushes, saltgrass and cattails line the creek mouth, where sandpipers, herons and egrets gather.

You can ford the creek mouth (rarely a problem except after winter storms) and continue south toward San Onofre State Beach and the giant domes of San Onofre Nuclear Power Plant. Or you can return the same way.

Or here's a third alternative, an inland return route: Walk under the train trestles and join the park service road, which is usually filled with surfers carrying their boards. The service road takes you up the bluffs, where you'll join the San Clemente Coastal Bike Trail, then wind through a residential area to an entrance to San Clemente State Beach Campground. Improvise a route through the camp-ground to the park's entry station and join the self-guiding nature trail (brochures available at the station). The path descends through a prickly pear- and lemonade berry-filled draw to Calafia Beach Park and the trailhead. The wind- and water-sculpted marine terraces just south of the trailhead resemble Bryce Canyon in miniature and are fun to photograph.

Doheny State Beach

DOHENY TRAIL

From Doheny State Beach to Capistrano Beach is 2 miles round trip; to San Clemente Pier is 10 miles round trip

San Juan Capistrano attracts swallows and tourists while Capistrano Beach, which bounds the old mission town, attracts sanderlings and locals. Capistrano Beach, along with Doheny Beach to the north and San Clemente Beach to the south, offers the beach hiker a mellow saunter along the strand.

In 1887, during one of the Southland's great land booms, a high-class subdivision called San Juan-By-the-Sea, was laid out on the mesa by San Juan Creek. It went bust, but was revived in 1925 as Capistrano Beach.

This hike begins just north of Dana Harbor at Doheny State Beach, a good place for family-style swimming and boogie-boarding because the harbor jetties gentle the surf here. Doheny attracts a lot of happy campers, though some seekers of peace and quiet complain that the campground is a bit too close to the highway.

Be sure to visit the Doheny State Beach Interpretive Center, which features an impressive tidepool exhibit, some aquariums and a photo gallery that highlights Orange County's longboard surfing era during the 1950s and 1960s. The interpretive center (open 10 A.M. to 4 P.M. daily) is located close to the park's entry station.

DIRECTIONS TO TRAILHEAD: From the San Diego Freeway (5) in San Juan Capistrano, exit on Camino Las Ramblas and drive a mile westward to

Doheny longboards, circa 1966.

Highway 1. Turn north and very soon reach an intersection and make a left on Harbor Drive, then another quick left into Doheny State Beach. There is a state park day use fee.

THE HIKE: Walk down to the shoreline and saunter south along the white sand beach. After 0.25 mile, you'll reach the mouth of San Juan Creek. In the summer, a sandbar closes off the creek mouth and forms a small lagoon patrolled by ducks and egrets. During the wintertime, or if the sandbar has been breached by the creek and is too high to cross, detour inland to the park road and follow it over the creek. Walk through the campground back to the beach.

After a bit more than a mile, you'll reach the end of Doheny and the beginning of Capistrano Beach, easily identified by the long, uninterrupted row of houses facing the beach. Lots of rock has been dumped near the tideline in an attempt to stabilize the beach and protect the houses from the surging waves; this translates into awkward passage and a less-than-aesthetically uplifting experience for the beach hiker.

At 2.75 miles, you'll reach undeveloped Poche Beach, a county park, and continue 0.5 mile to a development-crowded point that makes beach walking a challenge and thwarts all passage at higher tides. Detour inland, walk south along El Camino Real, then return to the beach by the MetroLink Station.

Resume your shore walk southward across the brown sands of San Clemente City Beach. San Clemente Pier and nearby refreshment opportunities suggest a turnaround point. Gung-ho hikers can continue another two miles or so downcoast across San Clemente State Beach to San Mateo Point and the Orange County/San Diego County line.

DANA POINT HARBOR

DANA POINT BEACH TRAIL
From Ocean Institute to Sea Cave is 1.5 miles round trip

"The most romantic spot in California," Richard Henry Dana called it in his classic seafaring account, *Two Years Before the Mast.*

Today, Dana Harbor's boosters are not at all shy about making that same claim for romance. Some visitors will certainly find romance in a sunset stroll by the yacht harbor and in enjoying a fine dinner at a waterside restaurant.

Other visitors, those who like to hike anyway, may just find some romance in traipsing a bit of old California—a boulder-strewn beach below the towering bluffs of Dana Point—a remnant of the wild coastline that greeted Dana when he arrived at the cove that in those bygone days was the only major harbor between Santa Barbara and San Diego.

The hike begins at Orange County's Ocean Institute, which offers marine life exhibits and classroom instruction to students of all ages. The Institute has an ambitious program of classes and field trips.

The *Pilgrim*, operated by Ocean Institute, is a full-size replica of the brig immortalized by Dana in his book. The tall ship is a favorite of the thousands of school children who come to visit.

Indoor fun at the Institute's touch tank.

DIRECTIONS TO TRAILHEAD: From the San Diego Freeway (I-5) in San Juan Capistrano, exit on Highway 1 and head west two miles. Turn left on Street of the Green Lantern and, after two blocks, make a left again on Cove Road. The road descends the cliffs to Dana Point Drive. Park at the base of the hill in the lot for Dana Cove Park.

THE HIKE: Begin alongside the *Pilgrim* and the monument depicting sailors of that era. Follow the concrete walkway behind the Ocean Institute's museum and descend green cage-enclosed stairs to the beach. If you didn't check the tide table before coming here to hike, here's a hint: if the tide is swirling at the bottom of the stairs, come back another time at a lower tide.

Head up-coast across the rocky beach. The intriguing conglomerate rocks, the towering cliffs, the waves crashing over the sea stacks offshore...a wilder coast than you might imagine. A sea cave marks your likely turnaround point. At very low, even minus tides, it's possible to continue around Dana Point to the beach at Salt Creek Park.

Dana Point Harbor: Beaches, bluffs and ocean research.

DANA POINT

BLUFF TOP TRAIL
From Ken Sampson Overview to Hide Drogher Statue is 1 mile round trip

Dana Point, Harbor and City are named for Richard Henry Dana, author of that classic 1840 sea narrative, *Two Years Before The Mast*. Dana's narrative chronicles the voyage of the merchant ship, *Pilgrim* from Boston around Cape Horn to the California coast.

"The most romantic spot on the California coast," is how Dana described Capistrano Bay, now known as Dana Point.

Dana detailed the sailors' arduous labor of tossing cow hides from the point that now bears his name to the beach below where they could then be loaded aboard longboats and rowed out to the ship. Maritime trade in that era revolved around vessels delivering finished goods to California coastal residents and picking up raw materials, such as hides from cattle raised near Mission San Juan Capistrano.

From Dana's account, we gather that pitching a hide from the bluffs down to the small beach below required a good aim. "Just where we landed was a small cover, or bight, which gave us, at high tide, a few square feet of sand-beach between the sea and the bottom of the hill. This was the only landing place. Directly before us, rose the perpendicular height of four or five hundred feet."

This walk's destination is a bronze statue of a hide drogher, captured in mid-toss. Very old dictionaries define "drogher" as the small vessel transporting goods from ship to shore and vice versa. Apparently a sailor who transported hides by tossing them from cliff to shore was referred to a drogher in those bygone days.

As you walk atop the tall bluffs, you'll observe that Dana Point is more than a point: it includes seven miles of bluffs, a city, located about halfway between L.A. and San Diego, with more than 35,000 residents, and a harbor with slips and moorings for 2,500 boats.

DIRECTIONS TO TRAIL-HEAD: From the San Diego Freeway

The *Pilgrim* in full sail.

The Hide Drogher captured in mid-toss.

(405) in San Juan Capistrano, exit on Beach Cities/Highway 1, and follow Pacific Coast Highway up-coast 2.5 miles to Street of the Blue Lantern. Turn left and follow it two blocks to its end at Ken Sampson Overview. Park along the street or along Santa Clara Avenue that parallels the coast one block inland.

THE HIKE: Check out the eye-popping view from the cliff-top park that honors its namesake, longtime (1957-1975) director of Orange County's park system. Below is the harbor, and to the south are Doheny State Beach, San Clemente Beach, and San Mateo Point (marking Orange County's southern boundary with San Diego County).

Walk inland a block to Santa Clara and then walk three blocks down-coast through a residential area to Street of the Amber Lantern. Turn right and walk a short block to the end of the street, an overlook and signed Bluff Top Trail.

Particularly impressive is a gorge-spanning wooden footbridge. (Why can't hikers ever find anything this elaborate out in the wilderness?) The path soon leads to a cement arch, about all that remains of the Dana Point Inn, a 1920s resort hotel, a business casualty of the Great Depression.

Climb the stairs to "The Hide Drogher" statue. It's a long way down to the shore and one wonders about the accuracy rate achieved by a top-notch hide-thrower. Just beyond the statue the path ends at the foot of Street of the Amber Lantern where it meets El Camino Capistrano.

SALT CREEK BEACH PARK

SALT CREEK BEACH TRAIL
From Bluff Park up and down the beach is 2 miles round trip

Salt Creek Beach is a popular surfing spot. Bluff Park, perched above the beach, offers great views of the surfers in action, as well as more distant views of Orange County's coastline and Catalina Island. During the winter months, the park's numerous benches and vista points are great places from which to observe migrating California gray whales.

Salt Creek Beach, located between the communities of South Laguna and Dana Point, is a great place for swimming, boogie boarding, sunbathing and strolling. It's particularly popular as a surfing spot, and has been since the early longboard days of the 1940s. A modest-size offshore reef creates high quality and dependable left swells. During the 1960s, the U.S. Surfing Association charged its members seventy-five cents per day to ride the waves. As the story goes, USSA members were required to drop their coins in a tiny cup handed over the top of a fence by a beach monitor.

Access to Salt Creek Beach is considerably more costly these days. Try a dollar an hour for parking in the large lot.

Overlooking—some would say dominating—the bluffs above the beach is the Ritz-Carlton Hotel. One of the cool things about this beach is that everybody from a diversity of backgrounds seems to mix so well—hotel guests, surfer, local

Salt Creek Beach: A ramble from the Ritz.

Whales and seabirds as viewed from the elegant terrace.

teens, families from all backgrounds from all over Orange County.

Salt Creek's many friends proved valuable during the "Save Salt Creek" conservation movement of the late 1960s that saved the beach from a massive residential development.

DIRECTIONS TO THE TRAILHEAD: From the San Diego Freeway (I-5) in Laguna Niguel, exit on Crown Valley Parkway and drive six miles south to Pacific Coast Highway. Turn left (down-coast), and proceed 0.5 mile to the signed entrance for Salt Creek Beach Park. Turn right on Ritz-Carlton Drive and park in the self-pay parking lot ($1 per hour).

You can also access the park from a second entrance off Silva Road. At a pedestrian gate, located just south of Ritz-Carlton Drive, you can join a paved path leading along the bluffs above Salt Creek Beach.

THE HIKE: From the parking lot, walk the park road, following it under Ritz-Carlton Drive to the wide grassy parkland that slopes to the sea.

Shortly before the access road reaches the beach, look left for the paved pathway that ascends the bluffs. This route leads along the Ritz-Carlton grounds to an overlook that offers inspiring views of the south Orange County coast.

Walk up-coast on the paved path that traverses the low bluffs. Connector trails and stairways connect this main trail to park facilities, as well as to a lower path leading along the seawall.

As the path approaches the golf course, you can choose to take a hike along Salt Creek (see description in this guide) or leave the main path in favor of a short descending trail that leads to the lower path that travels along the inland edge of the beach. Walk this path or the sand strand back down-coast.

SALT CREEK REGIONAL PARK

SALT CREEK TRAIL
From Salt Creek Beach Park to Chapparosa Community Park is 6 miles round trip with 400-foot elevation gain

Salt Creek Trail offers a tour of the good life, Orange County-style. It begins at Salt Creek Beach, a lovely, 1.5 mile-long sand strand, skirts the Ritz-Carlton Hotel grounds, turns inland and leads past the Monarch Beach Golf Links, then ascends through a long greenbelt park into the heart of Laguna Niguel.

Salt Creek Trail is popular with south Orange County locals, particularly exercise walkers. The paved path crosses the community of Dana Point, the city of Laguna Niguel, as well as three parks: Salt Creek Beach Park, Salt Creek Regional Park and Chapparosa Community Park.

While the trail is a multi-use path, and open to cyclists, it's mostly a travel corridor for those on foot—walkers, joggers, and stroller-pushing moms and dads. Beach-bound bicyclists prefer to zoom along the bike path paralleling Niguel Road—a far speedier route than Salt Creek Trail.

Salt Creek Trail goes by two other names: "Nature Trail" and Laguna Niguel Hike/Bike Trail. City and county park authorities, as well as homeowner groups have a say in how the trail is maintained.

Salt Creek Trail is that rare path that connects the beach to the coastal hills. While the California coast is blessed with many beach and bluff trails, as well as fine trails networks in the coastal mountains, Salt Creek is only one of a handful of trails along the 1,200 mile-long California coast that actually connects the shore with hills east of Coast Highway.

Southern Orange County's coastal hills, now almost completely covered by homes, have changed almost unimaginably since the 1840s when cattle grazed Juan Avila's sprawling Rancho Niguel. Still, a fragment of the area's natural heritage remains along Salt Creek.

Undoubtedly the nature trail set up along the upper two miles of Salt Creek Trail intended to interpret the area's natural history; however, this effort has been abandoned and no interpretive brochures are available to the hiker. Hikers will spot twenty numbered posts en route, but that's it—no information links to the numbers.

My guess is the nature trail intended to point out some of the remaining native flora. On drier slopes, look for prickly pear cactus and coast cholla. Shading the creek (but alas not the trail) are coast live oak, sycamore and willow. Trailside vegetation includes lots of sage, buckwheat, mustard and monkeyflowers.

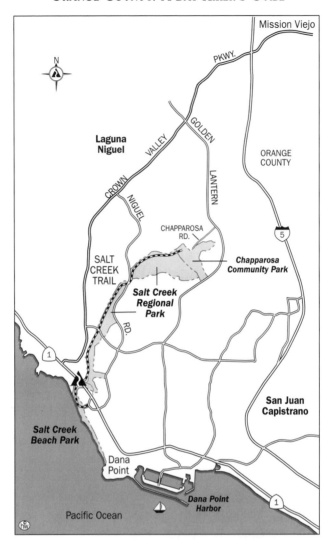

Although the hiker is never far from civilization on Salt Creek Trail, note that no water is available until trail's end at Chapparosa Park. With a car shuttle, those looking for an easy jaunt could make this a three-mile, all-downhill hike from Chapparosa Park to the beach.

DIRECTIONS TO TRAILHEAD: From the San Diego Freeway (I-5) in Laguna Niguel, exit on Crown Valley Parkway and drive six miles south to Pacific Coast Highway. Turn left (down-coast), and proceed 0.5 mile to the signed entrance for Salt Creek Beach Park. Turn right on Ritz-Carlton Drive and park in the self-pay parking lot ($1 per hour).

To the upper trailhead: From Crown Valley Parkway, a mile from the freeway, turn left on Street of the Golden Lantern and drive about two miles to Chapparosa Park Road. Follow this road through a neighborhood into Chapparosa Park. The signed trailhead is at the far western end of the park

THE HIKE: First resist the impulse to walk inland on the paved pathway leading from the parking lot through the Coast Highway underpass. Yes, you are going to follow a paved pathway and use a Coast Highway underpass, but not this pathway and this underpass.

Salt Creek Trail requires a leap of faith: you must walk west to go east. So join the surfers and sightseers and walk west down the paved coastal access path toward Salt Creek Beach. Admire the beauty of this beach and the often superb waves as you angle north (up-coast) on the promenade leading through Bluff Park. You'll pass below the ocean-facing side of the Ritz-Carlton Hotel, then curve inland.

Salt Creek Trail enters a tunnel below Coast Highway and emerges on the west side of Salt Creek and the far west side of Monarch Beach Golf Links. You'll ascend moderately for a mile alongside the golf course. Immediately after passing under Camino Del Avion, bear left at an unsigned junction. The path turns briefly west and you'll see an unsigned dirt trail descending to, and alongside, Salt Creek. (You can follow this dirt path a short half-mile before thick vegetation and swampy terrain make further passage impossible.)

Salt Creek Trail soon turns north again and the numbered posts (beginning with 20) belonging to the old nature trail appear. After another mile's ascent, through what signs proclaim is a "Wildlife Habitat Enhancement Area," the trail reaches the Clubhouse Plaza Shopping Center, whereupon it crosses beneath Niguel Road via another pedestrian underpass.

The last mile of trail has a bit wilder feel as it penetrates San Juan Canyon. From Salt Creek Regional Park, you'll pass into the city of Laguna Niguel's Chapparosa Community Park and reach trail's end at a small exhibit case that describes local flora.

ALISO & WOOD CANYONS WILDERNESS PARK

ALISO CREEK, WOOD CANYON TRAILS
To Wood Canyon is 3 miles round trip; through Wood Canyon to Sycamore
Grove is 6 miles round trip; loop of Wood Canyon is 9 miles round trip

Aliso & Wood Canyons Wilderness Park, the largest park in the hills above
Laguna Beach, preserves 3,400 acres of pastoral Orange County.

Most locals and other hikers refer to the low hills that back the Orange
County coast from Corona del Mar to Dana Point as the Laguna Hills or "the
mountains behind Laguna Beach." Actually, the northerly hills are the San
Joaquin Hills—their cousins to the south are the Sheep Hills.

Here's how nature writer Joseph Smeaton Chase described an outing in the
Sheep Hills in his classic 1913 book, *California Coast Trails:* "A few miles along a
road that wound and dipped over the cliffs brought us by sundown to Aliso
Canyon. The walls of the canyon are high hills sprinkled with lichened rock,
sprinkled with brush whose prevailing gray is relieved here and there by bosses of
olive sumac. Our camp was so attractive that we remained for several days."

Aliso & Wood Canyons Wilderness Park is a great place to hike, but it does
present a minor access problem: From the parking area to the mouth of Wood
Canyon is a less-than-scintillating 1.5 mile walk alongside a road. Some hikers

Stunning rock formations in OC hills.

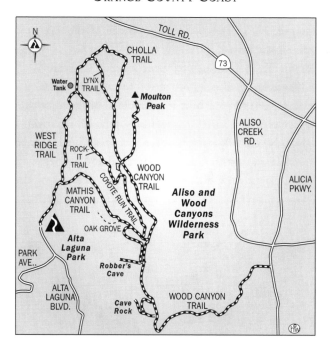

avoid this road walk by bringing their bikes—either mountain bike or standard bicycle will do—and cycling to the "true" trailhead. Cyclists can ride some of the park's trails (the wider dirt roads), then leave their bikes at conveniently placed racks and walk the narrower, hikers-only paths.

DIRECTIONS TO TRAILHEAD: From the San Diego Freeway (5) in Laguna Hills/ Mission Viejo, exit on Alicia Parkway and drive 4 miles south. Trailhead parking for Aliso & Wood Canyons Wilderness Park is located a quarter-mile south of Aliso Creek Road. Take a right into the parking lot, which is opposite Laguna Niguel Regional Park and near the Orange County Natural History Museum.

THE HIKE: From the parking area, hike along the paved road into Aliso Canyon. The road, and a parallel dirt path for hikers, heads southeast, and meanders just west of Aliso Creek.

After 1.5 miles of walking you'll arrive at the park's most significant signed junction (complete with restrooms no less). Join Wood Canyon Trail Trail (a dirt road) and begin a gentle ascent through Wood Canyon. Look left for the side trail leading to Cave Rock, where you'll find a number of caves, wind-sculpted into a substantial sandstone formation.

After rejoining Wood Canyon Trail, continue up-canyon to another left-branching side trail that leads to Dripping Cave a.k.a. Robbers Cave. The robbers who hid out here in the 19th century included cattle rustlers and highwaymen who held up stagecoaches. The "Dripping," much of the year anyway, refers to water seeping above the cave.

Wood Canyon Trail continues to meet Mathis Canyon Trail. A short distance up Wood Canyon Trail is an old sheep corral. You can turn around in this vicinity or choose to extend your hike in a couple of different ways.

If you want to leg it just a little more, head up Mathis Canyon, then north on Coyote Run Trail. Next, fork right to reconnect with Wood Canyon Trail. For a longer loop, bear left on northbound Rock-It Trail and connect with West Ridge Trail. (See Alta Laguna Park hike write-up for an account of the trails in the northern and western parts of A&W Canyons Wilderness Park.)

Trail to adventure in Aliso & Wood Canyons Wilderness Park.

ALTA LAGUNA PARK

WEST RIDGE, MATHIS, WOOD CANYON, CHOLLA TRAILS
Loop From Alta Laguna Park to Aliso & Wood Canyons Wilderness Park is
8 miles round trip with 600-foot elevation gain

Most park-goers use the Alicia Parkway entrance to Aliso & Wood Canyons
Wilderness Park to begin their self-propelled adventures from the canyon bottoms. Another, less crowded way to go is by way of a second trailhead at Alta
Laguna Park, perched atop a ridge on the big park's west boundary. This handsome little park offers every hiker amenity including water, restrooms, picnic
area, play area for the kids and plenty of parking.

Hikers should be forewarned that Aliso & Wood Canyons Wilderness Park
is extremely popular with mountain bicyclists. Beginning riders cruise the nearly
flat canyon bottoms in the main part of the park while advanced riders careen
down the steep ridgelines and along the rocky single tracks.

Vistas from Alta Laguna Park are superb. Hike the short trail to Carolynn
Wood View Knoll and admire the coastal panorama to the southwest: Laguna
Beach and the shoreline to the south, northward to the prominent Palos Verdes
Peninsula, then across the great blue Pacific to San Clemente Island and Santa
Catalina Island.

Gaze east to the San Joaquin Hills and the modern communities of Aliso
Viejo, Lake Forest and more. Behind the hills and suburbs rise the Santa Ana
Mountains and its two most distinctive peaks—Modjeska and Santiago—which

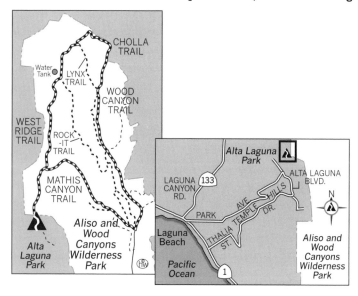

47

team together to form Old Saddleback. On a clear day, the observant hiker can pick out several San Gabriel Mountains high points including Mt. Wilson and Mt. Baldy.

This top-down approach to Aliso & Woods park that I've suggested can be shortened or lengthened to your time and inclination. Four trails extend from the park's West Ridge and offer the hiker several loop trip opportunities of varying lengths.

DIRECTIONS TO TRAILHEAD: From Pacific Coast Highway (1) in Laguna Beach, turn inland on Park Avenue and ascend two miles to Alta Laguna Boulevard. Turn left and after a block turn right into Alta Laguna Park.

THE HIKE: The most eager among us can get right to the walk by stepping out onto the wide West Ridge Trail, but I recommend following the more round-about trail to Carolynn Wood View Knoll and taking in the panoramic vistas. Thanks to some slope restoration efforts these hilltops are healing from the effects of off-road vehicle use that occurred prior to the creation of the park. While enjoying the view, realize that the knoll's "purpose" is actually more utilitarian than aesthetic: below ground is a reservoir containing some 3 million gallons of water.

From atop the knoll, a footpath corkscrews down to a spur road that, in turn, connects to West Ridge Trail. A half-mile northward descent leads to a park bulletin board, bench and signed intersection with Mathis Trail. If you're not up for a long hike, contemplate the park below, then retrace your steps back to the trailhead.

Mathis Trail drops southwest very quickly. It's a hairy mountain bike ride and even a steep route for hikers. The trail finally levels out and a better graded dirt road leads to the grassy, oak-dotted bottom of Mathis Canyon.

Turn north on Wood Canyon Trail through the heart of the park. Follow the mellow path along the seasonal creek on a gentle 2.5 mile ascent to the north end of the park and a junction with Cholla Trail. Bear left and head up Cholla Trail to the ridge line. A final 2.5 miles along West Ridge Trail returns you to the trailhead.

ALISO PEAK

OVERLOOK, ALISO PEAK TRAILS
From Seaview Park's Niguel Hill to Aliso Peak is 1.2 miles round trip with 300-foot elevation gain

Some hikers claim that the scenic overlook perched on a promontory in Seaview Park offers Orange County's best coastal view. Certainly the vistas from this obscure Laguna Niguel park are breathtaking, whether one is gazing down-slope to the hills back of Laguna Beach or down-coast all the way to San Clemente.

The park's overlook offers a particularly intriguing angle on Catalina Island, which appears so deceptively close on the horizon that you imagine you could hop in your kayak and in no time paddle right into Avalon Harbor. On clear nights, the isle's lights are quite distinct, too.

Along with the views, Seaview Park also boasts refreshing sea breezes and that Orange County rarity—secluded picnic tables—plus a sign-posted nature trail. With all these attractions, you'd think the park would be a more popular

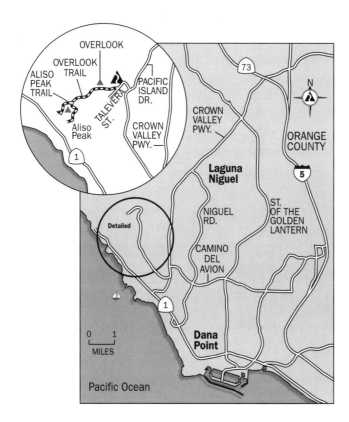

destination, but no, it seems to be completely off the radar of the throngs of beachgoers down at the coast, just a half-mile as the gull flies from Seaview Park.

While you're in the neighborhood (Laguna Niguel), drop by Niguel Botanical Preserve in Crown Valley Community Park, located at 29751 Crown Valley Parkway—or about midway between the coast highway and the San Diego Freeway. (See hike write-up.)

DIRECTIONS TO TRAILHEAD: To reach Seaview Park, exit the San Diego Freeway (I-5) in Laguna Niguel on Crown Valley Parkway and head south 5 miles to Pacific Island Drive. Turn right (west) and ascend to the crest of the hill. Turn left on Talavera Street and follow it to the end of the cul de sac and the entrance to Seaview Park.

From Coast Highway (1) in Laguna Beach, you can head inland on Crown Valley Parkway to Pacific Island Drive, turn left and head up to Talavera Street and the park.

THE HIKE: A wide, gentle pathway of decomposed granite leads past interpretive panels and name-tagged plants that highlight the characteristic native flora communities in these parts—coastal sage scrub and chaparral. Most visitors are content with stopping at the overlook, watching the hawks soar over precipitous Aliso and Wood canyons, admiring the sea views, and returning the way they came.

The intrepid may continue beyond the overlook on a narrower, rougher path known as Aliso Peak Trail. You'll pass two left-branching side trails: the first, sometimes called Valido Trail, drops down to West Street in South Laguna Beach, while the second descends to Ceanothus Drive. Aliso Peak-bound hikers stay right and ascend the railroad tie-stabilized trail to another wonderful overlook and more stunning coastal views.

The Good Life above the Badlands.

BADLANDS PARK AND SOUTH LAGUNA COAST

Badlands, Seaview, South Laguna Ridge Trails
To Overlook is 1 mile round trip; to Aliso Peak is 3 miles round trip

Laguna Beach has been a pioneer in preserving open space in south Orange County. More than a thousand acres of hillsides and canyonlands have been set aside.

The city has been very proactive in expanding its greenbelt and its blue belt (6.3 miles of shoreline). Badlands Park, named for its eroded sandstone cliffs, is located between the greenbelt and the blue belt on tall ocean bluffs that rise 700 feet above the beach.

From Badlands, trails lead across the clifftops and around the gated communities of South Laguna. The cliff-edge paths and overlooks give the hiker great views of the Laguna coast, Catalina Island and the wide blue Pacific. Hikers can follow trails from the Badlands to Aliso Peak trails (see hike write-up in this guide).

DIRECTIONS TO TRAILHEAD: From the San Diego Freeway (5) in Laguna Niguel, exit on Crown Valley Parkway and drive south 5.5 miles to Pacific Island Drive. Make a right and proceed a mile to Ocean Way. Make a left to reach Isle Vista in 0.2 mile and turn left. Find curbside parking where you can before reaching the gated entrance to the Monarch Point community.

If you're already at the coast, take Pacific Coast Highway (1) to South Laguna. Turn inland on Crown Valley Parkway and travel 0.75 mile to Pacific Island Drive. Turn left and follow directions from above.

THE HIKE: Walk Isle Vista to the Monarch Point entry and look right for steps leading to a vista point and junction with Seaview Trail. Make a left and shortly reach another junction. Seaview Trail continues straight 0.1 to its southern terminus a residential area, but you head right and descend steps to Badlands Park.

While the park has plenty of use trails, hike the main, wide Badlands Trail along the edge of the bluffs. After skirting residential streets, the path peters out atop a sharp ridge. Take in the coastal view then retrace your steps via Seaview Trail.

If you want to hike a bit more and/or head for Aliso Peak, instead of returning to the trailhead at Monarch Point, continue hiking northwest on Seaview Trail, forking right at a junction and traveling to the entry for another gated community–Laguna Sur. Follow the signs along Cannes, Marseille and St. Tropez to junction Aliso Peak Trail.

NIGUEL BOTANICAL PRESERVE

PRESERVE TRAILS
0.75 mile loop through preserve

From its humble beginnings in 1981 as a community vegetable garden, the garden has grown to become a botanical preserve admired as "A Mediterranean Climates Arboretum." Niguel Botanical Preserve is located within Crown Valley Park, a busy recreation center, complete with soccer fields, picnic grounds, YMCA facilities and a community pool.

The 18-acre preserve, located in Laguna Niguel, collects and displays plants from regions that share a Mediterranean climate similar to that of Southern California. In particular, the preserve emphasizes drought-resistant plants deemed garden-worthy—which is to say flora that will thrive in SoCal. Plant collections are grouped by region of origin: Mexico-California, Australia, Africa and South America.

DIRECTIONS TO TRAILHEAD: From the San Diego Freeway (5) in Laguna Niguel, exit on Crown Valley Parkway and head 2.5 miles southeast to Crown Valley Community Park. Niguel Botanical Preserve is located above the community center parking lot.

THE HIKE: A network of trails links the floral groupings, as well as viewpoints and tranquil seating areas. Wander at will from the unusual palms in Palm Canyon to a collection of cactus and succulents to jacaranda-dotted Girl Scout Canyon.

I particularly like the Eucalyptus Savanna with its Australian flora and taking in the views of the garden and Saddleback Valley from Australia Overlook.

Volunteers plant Labyrinth Garden at Niguel Botanical Preserve.

LAGUNA NIGUEL REGIONAL PARK

SULPHUR CREEK RESERVOIR TRAIL
1.5-mile loop around reservoir

The City of Laguna Niguel, located in the heart of south county about halfway between L.A. and San Diego, is proud of its parks. The planned community, incorporated in 1989 as Orange County's 29th city, offers its residents some two dozen neighborhood and community parks. By some estimates, one-third of this modern hillside town remains undeveloped open space.

Laguna Niguel Regional Park is a step apart in size and orientation from the various city parks. The park's 236 acres are oriented to picnickers, pedestrians, cyclists and anglers.

It's apparent that tree-planters have been busy over the years. The park is dotted with alder, acacia and sycamore.

The park is centered around Sulphur Creek Reservoir, which was created by a dam on the creek. Sulphur Creek is a tributary of Aliso Creek, which flows 19 miles from the foothills of the Santa Ana Mountains to the ocean south of Laguna Beach. Anglers like this manmade lake, which is stocked with blue gull, bass and catfish.

The reservoir is also something of a bird refuge for resident and migratory waterfowl. Local birders keep an eye out for some unusual migrants as well as the scores of ducks and geese. All of the residential streets on the east side of the park—including Canvasback Circle, Kite Hill Drive, Catbird Court and Nuthatch Lane—are named for birds.

During the mid-19th century, what is now parkland was part of Juan Avila's Rancho Niguel. As the story goes, the conservative Senor Avila was referred to as *El Rico* (The Rich) and ran a much-admired old California-style rancho. The Laguna Niguel Corporation donated land for the nucleus of a county park in 1970 and the regional park opened three years later.

The park, while including such amenities as an amphitheater, picnic areas that are both easy-to-access and more remote, volleyball courts and tennis courts, is also pedestrian friendly. Two pedestrian bridges over Sulphur Creek allow the hiker to circumnavigate the reservoir.

DIRECTIONS TO TRAILHEAD: From the Santa Ana Freeway (5) in Laguna Niguel, exit on La Paz Road and drive 4 miles west to the park. Beyond the entry, turn left. Park in the lot in the vicinity of Picnic Shelter #7.

THE HIKE: To travel clockwise around the reservoir, head down toward the creek and take the wide cement path to reach the dirt footpath. Head east along the shoreline trail, accompanied by the call of birds and the hum of traffic. The

Mid-afternoon at the oasis.

views include the tranquil waters of the reservoir and a havienda-covered ridge-line.

At the bridge over Sulphur Creek, you'll see a path leading southward along the creek to Crown Valley Community Park and Niguel Botanical Preserve (see write-up in this guide). But you'll continue with the shoreline trail to the boat dock area, then follow the park road back to the parking lot and trailhead.

LAGUNA BEACH AND BLUFFS

LAGUNA BEACH, HEISLER PARK TRAILS
From Main Beach to Crescent Bay is 2 miles round trip

One of California's finest resort towns, Laguna Beach includes more than seven miles of coast, tempting the explorer with cliffs, coves and lovely sand strands.

For most visitors, though, Laguna Beach's beach is Main Beach. It's a beauty with a lovely length of sand and a boardwalk promenade. The basketball and beach volleyball courts attract (how shall we say?) vigorous competitors. Players seem to be of semi-pro quality—but professional athletes have been known to join in the action, too.

This walk, designed to be completed in under two hours, offers a generous sampling of Laguna's tiny beaches, coves, vista points and surfing spots. Conspiring against longer coastal walks are the town's two-hour parking meters. Bring lots of quarters and don't let that meter expire!

From the blufftop path, you look down at extensive tidepools, completely covered at high tide and exposed at low, protected by the Laguna Beach Marine Life Refuge. When the surf's up, you're sure to spot lots of surfers, who ride a special break called Rockpile.

Many of those cliff-top strollers are visitors from across the nation and around the world. On a recent weekend walk, I overheard a half-dozen different languages.

Romantic Laguna: Wedded bliss at the beach.

A century ago, artists, inspired to paint in the plein air style like the French Impressionists, traveled from inland regions by horse and buggy to set up their easels on the beaches and bluffs. Some captured the shoreline and its soft south light in some amazing seascapes, paintings that are much admired and command very high prices these days.

Artists brought a Bohemian outlook and artistic sensibility that lingers today in the town, renowned for its galleries, Laguna Art Museum, Laguna Playhouse, and the Sawdust Art Festival. The annual summertime events include the Laguna Beach Festival of Arts, which features the Pageant of the Masters—the astonishing theatrical production of *tableaux vivants* ("living pictures").

Fortunately, some of the vistas that have inspired several generations of painters still remain for today's artists to capture and for the coastal rambler to savor. Heisler Park, which opened in 1927, now attracts an estimated half-million visitors a year.

All that foot traffic has an impact on the park of course, but it's really natural erosion that's slowly claiming the cliffs and threatening the park. One culprit is ice plant, which swells in the rainy season, dislodges from its roots, taking soil with it as it slides away. If left unchecked, this natural erosion could eventually undermine the park and even Cliff Drive. The city of Laguna Beach must find a way to halt this erosion with the added challenge of doing so in an aesthetically pleasing way (this is Laguna after all so a giant sea walls won't do) that fits with the character of the park and doesn't disrupt natural beach processes.

DIRECTIONS TO TRAILHEAD: Parking is the challenge for this walk. I prefer to park near downtown and Main Beach and walk up-coast to Heisler Park. However, if fortune favors you with a metered parking space on Cliff Drive near Crescent Bay, by all means take it and begin with a down-coast sojourn.

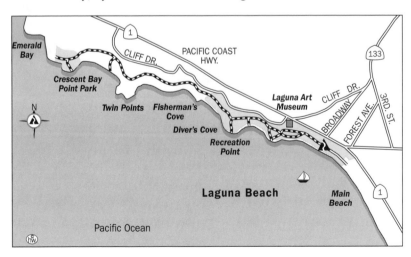

56

THE HIKE: Join the wooden boardwalk on Main Beach that begins at Forest Avenue and undulates between the sand and a grassy park. At the up-coast end of Main Beach, ascend stairs and a path to the top of the bluffs, Cliff Drive and a gazebo overlooking Bird Rock.

Follow the walkway along the landscaped bluffs, amidst palms, pines and picnic areas up-coast above Rockpile Beach and Picnic Beach. Note the stairways leading down to the shore at Fisherman's Cove and at Crescent Bay. This walk ends at an overlook above Crescent Bay

Laguna Coast Wilderness Park

Leave behind the modern OC for the pastoral Orange County
of the 19th century when you hike around this wonderful park
in the Laguna Hills. Begin by sauntering among sandstone
boulders sculpted by wind and water and traveling through
oak- and sycamore-shaded Laurel Canyon.
Emerge onto Bommer Ridge for grand vistas of Laguna Beach,
up and down the Orange Coast, as well as the coastal
mountains and a whole lot of suburbanopolis.
Don't miss park gem, Emerald Canyon, with its
oak woodlands and grassy meadows, in the most remote part
of the park. Shorter trails lead to grand vista points
above the Irvine Bowl and the city of Laguna Beach.

LAUREL CANYON

LAUREL CANYON, WILLOW CANYON TRAILS
Laurel-Willow canyons loop is 3.5 miles with 600-foot elevation gain;
to Bommer Ridge Overlook is 7 miles round trip

Laguna Coast Wilderness Park is the Orange County of the 19th century, a lovely diversity of landscapes highlighted by woodlands, grasslands and scenic ridgelines with handsome sandstone outcroppings. The 6,500-acre park also contains Orange County's only natural lakes, which provide habitat for fish as well as for such waterfowl as geese, grebes, coots, cormorants and kingfishers.

James Irvine and his partners purchased the one-time Rancho San Joaquin in 1865 and the company grazed cattle on it for more than a century. Now, with the Irvine Company's cooperation, substantial acreage in and around Laguna Canyon is becoming parkland under the stewardship of Orange County Harbors, Beaches and Parks.

That these hills and canyons don't resemble the developed Orange County of the 21st century is a tribute to three decades of exemplary work by local conserva-tionists, as well as state and local park agencies and municipalities. Preservationists, with the support of then-California Senator Alan Cranston attempted to create Orange Coast National Park in the late 1970s. In 1989, 8,000

The flowers that bloom in the spring at Laurel Canyon.

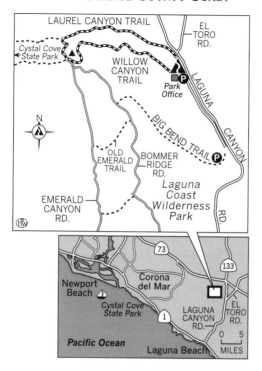

people marched along Laguna Canyon Road to show their commitment to pre-serving the Laguna Hills. A year later the citizens of Laguna Beach voted over-whelmingly to tax themselves $20 million in order to purchase land alongside Laguna Canyon Road and far up into the hills. Lengthy negotiations among pub-lic entities and private parties, as well as increased preservation efforts spearhead-ed by the Laguna Canyon Foundation took place during the 1990s.

For more than a decade, access was restricted to an extent that only the most connected local hikers were able to figure out when, where and how to hike this park. Currently the park is open for hiking seven days a week.

Laurel Canyon is a hiking-only trail, in contrast to the park's many multi-use trails, including Willow Canyon road, your return route on this hike. The canyon has plenty of the laurel sumac that inspired its name, lots of old oaks, a wonderful-ly aromatic coastal sage community of flora, intriguing rock formations, and even a seasonal waterfall. No wonder Laurel Canyon is one of the very best places to take a guided nature hike.

DIRECTIONS TO TRAILHEAD: From the San Diego Freeway (405) in Irvine, a few miles north of this freeway's junction with the Santa Ana Freeway (5), exit on Laguna Canyon Road (133) and head south toward the coast and Laguna Beach. Look for the main (Laurel Canyon) entrance to the park on the right (west) side of the road.

THE HIKE: Join the path leading north parallel to Laguna Canyon Road and soon pass a sandstone boulder sculpted by wind and water into a very small cave. Keep an eye out for more such caves and rock formations crowning the park's ridges.

The trail traverses an open slope that, with an end to cattle grazing, is making the environmental transition from annual grassland to coastal sage scrub. Buckwheat and sage line the path which turns away from Laguna Canyon Road and enters the quiet of Laurel Canyon.

Begin a westward ascent among live oaks and sycamores. The oaks appear to have recovered far better than the sycamores from the terrible 1993 Laguna Fire that blackened Laurel Canyon and thousands of acres around it. Certainly the vegetation in the canyon bottom regenerated quickly: what is now a brush-crowded narrow footpath up Laurel Canyon was actually a fairly wide ranch road before the fire.

The path leads by a seasonal creek (look for an ephemeral waterfall during the rainy season) and ascends to meet a dirt road. Turn left on this road and begin an ascent to a saddle on Willow Ridge and another junction. Go left again and descend Willow Canyon Road.

Most of the view on your descent east is of parkland, with the major exception of the San Joaquin Hills Toll Road which, alas, bisects Laguna Coast Wilderness Park. Your journey ends at the park office, a short walk from the trailhead and parking area.

EMERALD CANYON

WILLOW CANYON, BOMMER RIDGE, EMERALD CANYON TRAILS
From Visitor Center to Emerald Canyon is 9 miles round trip

With its venerable oaks, sandstone outcroppings and even a seasonal waterfall, Emerald Canyon is the jewel in the crown of Laguna Coast Wilderness Park.

When you're out hiking the park's ridges, and gaze out at the not-so-far-away Toll Road and the surrounding suburbanopolis, you might start to think Laguna Coast is a "Wilderness" in name only. Ah, but when you descend into the park's Emerald Canyon, and lose all sights and sounds of OC civilization, you experience the wilderness in the park's name.

When you study the park map, you may wonder why you can't simply hike up Emerald Canyon from the bottom (Laguna Beach) mouth of the canyon. Yes, it would be a much easier way to experience Emerald Canyon's charms than the trek I describe from the top down. Unfortunately, at this time, there is no legal public access to the canyon from this direction.

I've charted a fairly direct course to Emerald Canyon, but a number of longer, return options are available to the curious hiker. My mileage figure presumes you might wish to return to the visitor center via Laurel Canyon. If you want to return the way you came—by way of Willow Canyon—subtract 0.75 mile from the hike distance.

Big sky country at Laguna Coast Wilderness Park.

DIRECTIONS TO TRAILHEAD: From the San Diego Freeway (405) in Irvine, a few miles north of this freeway's junction with the Santa Ana Freeway (5), exit on Laguna Canyon Road (133) and head south toward the coast and Laguna Beach. Look for the main (Laurel Canyon) entrance to the park on the right (west) side of the road.

THE HIKE: From the park visitor center, take signed Willow Canyon Trail (a dirt road) and soon leave the shady part of the canyon behind and make a rather steep ascent up the south canyon wall. About 1.5 miles from the trailhead, you'll reach a ridgeline junction. A connector trail leads right to Laurel Canyon, but you continue straight (south) 0.1 miles to a signed junction with Bommer Ridge Road. Hike right another 0.1 mile and look left for Emerald Canyon Road (more of a trail, really).

After a mile-long descent on the sage-scented trail (steep in places), you reach the bottom of Emerald Canyon. Notice Old Emerald Trail taking off to the left (east), but continue your descent down-canyon on the road. Travel the oak- and sycamore-lined road past grassy pocket meadows that invite a picnic.

A bit more than a mile and a half from the junction with Old Emerald Trail, watch for a waterfall on the right. The rainfall-generated 20-footer is a real looker after a few days of precipitation; otherwise, it's a dry-fall. This is a good turnaround point because Emerald Canyon Road descends steeply from here to a locked gate and a no-exit point for hikers.

Retrace your steps back to Old Emerald Trail and take this narrow path across a footbridge. Next you'll tackle a quite steep mile-long ascent of Emerald Canyon's east wall. Phew!

When the trail intersects Bommer Ridge Road, catch your breath, enjoy the views from atop the ridge and head north. As the road curves left, look left down at Emerald Canyon and bid it adieu, then meet Willow Canyon Road for the descent back to the trailhead. (You can also take the left-forking connector trail over to Laurel Canyon and descend lovely Laurel Canyon Trail back to the visitor center and trailhead.)

LAGUNA COAST OVERLOOK

BOAT SPUR TRAIL
From Dartmoor Gate to Laguna Coast Overlook is 2 miles round trip with 400-foot elevation gain

If The Trailmaster had his way, Laguna Coast Wilderness Park would have its own "Mountains to Sea" Trail that would connect Laguna Beach and the Laguna Hills. Alas, hikers cannot saunter from between Laguna's two lovely landscapes.

Perhaps the next best thing is to start hiking from a trailhead near the coast and ascend to great coastal vistas. To hike up Boat Canyon Trail is to ascend Laguna's greenbelt to look down at its blue belt. Let me explain.

The city of Laguna Beach, which has so far managed to preserve more than a thousand acres of open space in the city's hillsides and canyon comprising its greenbelt, also has been an effective advocate and steward for its "blue belt"—the 6.3 miles of city coastline. The entire coastline is considered part of the city's open space and is designated a marine left refuge.

And Laguna has been vigilant in protecting creatures great and small including the many sea lions hauling out on Sear Rock. Glenn E. Vedder Ecological Reserve, which extends north from Main Beach to Divers Cove, protects the Laguna's abundant marine life. The entire city of Laguna Beach was designated a bird refuge more than two decades ago.

Take this lovely little hike on fog-free mornings or near sunset. And you want to know a secret? I love the hike up Boat Canyon to connect with Bommer Ridge and then down into Emerald Canyon. (See the Emerald Canyon hike write-up in this guide.)

DIRECTIONS TO TRAILHEAD: From Pacific Coast Highway (1) in Laguna Beach, a mile or so up-coast from Laguna Canyon Road (133), turn inland on San Joaquin Street and drive one block to Hillcrest Drive. Turn right then, make a quick left onto Dartmoor Street, which you follow to its end at the gated fire road. Find curbside parking along Dartmoor.

THE HIKE: Begin your ascent on the fire road, which briefly extends east before bending north. The coastal vistas get better and better as you climb.

Your Boat Spur intersects Boat Road. Here you make a sharp left and make your way to the viewpoint. You can return the same way or continue north up the main Boat Road to a junction with Laguna Bowl Road. (See Irvine Bowl hike write-up). You could then descend to Irvine Bowl and Laguna Canyon Road by downtown Laguna Beach and improvise your way by commercial/residential streets back to the trailhead.

IRVINE BOWL PARK & BEYOND

WATER TANK, LAGUNA BOWL TRAILS
Loop from Irvine Bowl Park is 3.8 miles round trip with 600-foot elevation gain

Irvine Bowl Park hosts Laguna Beach's internationally acclaimed Festival of the Arts and Pageant of the Masters. The late James Irvine II, widely recognized as a pioneer rancher and major Orange County landowner, was also a patron of the arts and donated the six-acre bowl site to Laguna Beach in 1941.

During July and August, the bowl is the scene of theatrical re-creations of the world's great artworks. "Living pictures" of both classical and contemporary work are accompanied by a narrative and live orchestra. Irvine Bowl and its environs, now a city park, host other arts and cultural events during the year.

Take a walk on the wild side above Irvine Bowl Park for a good cardio work-out and fine coastal views. Fire roads make a horseshoe-shaped route around the bowl and you complete the route by strolling the sidewalks of Laguna Beach.

Parking is at a premium in Laguna Beach so if you find a good space in the downtown area, consider walking to the trailhead.

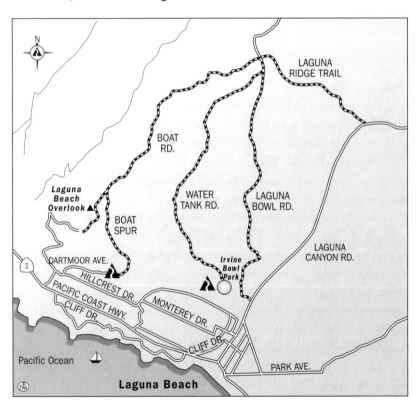

On the trail to the overlook.

DIRECTIONS TO TRAILHEAD: From the San Diego Freeway (405) in Irvine, a few miles north of this freeway's junction with the Santa Ana Freeway (5), exit on Laguna Canyon Road (133) and head south toward the coast and Laguna Beach. Look for the entrance to Irvine Bowl on the right (west) side of the road and then proceed another 0.25 mile to Acacia Drive. Turn right and make a second, very quick right on High Drive and proceed another 0.25 mile to Poplar Street. Turn right and look for parking along the street. The hike begins at the gated fire road at the end of Poplar Street.

THE HIKE: After stretching to get those leg muscles loose, launch yourself up an extremely steep paved road and ascend a few hundred yards to a fence-surrounded water tank and cellphone towers. Bear right on a dirt track and soon connect with Water Tank Road. About a half mile from the trailhead you'll enter Laguna Coast Wilderness Park and continue another mile onward and upward to a junction with another dirt road.

To the left (north) the road is known as Bommer Ridge Road, and is the main ridge-running route across Laguna Coast Wilderness Park. If you were to head left, you would soon connect with Boat Road (see Laguna Beach Overlook hike description).

But you turn right on the road, on the leg known as Laguna Bowl Road and hike south along the ridge. After about 0.75 mile, stay right at a fork, and plummet down past the fenced-off Irvine Bowl to Laguna Canyon Road.

Extend your outing by walking into town for food or refreshment. Otherwise you repeat the driving route to the trailhead: Walk coastward 0.25 on the sidewalk by Laguna Canyon Road to Acacia Drive, Turn right and then make a quick right onto High Drive and walk another 0.25 mile to Poplar Street. Turn right and retrace your steps back to your vehicle.

JAMES DILLEY PRESERVE

CANYON, EDISON, TO THE LAKE TRAILS
From Laguna Canyon Road to Barbara's Lake is 3.5-mile loop with 300-foot elevation gain

Lakes are few and far between in Orange County, and for the most part are decorative contrivances created for city parks, golf courses and suburban neighborhoods.

Orange County's only natural lakes are the Laguna Lakes in Laguna Canyon. The largest of the three lakes is delightful to visit, particularly for the hiker, because it's accessible only by a trail through the engaging James Dilley Preserve.

Early maps referred to the lakes as *laguna*, Spanish for pond, while modern maps generally opt for the rather redundant Laguna Lakes. The lakes are replenished by rainfall and possibly some water from underground springs.

Barbara's Lake, largest of the lakes, honors conservation activist Barbara Stuart. Fringed by bulrush, cattail and willows, the lake offers habitat for coots, grebes and mallards.

From the preserve's high points, hikers get good views of Bubbles Lake, named for the hippopotamus named Bubbles who escaped from Lion Country Safari in the mid-1970s and took up residence in the little lake located on the west side of Laguna Canyon Road. For a time, the wayward hippo eluded capture, staying underwater by day and emerging only at night. Alas for Bubbles, she was shot

OC ranger tends to a Dilley of a Preserve.

68

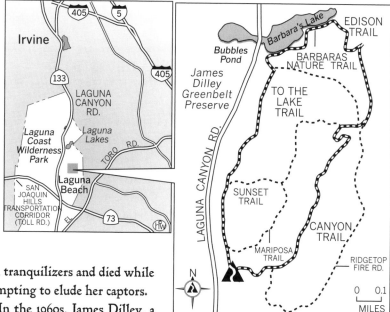

with tranquilizers and died while attempting to elude her captors.

In the 1960s, James Dilley, a Laguna Beach bookseller, began promoting his vision: the creation of a band of parks and preserves surrounding Laguna Beach. Dilley's notion of a greenbelt ringing the coastal town was enthusiastically supported by local conservationists, and a broad cross-section of the community.

Thanks to "The Father of the Greenbelt," plus four decades of cooperative efforts among conservation groups, park agencies and the area's major landowner, the Irvine Company, Laguna Beach is green on three sides and Pacific blue on the fourth. All Southland communities should be so fortunate!

The preserve, owned by the city and managed by the county's parks department was established in 1978 and is the oldest portion of Laguna Coast Wilderness Park. Spearheaded by the nonprofit Laguna Canyon Foundation, conservation efforts continue in order to expand the park, preserve other hills and canyons, and open up the greenbelt to increased public use.

The preserve is something of an island on the land. It's bordered by Laguna Canyon Road on the west, El Toro Road and Leisure World on the east and the San Joaquin Hills Transportation Corridor (toll road) on the south. The Laguna Lakes form the preserve's north boundary. James Dilley Preserve's "islandness" is apparent from looking at the map and even more obvious when contemplating the landscape from atop the preserve's ridges.

Canyon Trail, part of my suggested loop around the preserve, is the first leg of a nature trail with numbered wooden markers keyed to an interpretive pamphlet

One-time bookseller James Dilley artistically immortablized in park that bears his name.

(sometimes available at the trail-head). The pamphlet is by no means necessary to enjoy the hike.

DIRECTIONS TO TRAILHEAD: From the San Diego Freeway (405) in Irvine, exit onto the Laguna Freeway (133), which soon becomes Laguna Canyon Road. Drive south miles to the signed entrance for James Dilley Preserve on the left (east) side of the road and park in the dirt lot. The preserve entrance is just north of San Joaquin Hills Transportation Corridor (toll road).

THE HIKE: From the parking area, take the dirt road east and soon join Canyon Trail. The path swings north up the canyon, which is lined with coastal live oak and sycamore, white sage, black sage and buckwheat.

Leaving the moist canyon bottom, the path climbs higher slopes with a change in elevation to prickly pear cactus, lemonadeberry and monkeyflower. Near a ridgeline the path forks. The left branch, sometimes called the Eagle Scout Trail, descends south toward the trailhead.

Continue up the remains of a dirt road to the top of the hill and you'll see a gravel road leading downhill west toward Laguna Canyon Road and a steep Edison fire road Edison Trail) heading north. I prefer taking the Edison Trail for the views, which can include the San Gabriel Mountains on a clear winter day.

The more immediate view from the trail is of Orange County's largest natu-ral lake, with a surface area of about 12 acres. Cattle grazed the slopes back of the lake for more than 150 years.

Barbara's Nature Trail, another interpretive trail, leads along the lakeshore to an old pump house, and an intersection with To The Lake Trail, which heads south, parallel to Laguna Canyon Road back to the trailhead.

Crystal Cove State Park

Extending more than three miles along the coast between
Laguna Beach and Corona del Mar, and inland over the
San Joaquin Hills, the 3,000-acre park is a great place
to take a hike. Bold bluffs, sandy beaches and coves
are some of the highlights of the park's coastline,
and such attractions as Pelican Point, Reef Point and
Moro Beach, plus the Crystal Cove Historical District,
a collection of vintage coastal cottages dating from
the 1920s and 1930s, some of which are now available
as overnight accommodations. The park's backcountry
boasts a terrific trail system, with a "must hike" trail
through Moro Canyon, the main
watershed of the park.

CRYSTAL COVE BEACH AND BLUFFS

CRYSTAL COVE TRAIL
From Reef Point to Pelican Point is 4 miles round trip (shorter and longer options possible)

Between the Pacific Coast Highway and the wide blue Pacific, and between Laguna Beach and Newport Beach, lie the beautiful blufftops of Crystal Cove State Park.

A paved, multi-use path extends along most of the 3.2-mile length of the bluffs. (This is the rare bike path used by far more pedestrians than cyclists, most of whom opt for traveling the bike lane alongside PCH.) Eight connector trails—dirt and paved ones as well as a boardwalk—invite the hiker to leave the main route and explore tide pools, rocky coves and sand strands and check such intriguingly named topography as Pelican Point and Little Treasure Cove.

Be sure to detour from Bluff Trail through Los Trancos Canyon to the Crystal Cove Historical District. The funky wood-frame beach houses are in marked contrast to Newport Coast, the upscale community of luxury villas and custom homes arising on the inland side of the highway.

At low tide, the beach is passable; with judicious use of a tide table, the hiker can travel the bluffs one way and the beach the other. This beach attracts its share

The real thing: California beach culture at Crystal Cove.

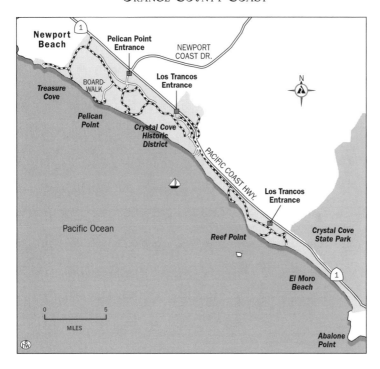

of surfers, swimmers and sun-bathers but still gives the feeling of being away from it all and by no means resembles one of SoCal's mass use sandlots.

Park boundaries extend beyond the tideline A portion of Crystal Cove's waters are protected in an underwater park, which attracts divers. Local conservationists planted kelp to provide habitat for the native marine life.

Bottlenose dolphins are frequently sighted in these waters and even been known to give birth here. The creatures form birthing circles, a marvelous natural drama to witness should you be so lucky.

DIRECTIONS TO TRAILHEAD: Crystal Cove State Park's Reef Point entrance is located off Pacific Coast Highway, three miles north of Laguna Canyon Road in Laguna Beach and 3.5 miles south of MacArthur Boulevard in Newport Beach.

The park's Pelican Point Entrance boasts four parking lots, each with restrooms. At the Los Trancos entrance, a parking area on the inland side of PCH and a pedestrian tunnel leading under the highway facilitate access to the Crystal Cove Historical District.

THE HIKE: Walk up-coast on the Bluff Trail. Our first invitation to visit the beach comes in the form of a stairway that descends to popular Scotchman's Cove.

The Reef Point area is a native plant-lover's paradise. Saltbush, toyon, buckwheat, California sagebrush, mulefat, coast prickly pear, deer weed, lemonade

73

berry, coyote bush and encelia. Of course, plenty of non-natives cling to the bluff tops, too, including scads of ice plant, Australian salt bush and mustard.

Bluff Trail travels close to PCH (a little too close in this hiker's opinion) and delivers you to the counter of the Shake Shack, located on the bluffs above Crystal Cove. This roadside refreshment stand has been a landmark to locals and coastal travelers since 1945. It was recently purchased by Ruby's Diner, repainted, and had its menu revamped. Rumor has it that the old favorites live on, however, and those in the know still order the ever-popular Monkey Flip, the Date Shake, or even a peanut butter, banana, and honey sandwich.

A bit beyond the Shake Shack, you'll spot the service road that descends to

Crystal Cove Historic District. Most of the cottages on Crystal Cove's beach and bluffs were built in the 1920s and 1930s. Families added-on to these vacation homes, enlarging them a little at a time—decks, bedrooms, second stories. The landowner, the Irvine Company, required the cottage owners to either move their beachside domiciles or lease them back from the company. Most took the lease option, which had the (perhaps unintended result) of effectively protecting the cottages and keeping this unique SoCal beach architecture frozen in time.

In 1979, California State Parks acquired the Crystal Cove area as parkland, and the cottages as well. Several cottages have been renovated, frozen in time with vintage furnishings and historical details. Since mid-2006 they've been in high demand as vacation getaways. The Beachcomber Café is also located here.

Crystal Cove is a very pretty place; however, it's not a cove and there appears to be no coastal indentation of any kind here. Certainly it's no more crystalline-appearing than any other Southland beach.

Back on Bluff Trail, the hiker is soon tempted with more trails leading down to Crystal Cove and a boardwalk descending to Pelican Point. Continue to the edge of the blufftops at the park boundary and curve coastward to join View Point Path. Enjoy vistas from above Little Treasure Cove and Treasure Cove.

Return to the Reef Point parking area and trailhead the way you came or via the beach. To extend your walk from Reef Point, descend the bluffs on a steep path leading to Scotchman's Cove. Head down-coast along El Moro Beach, long lined by a trailer park. The trailers are scheduled to be removed from the state park. A future state park campground will be connected to this beach by a tunnel under the coast highway.

Emerald Bay Viewpoint

EMERALD RIDGE TRAIL

From Park Visitor Center to Emerald Bay Viewpoint is 3.5 miles round trip with 500-foot elevation gain; return via Moro Canyon is 5 miles round trip

All of Crystal Cove State Park's ridgelines offer inspiring Pacific views, but surely the grandest of panoramas are to be found from a perch atop Moro Ridge. Emerald Bay and Laguna Beach are the most obvious sights to see from this little lookout located less than a half mile as the seagull flies from the Pacific breakers.

That's just a start. Down-coast lie Dana Point, Point Loma and, south of the border, Mexico's Coronado Islands. Santa Clemente floats gently on the seas to the southwest while Catalina, looking quite rugged and mountainous, rises boldly in your face in the west. Up-coast, the Palos Verdes Peninsula, too, rises dramatically above the shoreline. On particularly clear days the Santa Monica Mountains and the Ventura County coastline are visible.

You might expect a considerable trek to a high elevation peak to get such a view, but no, the hiker gains this awesome vista with a very modest climb to a promontory that measures but 594 feet above sea level. Sea is certainly an operative word here because you see so much of it, as well as some 200 miles of coastline, from the vista point.

The point has two distinctly utilitarian functions—as an antennae site (small low ones) and as a reservoir site with some 400 thousand gallons of water stored underground.

DIRECTIONS TO TRAILHEAD: Crystal Cove State Park is located off Pacific Coast Highway, about two miles south of the town of Corona del Mar or one mile north of Laguna Beach. Turn inland on the park road, signed El Moro Canyon. Drinking water, restrooms, interpretive displays, park maps, a picnic area and plenty of parking are available at the visitor center. Check out the schedule of ranger- and docent-led interpretive walks, which explore both inland and coastal sections of the state park.

THE HIKE: From the visitor center, head down to the coastward side of the parking lot, join the fire road and file south past the El Morro School and also past a longtime trailer park currently in the process of conversion into a state park campground. The road drops into the canyon.

At a junction you meet a connector trail, long called BFI, and now referred to more lyrical Emerald Ridge Trail, which continues south, climbing steeply at first, then leveling and serving up good coastal views.

The path intersects Moro Ridge Trail at a spot, very low on the ridge (scarcely

0.1 mile above Pacific Coast Highway). Hike uphill on the steep road, which alternates between pavement and gravel, eventually deevolving into eroded dirt.

When you reach Moro Ridge, you'll travel to an unsigned road (paved for a short distance, then dirt) and then head coastward. Disbelieving that you're traveling downhill to get a good view, but that's the case. Savor the terrific views

Extend the hike to a 5mile or so loop by continuing another 0.8 mile up Moro Ridge to the East Cut Across Trail, descending to El Moro Canyon Trail and following this major route downcanyon and back to the trailhead parking lot.

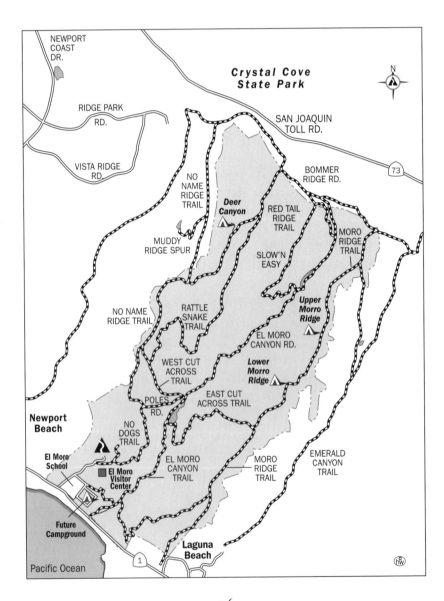

MORO CANYON

MORO CANYON TRAIL
From Park Headquarters to the top of Moro Canyon is 7 miles round trip
with 700-foot elevation gain

Extending three miles along the coast between Laguna Beach and Corona del
Mar, and inland over the San Joaquin Hills, 3,000-acre Crystal Cove State Park
attracts bird-watchers, beachcombers and hikers.

The backcountry of Crystal Cove State Park is part of the San Joaquin Hills,
first used by Mission San Juan Capistrano for grazing land. Cattle raising continued under José Sepúlveda when the area became part of his land grant, Rancho
San Joaquín, in 1837. In 1864, Sepúlveda sold the land to James Irvine and his
partners and it became part of his Irvine Ranch. Grazing continued until shortly
after the state purchased the property as parkland in 1979.

Former Irvine Ranch roads now form a network of hiking trails that loop
through the state park. An especially nice trail travels the length of Moro
Canyon, the main watershed of the park. An oak woodland, a seasonal stream and
sandstone caves are some of the attractions of a walk through this canyon. Bird-
watchers may spot the roadrunner, quail, Cooper's hawk, California thrasher,
wrentit and many more species.

After exploring inland portions of the state park, allow some time to visit the
park's coastline, highlighted by grassy bluffs, sandy beaches, tidepools and coves.
The Pelican Point, Crystal Cove, Reef Point and Moro Beach areas of the park
allow easy beach access.

DIRECTIONS TO TRAILHEAD: Crystal Cove State Park is located off
Pacific Coast Highway, about two miles south of the town of Corona del Mar or
one mile north of Laguna Beach. Turn inland on the short park road, signed "El
Moro Canyon." Drinking water, restrooms, interpretive displays and plenty of
parking is available at the ranger station.

THE HIKE: Below the ranger station, near the park entry kiosk pick up the
unsigned Moro Canyon Trail, which crosses the grassy slopes behind a school and
former trailer park down into Moro Canyon. At the canyon bottom, you meet a
fire road and head left, up-canyon.

The hiker may observe such native plants as black sage, prickly pear cactus,
monkeyflowers, golden bush, lemonade berry and deer weed. Long before Spanish
missionaries and settlers arrived in Southern California, a Native American population flourished in the coastal canyons of Orange County. The abundance of
edible plants in the area, combined with the mild climate and easy access to the

A fine place to hike—and bike. Be forewarned that mountain bikers usually
outnumber hikers in Moro Canyon.

bounty of the sea, contributed to the success of these people, whom anthropolo-
gists believe lived off this land for more than four thousand years.

The canyon narrows, and you ignore fire roads joining Moro Canyon from
the right and left. Stay in the canyon bottom and proceed through an oak woodland, which shades a trickling stream. You'll pass a shallow sandstone cave just off
the trail to the right.

About 2.5 miles from the trailhead, you'll reach the unsigned junction with a
fire road. If you wish to make a loop trip out of this day hike, bear left on this
road, which climbs steeply west, then northeast toward the ridgetop that forms a
kind of inland wall for Muddy, Moro, Emerald and other coastal canyons.

When you reach the ridgetop, unpack your lunch and enjoy the far reaching
views of the San Joaquin Hills and Orange County coast, Catalina and San
Clemente Islands. You'll also have a raven's-eye view of Moro Canyon and the
route back to the trailhead. After catching your breath, you'll bear right (east)
along the ridgetop and quickly descend back into Moro Canyon. A 0.75-mile walk
brings you back to the junction where you earlier ascended out of the canyon. This
time you continue straight down-canyon, retracing your steps to the trailhead.

NO NAME RIDGE

NO NAME RIDGE TRAIL
Loop from El Moro Visitor Center to Moro Canyon is 3.5 miles round trip
with 300-foot elevation gain; to Deer Canyon Campground is 7 miles round
trip with 600-foot gain

The classic family hike, a great introduction to the park, the interpretive walk led
by rangers is the jaunt from the visitor center up No Name Ridge and a return
via the park's main thoroughfare, Moro Canyon.

It offers a sampling of the park's natural attractions including great views,
descends a shrub-smothered slopes of lower Moro Canyon, then along the Moro
Creek watershed lined by oak, sycamore and willows.

A longer loop offers even better views, as well as a visit to a backcountry
campground.

A word of appreciation for the park's trail signs that appear at the most critical backcountry junctions. Complete with the "You are Here" dot, they make this
park easier to navigate, although it's relatively easy to navigate to begin with.
Moro Canyon is in the middle, which you can see from the trails on the ridge
above the canyon.

A distinct ridgetop on the San Joaquin Hills marks the northern boundary,
the ocean the south boundary. Moro Ridge is on the east and No Name Ridge on
the west. I guess they could have called the ridges East Moro Ridge and West
Moro Ridge, but then again,
there are already too many park
features with Moro in the name.

Perhaps no-name ridge should
be named, as have the other trails,
with such colorful names. It's fun
to guess how some of these names
came into being. Sure enough,
Poles Road is lined with poles.
Perhaps Ticketron Trail that leads
to Deer Canyon Campground
takes the company name of the

"No Dogs Trail" – Guess how this pathway got its
name? Actually dogs aren't allowed on State Park trails.

former state park campsite reservation service. Slow 'n Easy and Mach One are no
doubt suggestive of the speeds realized by the mountain bikers who use them.

DIRECTIONS TO TRAILHEAD: Crystal Cove State Park is located off
Pacific Coast Highway, about two miles south of the town of Corona del Mar or

one mile north of Laguna Beach. Turn inland on the short park road, signed "El Moro Canyon." Drinking water, restrooms, interpretive displays and plenty of (fee) parking is available by the ranger station.

THE HIKE: Head up No Name Ridge Trail, the first part of which is still popularly referred to as No Dogs Trail. Enjoy the views from the ridge up and down Moro Canyon as well as over your shoulder back to the coast. The path wastes no time climbing to a junction with Poles Road.

Those of you opting for the short loop, should descend this absurdly steep road down to Moro Canyon. Enjoy tramping El Moro Canyon Trail on a gentle descent to a connector trail that in turn leads back to El Moro Visitor Center and the trailhead parking lot.

Those bound for the park's upper heights will continue the brisk ascent up No Name Ridge. Rising in French Riviera-fashion on the eastern park boundary above Muddy Canyon is the new community of Newport Coast.

At a signed junction, a narrow path descends steeply to the bottom of Deer Canyon, then heads north, up-canyon to pleasant Deer Canyon Campground. Relax at one of the picnic tables, then rise steeply, but briefly, on the connector path leading to Red Tail Ridge Trail. Turn right, south, on the narrow ridgetop path, which offers grand vistas of the parks, and the hills and canyons up and down the coast.

Red Trail Ridge Trail merges into Rattlesnake Trail, which descends the ridge into Deer Canyon, then rises again to meet West Cut Across Trail. Turn left, southeast for the brief descent into Moro Canyon. You can follow the park's main thoroughfare (as described above) back to the visitor center or get your motor running and ascend the very steep, but mercifully brief Poles Road to regain No Name Ridge Trail. Enjoy the great coastal vistas as you retrace your steps down No Name Ridge back to the trailhead.

CORONA DEL MAR

CROWN OF THE SEA TRAIL
From Corona del Mar Beach to Arch Rock is 2 miles round trip; to Crystal Cove is 4 miles round trip; to Abalone Point is 7 miles round trip

In 1904, George Hart purchased 700 acres of land on the cliffs east of the entrance to Newport Bay and laid out a subdivision he called Corona del Mar ("Crown of the Sea"). The only way to reach the townsite was by way of a long muddy road that circled around the head of Upper Newport Bay. Later a ferry carried tourists and residents from Balboa to Corona del Mar. Little civic improvement occurred until Highway 101 bridged the bay and the community was annexed to Newport Beach.

This hike explores the beaches and marine refuges of "Big" and Little Corona del Mar beaches and continues to the beaches and headlands of Crystal Cove State Park. Snorkeling is good beneath the cliffs of "Big" and Little Corona beaches. Both areas are protected from boat traffic by kelp beds and marine refuge status.

Consult a tide table. Best beach-walking is at low tide.

DIRECTIONS TO TRAILHEAD: From Pacific Coast Highway in Corona del Mar, turn oceanward on Marguerite Avenue and travel a few blocks to

"Little Corona": Known for its gentle surf and excellent tide pools.

Play by the rules to protect Little Corona.

Ocean Boulevard. Turn right and you'll soon spot the entrance to the Corona del Mar State Beach parking lot.

THE HIKE: Begin at the east jetty of Newport Beach, where you'll see sailboats tacking in and out of the harbor. Surfers tackle the waves near the jetty. Proceed down-coast along wide, sandy Corona del Mar State Beach.

At the south end of the beach, take the paved walkway and ascend to Inspiration Point, an overlook offering excellent views of the Orange County coast. Continue down-coast a few blocks on the sidewalk alongside Ocean Boulevard to the walkway leading down to Little Corona Beach. Highlight of this beach is well-named Arch Rock, which is just offshore and can be reached at very low tide.

The beach from Arch Rock to Irvine Cove, 2.5 miles to the south, is passable at low tide and is part of Crystal Cove State Park. Trails lead up the bluffs which, in winter, offer a good vantage point from which to observe the California gray whale migration.

Continuing your stroll down the undeveloped beach and past some tidepools brings you to the onetime resort community of Crystal Cove, site of a few dozen funky beach cottages. The wood frame cottages, little altered since their construction in the 1920s are on the National Register of Historic Places. Some of the cottages are restored and rented out by the night by advance reservation only as vacation getaways.

While "Cove" is something of a misnomer here because the beach here shows almost no coastal indentation, it sure is a pretty place. Rounding Reef Point, you'll continue along El Moro Beach, a sand strand that's sometimes beautifully cusped. The state park is transforming what was once a beach lined with private trailers into a day use area with beach access from a campground and the other side of Highway 1.

El Moro is a misspelling of the Spanish word *moro*, meaning round, and describes the round dome of Abalone Point, which lies dead ahead. The point, a

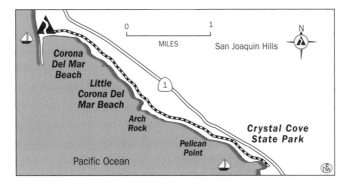

rocky promontory located just outside Laguna Beach city limits, is made of eroded lava and other volcanic material distributed in the San Joaquin Hills. It's capped by a grass-covered dome rising two hundred feet above the water.

Return the same way or ascend one of the coastal accessways to the blufftops of Crystal Cove State Park. Blufftop trails offer a scenic alternative for a portion of your return route.

BALBOA ISLAND

BALBOA BEACH TRAIL
From Newport Pier to Balboa Island is 3 miles round trip

Miles of sandy beach, one of California's largest pleasure craft harbors, and some colorful coastal history are attractions of a walk along Balboa Beach. Balboa—the town, beach and island—was long ago (1906) incorporated into the city of Newport Beach, but has managed to hold onto a different look, feel, vibe than chic Newport.

Local boosters and real estate promoters built the Balboa Pier and Balboa Pavilion in 1905 with hopes of luring both tourists and well-heeled settlers. They succeeded on both counts. Today, Balboa's sand strand hosts huge crowds of surfers and sunworshipers and as one harbor cruise company boasts, "You'll see some of the most expensive coastal real estate in the world."

On the Balboa beach-hike you'll also encounter two historic piers and a chance to take the ferry to Balboa Island.

For those weekend warriors who scoff at the mere 3-mile round trip distance between Newport Pier and Balboa Pier, I recommend starting your beach-walk at popular Huntington State Beach, 3 miles north.

If you trek this longer option, you'll begin your 10-mile hike by heading down-coast on Huntington Beach, once called Shell Beach because millions of

Balboa's Fun Zone – more serious with the addition of the Newport Harbor Nautical Museum.

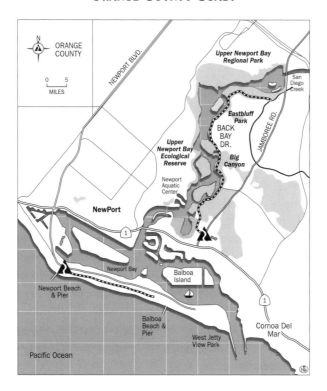

small bean clams were washed up on its sands. In recent years, Pismo clamming has undergone something of a revival here.

At the south end of the beach you'll cross the Santa Ana River on the coast highway bridge. Formerly, the river emptied into the ocean at Newport Bay, but was diverted to shore at this point in order to reduce silting after the bay became a great yacht harbor. Next you'll head shoreward over some sand dunes on the east side of the river, then walk down-coast on Santa Ana River County Beach to Newport Pier.

DIRECTIONS TO TRAILHEAD: Head southwest on the Costa Mesa Freeway (Highway 55) toward Newport Beach. In Costa Mesa, the highway empties out onto Newport Boulevard, which you'll follow to its end a the beach. Just as Newport Boulevard angles sharply southeast and puts you on Balboa Boulevard, you'll spot Newport Pier and a number of parking lots. Parking in these parts is mostly metered. Beware that some of the meters give you only an hour; you'll need more time to enjoy this hike.

THE HIKE: Begin at the historic Newport Pier, oldest in Southern California. A wharf built here in 1888 served as a railway shipping point for Orange County produce. The railroad also carried passengers here from Santa Ana and helped foster the development of the city of Newport Beach.

In 1889, the Newport Dory fishing fleet began working the waters off Balboa Peninsula. The fishermen are still at it, still headquartered at the foot of what's officially known as Newport's McFadden Wharf. Each dawn, the fleet heads out to sea and returns to the pier in mid-morning to sell its catch of rock fish and sea bass, crab and lobster. The site is a City Historical Landmark.

Walk down-coast along the beach. The beach, particularly the stretch north of the pier looks like a quintessential postcard-perfect promised sand, but has occasionally suffered from erosion and lack of sand. Orange County's inland building booms diverted many streams from their normal paths to the sea; the streams were unable to perform their natural function of carrying a cargo of sand to the Pacific. More sand is lost to the Newport Submarine Canyon, located just offshore.

About 1.5 miles of beach-walking brings you to the Balboa Pier, where a plaque commemorates the site of the first water-to-water flight in 1912. Glenn L. Martin flew a hydroplane from the waters here to Avalon Bay at Catalina Island.

Near the pier is Peninsula Park with picnic tables. Walk into town on Main Street, crossing East Balboa Boulevard and coming to the marina. Harbor tour companies are based here. You can join a short cruise of Newport Harbor or do it yourself by renting a pedal-boat or kayak.

Walk along the historic Balboa boardwalk. Remodeling and new construction have obliterated most of the the early building prompted by the extension of electric railway service from Los Angeles in 1905. Still standing is that landmark of Victorian architecture, the Balboa Pavilion. The Pavilion has served as a Pacific Electric Railway Terminal, a seaside recreation center and a 1940s dancehall. Next to the Pavilion is the longtime home of the Fun Zone, a small collection of rides and arcades, beloved in these parts since 1936. Plans to replace the Fun Zone with the Newport Harbor Nautical Museum are in the works—but the new property owners promise to save at least the Ferris Wheel.

From the foot of Palm Street, right along the boardwalk, you can catch the Balboa Ferry, which runs frequently. Ferry service was inaugurated in 1907 by a genial African-American boatman named John Watts, who encouraged his open launch, *The Teal,* with great draughts from an oil can. Today's small auto ferries make the 200-yard or so voyage in fewer than five minutes.

On Balboa Island, you can follow a scenic boardwalk to boat slips and small sandy beaches. Balboa Island had its beginning in 1906 when W.S. Collins dredged bay mud onto a sand flat that appeared in Newport Bay during low tide. He subdivided the island and buy 1914, more than one-half the 1,300 lots were sold.

After you've enjoyed the island, take the ferry back to the peninsula and return the same way.

BONITA CANYON

BONITA CANYON TRAIL
From Ford Park to Arroyo Park is 1.5 mile round trip with foot elevation gain

The path traversing Newport Beach's Bonita Canyon is very much a "neighbor-hood trail." While it's likely to appeal to those who live nearby and are looking for an after-dinner stroll, it's unlikely to draw hikers from other OC locales.

Still, there are two sights-to-see: A small waterfall tumbling into a grotto, and the many mud swallow nests stuck high up on the underside of the Bonita Canyon Road overpass.

DIRECTIONS TO TRAILHEAD: From the San Diego Freeway (405), take Highway 73 south and, shortly before the highway turns tollway, exit on MacArthur Boulevard. Head south 0.8 mile to Bonita Canyon Road. Turn left and drive over the Bonita Canyon bridge and make a right on Mesa View. Turn right on Ford Road. Not far past the ballfields and restrooms (but before the phone company building) look for roadside parking and the trailhead on your right.

THE HIKE: The path plunges very steeply into the canyon. Keep an eye out for the little waterfall and grotto just off a lower switchback. This neglected spot could be pretty but is often graffiti-marred and the water is polluted.

The path continues under the Bonita Canyon Bridge (look up at those swallow nests), passes a junc-tion with a cement walkway com-ing down from the residences lin-ing the west side of the canyon, and ends at a paved walkway near a softball field.

Unlikely waterfall in Bonita Canyon.

87

NEWPORT'S BACK BAY

BACK BAY TRAIL
Along Upper Newport Bay Ecological Reserve is 3.5 miles one way

Southern California's coastal wetlands have suffered severely from the pressures of the expanding metropolis but one wetland, partially spared from development, is Upper Newport Bay in Orange County. In 1974, Orange County and the Irvine Company reached an agreement calling for public ownership of Upper Newport Bay, most of which has become a state-operated ecological reserve.

The Upper Bay is a marked contrast to the huge marina complex, one of the world's largest yacht harbors, of the Lower Bay—developments once planned for the Upper Bay. The preservation of Upper Newport Bay is one of Southern California conservationists' success stories.

The wetland is a premiere bird-watching spot. Plovers stand motionless on one

leg, great blue herons pick their way carefully across the mudflats, flotillas of ducks patrol the shallows. Out of sight, mollusks, insects, fish and protozoa provide vital links in the complex food chain of the estuary.

This hike follows one-way Back Bay Road which really should be closed to motorized traffic. However, on weekdays, there's rarely much traffic and on weekends, there's seldom more auto traffic than bike traffic. The tideland is fragile; stay on established roads and trails.

DIRECTIONS TO TRAILHEAD: From Pacific Coast Highway in Newport Beach, turn inland onto Jamboree Road, then left on Back Bay Drive. The one-way road follows the margin of the bay. Park along the road.

Back Bay's feathered friends.

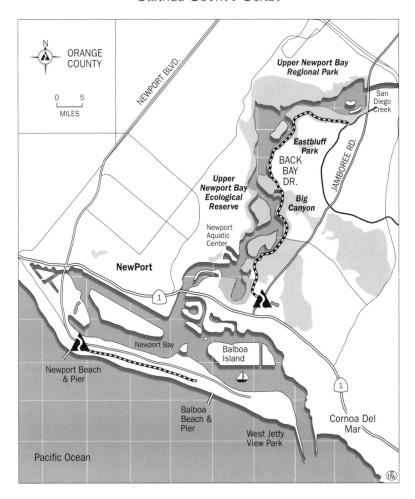

THE HIKE: As you walk along the road, notice the various vegetation zones. Eel grass thrives in areas of almost constant submergence, cord grasses at a few feet above mean low tide, salt wort and pickleweed higher on the banks of the estuary. Keep an eye out for three of California's endangered birds: Belding's Savannah Sparrow, the California least tern, the light-footed clapper rail.

Old levees and an occasional trail let you walk out toward the main bodies of water. Also, a trail from UC Irvine runs along the west side of the reserve.

UPPER NEWPORT BAY NATURE PRESERVE

WEST BLUFF TRAIL
From Interpretive Center to South Boundary is 2 miles round trip

Several hundred thousand visitors a year walk or cycle around Upper Newport Bay, but very few hike the trails on the west side of the bay. Upper Newport Bay Nature Preserve, which preserves the bluffs surrounding Upper Newport Bay, offers the hiker a special vantage point for observing one of the more pristine of Southern California's estuaries.

From the bluffs look down on birds that gather here in large numbers—more than 35,000. The estuary is home to nearly 200 species of birds, including several endagred ones. Three uncommon bird species have spotted by the bluffs, including the burrowing owl, San Diego cactus wren and the California gnatcatcher.

The interpretive center, built into the bluffs on the northwest side of Upper Newport Bay, offers great panoramic views to visitors, who learn about the bay and the California coast's precious wetlands from an excellent assemblage of exhibits and interactive displays. Kids enjoy Tunnel of Mud, a worm's eye view of the bay.

During the 1960s, conservationists rallied to thwart a developer's plan to use the bay for a waterskiing complex and to preserve the undeveloped portions of

The real OC: High-rises and wildlife reserves.

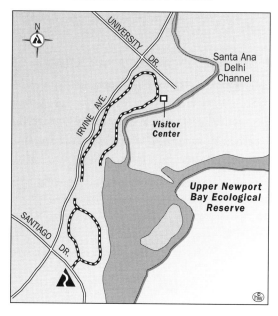

Upper Newport Bay. In later years, the bluffs on the northwest and north sides of the bay were added to a regional park, which in 2000 was rededicated as a preserve.

Numerous informal trails used to weave along the west side of the bay. Some of these trails have been closed off to restore native plant life, and for other ecological reasons. Please heed the signs.

DIRECTIONS TO TRAILHEAD: From the San Diego Freeway (405) southbound, take the 73 South and take the Campus/Irvine exit. Merge right and turn right on Irvine Avenue. Turn left on University Drive, then make the first right into the parking lot. The Peter & Mary Muth Interpretive Center is located at 2301 University Drive in Newport Beach

From the San Diego Freeway (405) northbound, exit on Jamboree and make a left. Turn right on Campus Drive, which becomes Irvine Avenue. Turn left on University Drive, then make the first right into the parking lot.

THE HIKE: From the visitor center, you can scope out the hiking trails. One path leads up to the blufftop by Irvine Avenue. Another path travels the base of the bluffs closer to water's edge.

I suggest following the sometimes muddy pathway at the base of the bluffs, which in places leads close to waters edge. Keep alongside the mudflats until either your forward progress is halted by mud, water or reaching the south boundary of the preserve and a residential area.

Return via the path atop the bluffs, which offer great views as well as interpretive signs that tell of the history and ecological complexity of the estuary.

SAN JOAQUIN WILDLIFE SANCTUARY

TREEHILL, SOUTH LOOP, MIDWAY TRAILS
2 mile loop; longer and shorter options possible

Long ago, freshwater wetlands spread over much of Orange County's floodplain, but few of these wetlands remains. One of the larger remaining marshlands in Southern California, the 200-acre San Joaquin Wildlife Sanctuary, owned by the Irvine Ranch Water District and managed by sanctuary staff and volunteers.

Size certainly matters in terms of supporting huge populations of birds, but not necessarily in attracting great numbers of species. SJWS's bird-list numbers more than 230 kinds of birds.

For about a hundred bird species, the marsh is a vital stopover on the Pacific Flyway. The sanctuary attracts a variety of ducks and more than 30 species of shorebirds. Birds attract more birds—raptors such as the red-tailed hawk and Coopers hawk, falcon, white-tailed kite and osprey.

On March 19 every year, the swallows actually return to . . . San Joaquin Marsh. While the arrival of these swallows is certainly far less heralded and cele-brated than that of the swallows returning to San Juan Capistrano, the (count 'em) five species of swallows that the skilled bird-watcher can distinguish on a spring day are quite a sight.

THE HIKE: Exercise walkers, birders and lunchtime strollers, as well as faculty and staff from the nearby University of California Irvine all have their favorite routes and parking places. If you looped every loop, you could walk 10 miles in the sanctuary.

The L-shaped preserve consists of some 18 man-made ponds of varying size. Five of the largest ponds are what's left of the historic freshwater marsh. Thirteen shallow duck ponds, originally constructed by a local hunting club.

The San Joaquin Gun Club leased what is now sanctuary land in the early 1900s from James Irvine and diverted water from San Diego Creek into a series of ponds.

Restoration efforts of the native flora and of the ponds and waterways began as far back as 1970, when the remnant San Joaquin Marsh was incorporated into the University of California Natural Reserve System, and continues today.

A sanctuary indeed, one that's all the more precious for its location—a 10-minute walk from UC Irvine and across the street from Fletcher Jones Motorcars, world's largest Mercedes-Benz dealer. More than once I've observed a graceful heron on the shoreline of a pond, while in the background a crane (a *building* crane) was at work on an office building.

One of my favorites is the true-to-its-name Treehill Trail that connects to two of the more enjoyable and better-signed paths are the 1.2-mile North Loop Trail and the 1.4-mile South Loop Trail.

DIRECTIONS TO THE TRAILHEAD: From the San Diego Freeway (405), exit on Jamboree Road and head south to Michelson Drive. Turn left. In just 0.25 mile, turn right on Carlson Avenue and park along the street. You'll spot the obvious signed entrance to the sanctuary.

To reach the east side of the sanctuary, you'll make the second right, on Riparian Avenue and follow it to a parking area. An information panel offers a map and natural history notes. Sometimes a sanctuary map-pamphlet is available at this trailhead.

TALBERT NATURE PRESERVE

TALBERT TRAIL
Loop around Talbert Nature Preserve from Fairview Park is 2 miles round trip

You don't need to be a Professor of Ecology to know it's better to preserve an ecosystem in its original state than restore it after it's been degraded. Still, while restoration is a far poorer choice than preservation, we who appreciate Orange County's natural environments can be appreciative of the considerable efforts made to restore the region's coastal areas.

Seen in this light, we can be thankful for Talbert Nature Preserve, a coastal wetland located alongside the Santa Ana River about a mile and a half inland

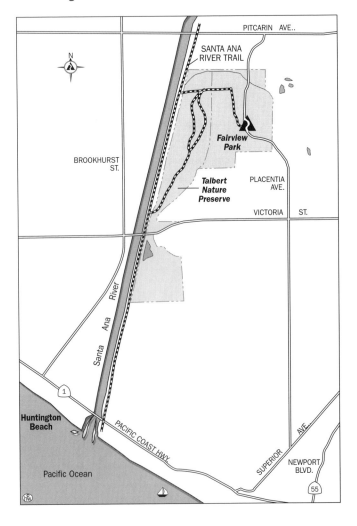

from Huntington Beach. Native plant communities, including grassland, wet-land, woodland and riparian, have been reintroduced to the Santa Ana River floodplain, and trails constructed to explore them. The northern part of the pre-serve has been "restored" and the southern section's re-vegetation process is underway.

Talbert Nature Preserve is mostly a locals-only attraction for joggers, exercise walkers and parents pushing strollers. Bird-watchers sight a considerable number of species, and even the most casual observer will observe the many waterfowl, including the great blue heron and snowy egret.

Cyclists—and some walkers—enter Talbert Nature Preserve via Santa Ana River Trail, which begins inland at Prado Dam in Corona and parallels both banks of the river to Highway 1 and the shore at Huntington Beach, just north of Newport Beach. A bridge over an adjacent storm channel allows passage from the bike path to the preserve.

From the preserve's main trail, side trails offer opportunities to meander amongst the native and introduced flora groupings; getting off the beaten path is also a way for increased solitude.

The best way for hikers to enter the preserve is by starting at Fairview Park, a mostly undeveloped blufftop park.

DIRECTIONS TO TRAILHEAD: From the San Diego Freeway (405) in Costa Mesa, exit on Harbor Boulevard. Head south a mile to Adams Avenue. Turn right and drive west a mile to Placentia Avenue. Turn left (south) and pro-ceed a half-mile to the park entrance and turn right into the parking lot.

THE HIKE: Dirt trails with interpretive signs ring Fairview Park. You can look down at lower Fairview Park which, like neighboring Talbert Nature Preserve, is part of the Santa Ana River and is also undergoing environmental rehab.

If you want to get right to it—that is to say go directly to Talbert Nature Preserve, begin on the paved path and follow it briefly and steeply downhill to the preserve, which welcomes you with drinking fountains, restrooms and an infor-mation kiosk.

Next take the wide gravel path south, skirting a bluff. Sand dunes, grasslands and shrub islands are among the ecological communities you'll pass as you traipse along the fenced trail.

Continuing south you'll intersect Santa Ana River Trail. If you follow the bikeway under Victoria Avenue, you'll discover a pond patrolled by mallards and other waterfowl. It's another mile or so walk to Pacific Coast Highway and to the beach, if you're so inclined.

HUNTINGTON AND BOLSA CHICA STATE BEACHES

HUNTINGTON BEACH TRAIL
From Huntington State Beach to Bolsa Chica State Beach is 6 miles round trip; to Bolsa Chica north boundary is 7.5 miles one way

Huntington and Bolsa Chica are the perfect locations for a beach party. They're wide and long, and dotted with numerous fire pits for summertime fun long after the sun has set. The state beaches (with Huntington City Beach sandwiched in the middle) extend some 9 miles along northern Orange County's coast, from the Santa Ana River to just-short of the San Gabriel River.

In many ways, Huntington/Bolsa Chica has always been a kind of blue-collar beach. Until Bolsa Chica beach came under state control in 1961, nobody did much to keep the beach clean—hence its once-popular name of Tin Can Beach. Despite a couple of boutiqued blocks where Main Street meets the shore, and some upscale subdivisions more in keeping with OC inland 'burbs, Huntington Beach still has rough edges, including bad-boy surfers and shoulder-to-shoulder oil wells.

Before Huntington Beach received its present name, the long shoreline was a popular camping spot. Millions of small clams were washed up on its sands and old timers called it Shell Beach. In 1901 a town was laid out with the name of Pacific City, in hopes it would rival Atlantic City. In 1902, Henry E. Huntington,

Oil wells everywhere—Bolsa Chica and Huntington Beach circa 1930s.

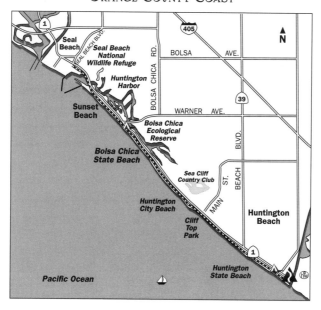

owner of the Pacific Electric Railroad, bought a controlling interest and renamed the city after himself. Today, though, it's known by the officially trademarked name, "Surf City USA."™

This hike takes you north along wide sandy Huntington State Beach to Bolsa Chica State Beach and adjacent Bolsa Chica Ecological Reserve. You can also make this a one-way jaunt by taking advantage of OCTD Bus #1 which makes several stops along Pacific Coast Highway.

This is an ideal beach trail to bike and hike. A bike path extends the length of Bolsa Chica Beach to the Santa Ana River south of Huntington Beach. You can leave your bike at Bolsa Chica State Beach and hike up to it from Huntington Beach.

DIRECTIONS TO TRAILHEAD: From the San Diego Freeway (405) in Huntington Beach, exit on Beach Boulevard and travel 5.5 miles south to the boulevard's end at Huntington State Beach.

THE HIKE: Walk north along the northernmost mile of the three-mile-long sandy state beach. The state beach blends into Huntington City Beach just before the pier. The beach is best known as the site of international surfing competition. Eighteen-hundred foot Huntington Pier was built in 1914.

Beyond the pier is Bolsa Chica State Beach. The southern end has steep cliffs rising between Pacific Coast Highway and the beach. Huntington Beach Mesa or "The Cliffs" is popular with surfers and oil well drillers.

The northern three miles of the beach packs in all the facilities: showers, food concessions, picnic areas and more.

BOLSA CHICA ECOLOGICAL RESERVE

BOLSA CHICA LAGOON TRAIL
3 miles round trip

Bolsa Chica Wetlands, a 1,800-acre tidal basin surrounded by the city of Huntington Beach, is one of Southern California's most valuable oceanfront properties. The somewhat degraded marshland was the scene of a long dispute between Signal Oil Company, the principal landholder, which desired to develop a marina and suburb and Amigos de Bolsa Chica, who wanted to preserve the marsh as a stopover for migratory birds on the Pacific Flyway and as habitat for endangered species.

For many centuries, the wetlands were the bountiful home of Indians until a Mission-era land grant gave retiring Spanish soldier Manuel Nieto title to a portion of Bolsa Chica. Although the coastal marsh proved useless for farming and ranching to Nieto and succeeding owners, the abundant wildlife attracted game hunters from all over Southern California. In order to stabilize their duck pond, they dammed off the ocean waters, thus starting the demise of the wetland.

During the 1920s, oil was discovered at Bolsa Chica. Dikes were built, water drained, wells drilled, roads spread across the marsh. In fact, oil production is scheduled to continue through the year 2020.

Portions of the marsh bordering Pacific Coast Highway have been restored by the state and are now part of an ecological reserve under Department of Fish and Game management. This loop trail takes you on a tour of the most attractive section. Bring your binoculars. Bird-watching is often quite good here.

DIRECTIONS TO TRAIL-HEAD: Bolsa Chica Ecological Reserve is located just opposite the main entrance of Bolsa Chica State Beach on Pacific Coast Highway. From the San Diego Freeway

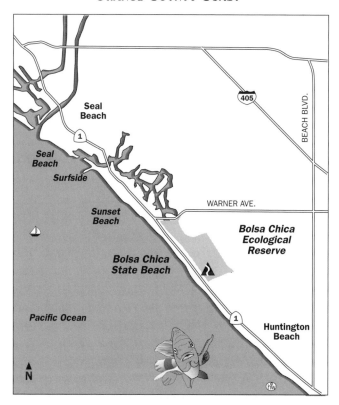

(405), exit on Beach Boulevard and follow it to the beach. Head north on Pacific Coast Highway for 3 miles to the Reserve entrance.

THE HIKE: At the trailhead is a sign imparting some Bolsa Chica history. Cross the lagoon on the bridge, where other signs offer information about marsh-land plants and birds. The loop trail soon begins following a levee around the marsh. You'll pass fields of pickleweed and cordgrass, sun-baked mudflats, the remains of oil drilling equipment. Three endangered birds—Savanannah sparrow, light-footed clapper rail, California least tern—are sometimes seen here.

At the north end of the loop, you may bear right on a closed road to an over-look. As you return, you cross the lagoon on another bridge and return to the parking area on a path paralleling Pacific Coast Highway.

CHAPTER TWO

North County Parks & Preserves

Conservationists describe this part of OC as open-space starved.
North Orange County offers only one acre of open space for
every 246 people; the National Recreation and
Park Association recommends one acre or more for every
100 people. Therefore, the parks and trails that do exist—
such regional parks as Craig and Clark, as well as the
parks and preserves in the city of Fullerton—
are precious resources for an area with more than
its share of traffic and congestion.
For decades a battle has been waged to stop plans
for a massive subdivision in the West Coyote Hills,
the only remaining unprotected natural landscape
left in north Orange County.

RALPH B. CLARK REGIONAL PARK

PERIMETER TRAIL
From west park boundary to Camel Hill is 1.5 miles round trip with 100-foot elevation gain

Located in the northwest corner of Orange County on the Buena Park/Fullerton border, this park owes its origin to our fascination with fossils. It seems 12,000 years or so ago, the ring-tailed cat, ground sloth, and ancient mammoth roamed a region of meadows, marshes and woodlands, an environment altogether different from present-day Orange County.

Extensive fossil beds were discovered when sand and gravel was excavated during the 1950s and 1960s for construction of the Santa Ana and Riverside freeways by the California Division of Highways (now Caltrans). Paleontologists identified the remains of prehistoric whales, bison and even a camel. By public demand, Emery Borrow Pit, as the excavation site was known, was purchased by Orange County in 1974, and opened as Los Coyotes Regional Park in 1981. It was later

renamed for Ralph B. Clark, a county supervisor who retired in 1987 after 16 years of public service and was devoted to the creation of this 105-acre park.

Exhibits in the park interpretive center tell the intriguing tale of prehistoric Orange County. The discovery of turtles, tapirs, turkeys and an unusual number of vertebrates prompted some researchers to mention the site in the same breath with the legendary La Brea Tar Pits. Other exhibits suggest what the OC was like from way, way back in time—the Pleistocene period of 100,000 years ago and the Late Cretaceous period of 75 million years ago.

The prehistoric record revealed at the park's interpretive center.

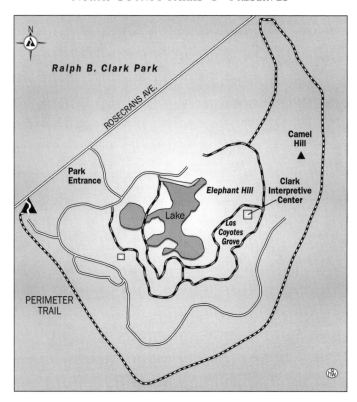

The park also provides lots of ball fields and a lake stocked with largemouth bass, bluegill and catfish. Hikers have Perimeter Trail, which winds halfway around the park, some dirt paths around Camel Hill, plus some cement walkways that lead to the lake and picnic grounds. Perimeter Trail is that rare county trail is that is not multi-use; no bikes are allowed!

DIRECTIONS TO TRAILHEAD: From the Santa Ana Freeway (5) in Buena Park, exit on Beach Boulevard and drive 2.2 miles north to Rosecrans Ave. (Or from the Artesia Freeway (91), exit on Beach Boulevard and drive 3 miles north to Rosecrans.) Turn right (east) and head 0.5 mile to the entrance of Ralph P. Clark Regional Park on the right. Turn right on the park road, then right again just past the tennis courts. Park in the lot located by the tennis courts or curbside along the park road. Perimeter Trail extends along the top of an embankment, where the park borders a neighborhood.

THE HIKE: Head south on Perimeter Trail. Pine trees partially screen the trail from the nearby housing and park maintenance yard. The trail bends east, staying with the boundary between the park and neighborhoods.

Perimeter Trail meets a dirt road leading up Camel Hill which in turn divides. The left branch climbs right up the hill while the right branch circles

Artist's rendition of Clark Park's ancient past.

around the back side of the hill. Choose either one and gain the top. Enjoy the good clear-day views of northern Orange County and the San Gabriel Mountains.

Two dirt trails descend Camel Mountain: one path descends alongside Rosecrans to the northern end of the softball diamonds; a second path drops more directly to the south side of the ball diamonds.

Make your way to the interpretive center, tucked between Elephant Hill and the lake. After learning about Orange County's fossil record, walk past play-grounds and picnic grounds back to the trailhead.

PANORAMA NATURE PRESERVE

PANORAMA TRAIL

From Summit House Restaurant to Vista Points is 1 mile round trip with 200-foot elevation gain; to Brea Boulevard is 3 miles round trip

You could take advantage of the drive-through vista point on State College Boulevard just north of Bastanchury Road and skip the hike that begins nearby, but then you wouldn't be a hiker, would you?

Besides, the hiker's-only view you can get from Fullerton's Panorama Trail is better than anything you can get from in—or near—a car. In fact, exactly what you see from the viewpoints atop this end of the Coyote Hills is detailed on signs. You will know and not have to guess that the view to the northeast includes Placentia, Yorba Linda, Brea and the Chino Hills, and that the view to the southeast includes Orange, Tustin, Irvine, Huntington Beach and Newport Bay.

Panorama Nature Preserve, located at the top of the hill, was set aside to safe-guard the panoramic views, as well as a slice of coastal sage scrub habitat. The lit-tle refuge is habitat for many birds, including two rare ones, the coastal cactus wren and the California gnatcatcher.

From the hiker's perspective, Panorama Trail is one of those pathways that start well and finish poorly. Once you've conquered the hill and taken in those

No question about how this trail got its name.

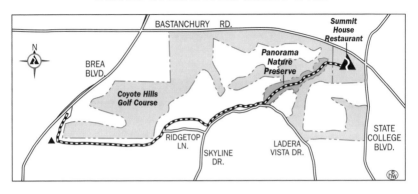

great views, it's all downhill, literally and figuratively—a descent into suburbia and around a golf course.

DIRECTIONS TO TRAILHEAD: From the Riverside Freeway (91), exit on State College Boulevard. Head north 3 miles to Bastanchury Road. Turn left and then make a quick second left into the large parking lot of the Summit House, an upscale, English inn-style restaurant. Look for the beginning of the trail on the far west side of the parking lot at a gate leading into the Coyote Hills Golf Course.

THE HIKE: Follow the paved drive into the golf course. The "Nature Trail" veers off from the golf cart track and soon passes an active oil well. Before long you'll junction a signed equestrian trail on your left and follow this dirt road on an ascent up the hill.

The hilltop vista points are connected by Vista Loop Trail, which branches from the Panorama Trail. Be sure to get those panoramic views from both sides of the hill.

If views are all you want, turn around here. Otherwise, follow Panorama Trail on a descent into suburbia, where it passes through a gate and continues as a wide walkway in front of homes. At Ridgetop Lane, the path leads alongside a white fence and drops to the fenced boundary of the golf course. The trail reverts to dirt and, sandwiched between homes and golf course ascends to the Golden Hill Little League's baseball diamonds and Brea Boulevard.

THE FULLERTON LOOP

FULLERTON LOOP TRAIL
12-mile loop around the city of Fullerton with 300-foot elevation gain

Fullerton is full of trails if you know where to find them—and most people don't. The city boasts more than 28 miles of trail and about 20 named ones.

A half-dozen or so of these trails, along with paths along railroad tracks and through several parks, form Fullerton Loop, a *grand randonée* through town and country. Some of the paths are former electric car transit routes, and thus make for easy walking.

Fullerton Loop certainly doesn't fall in the "Undiscovered Hikes" category. It's a popular ride for northern Orange County cycling enthusiasts. The trail has some ups and downs, and links a lot of different parts of Fullerton. You might be surprised at what you find en route. Of course, no one's forcing you to do the whole loop and it's easy enough to use city streets to get back to start.

Download the latest map from the city of Fullerton parks department and hit the trail. Expect to lose the trail a couple of times and have to improvise. The account below is merely a broad summary not a highly detailed description.

Frankly, the best way to do this trail is go with a local—someone who knows the route.

DIRECTIONS TO TRAILHEAD: From the Riverside Freeway (91) in Fullerton, exit on Harbor Boulevard and head north past Chapman Avenue to Berkeley Avenue. Turn left (west) on Berkeley, which soon turns north. Look for the path (actually the unsigned south end of Juanita Cooke Trail on the left (west) side of Berkeley. Find the best dependable parking by following Berkeley a short distance north to Valley View Drive and a city parking lot.

THE HIKE: Mostly level Juanita Cooke Trail leads to signed Hiltscher Trail, which descends along a creek. Next comes a step ascent, followed by sidewalk strolling and negotiating busy Bastanchury Road, then a walk north along railroad tracks. Parks Trail leads through the three "astronaut parks." The parks are named for the three Apollo One astronauts—Edward White, Roger B. Chaffee, and Gus Grissom—who perished in a fire in 1967. The City of Fullerton was vital to the aerospace industry in the 1960s and 1970s. Executives and engineers lived and worked in the city as they developed the Apollo and Space Shuttle programs.

Then it's on to West Coyote Hills Tree Park, a shady place to rest, if you'd like to take a seat under a tree. Onward on Rosecrans Trail, which has both paved and unpaved sections, then onto Castlewood Trail and Nora Kuttner Recreational

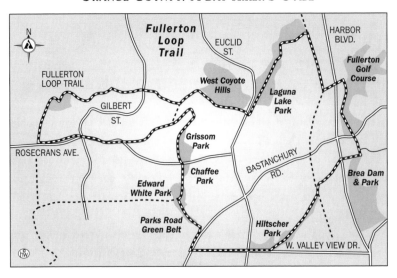

Trail, which extends to Euclid Street and Bud Turner Trail, which goes along the east side of Euclid.

Entering Laguna Lake Park, the path passes through a wooded are. Crosses Lakeside Drive and meets Junita Cooke Trail. Now it's over an old railroad trestle and a path near the tracks and then around Fullerton Golf Course. The path heads up to the edge of Brea Dam and over to meet Harbor Boulevard. A walk south on Harbor Boulevard returns you to where you began your Fullerton adventure.

WEST COYOTE HILLS

WEST COYOTE HILLS TRAILS
Guided hikes of 2 to 5 miles round trip

Rising above inland valleys and the San Gabriel River plain, the West Coyote Hills are a thriving ecosystem that hosts a wide diversity (more than 130 species) of plants and animals. The hills have the dubious distinction of being the only remaining unprotected natural landscape left in densely urbanized/suburbanized north Orange County.

Landowner Chevron Texaco, through its subsidiary Pacific Coast Homes, intends to construct 760 homes, plus commercial buildings on the last 510 acres of undeveloped land. In previous decades, the company subdivided another 1200 acres of hills with homes and golf courses.

Conservationists, particularly Friends of Coyote Hills, and the Sierra Club's Coyote Hills Task Force, have spearheaded the drive to save the hills as a park/nature preserve. Saving the hills, they argue, will be of great benefit to a part of Orange County that by all accounts is "open-space starved." The would-be developer claims its latest subdivision proposal will leave 280 acres as natural open space and add eight miles of multi-use trail.

Chevron first proposed building homes in the hills in 1977, sparking what

OC activists take to the streets to save their open space.

Natural land in short supply in these parts.

has become one of Southern California's most prolonged conservation battles. As oil production faded away, local conservationists pushed a pro-park/open space platform for the Coyote Hills. One success occurred in 1983, when the city of Fullerton acquired 72 acres to create a nature preserve. Robert E. Ward Nature Preserve, also called West Coyote Hills Nature Preserve on some maps, honors a Fullerton mayor/council member who worked to retain a portion of the hills in a natural state.

As conservationists see it, the hills are the last of the wild for four now scarce plant communities in northern Orange County: coyote brush, southern willow scrub, coast prickly pear and California sagebrush. For a century, the West Coyote Hills were dotted with oil derricks, but since oil drilling operations ceased, the landscape is regenerating, and can even look lovely at times. In springtime, the Coyote Hills are colored by purple phacelia, yellow sun cups and orange monkeyflowers.

The hills are habitat for many bird species including two threatened ones-the California gnatcatcher and coastal cactus wren. Towhees, Bewick's wrens and California Quail are among the more commonly sighted birds. The hills are a stopover on the Pacific Flyway for migratory birds, and a wintering ground for hawks and harriers.

As for the hiking, well, most of the West Coyote Hills and trails are not in the public domain so no trail descriptions will be provided in this guide. (You do get a pretty good look at the hills via the Fullerton Loop; see the hike write-up in this book.)

For a great introduction to the hills and the importance of saving them, I sug-gest you join one of the free naturalist guided hikes sponsored by the Friends of the Coyote Hills. Find out about these hikes, usually offered the second Saturday of every month, by visiting www.coyotehills.org. The summer hike schedule varies.

One attraction for hikers to the top of the hills are the 360-degree panoramic views that take in the San Gabriel and San Bernardino mountain ranges, down-town Los Angeles, the Santa Monica Mountains and Catalina Island.

DIRECTIONS TO TRAILHEAD: From the Riverside Freeway (91), exit on Euclid Street and drive about three miles north to Lakeview Drive and entrance to Laguna Lake Park on the right. Guided hikes begin at the park's equestrian center.

The small, publicly accessible part of the hills are just south of Laguna Lake Park. A westbound trail departs from Euclid Street.

CRAIG REGIONAL PARK

CRAIG PARK WALKABOUT
2.5-mile loop

An oil boom began in Brea and Fullerton at the beginning of the 20th century, for decades oil derricks and tanks dotted what is now 124-acre Craig Park. Floods of the 1930s prompted the U.S. Army Corps of Engineers to construct Fullerton Dam, as well as a flood basin, to guard against future flooding of the flatlands below. Such flood basins are often transformed into parks—which happened in the case of Craig Park in 1974. In later years, a small waterfowl refuge was created in an area swollen with water by winter storms.

While the park does have a "Natural Area" at the south end of the park by the Fullerton Reservoir dam, most of the park is green grass, shaded with trees. A little lake offers fishing for bluegill and catfish. Craig also has plenty of ball fields and a sports complex for volleyball, basketball and racquetball.

A small nature center, located behind the park office, offers an introduction to Orange County's native wildlife and ecological habitats. One display I've dubbed "Survival of the Fittest" presents nature as a great big cafeteria: a coyote eats a squirrel; a raccoon hunts a coot; a gopher snake snags, well, a gopher. After your

Craig Regional Park: Just the place for a walk in the park.

natural history lesson, be sure to stroll the lovely rose garden, also located behind the park office.

Sign of the times

If Craig Park, like Clark Park, had a signed "Perimeter Trail" it might be a more compelling destination for hikers. As it is, a walk around the park's perimeter requires some improvisation. However, by linking walkways, dirt trails and park roads, the hiker can create an enjoyable walk in the park. Figure a hilly loop of about 2.5 miles.

DIRECTIONS TO TRAILHEAD: From the Orange Freeway (57) in Fullerton, exit on Imperial Highway and proceed very briefly west to State College Boulevard. Turn left (south) and almost immediately turn left into Craig Regional Park. Leave your car at the first available space beyond the park entrance station.

THE HIKE: For a basic, clockwise tour of Craig Park, begin by walking over to the north side of park and paved walkway east. The walkway turns south and you'll hear the roar of the nearby Orange Freeway. You'll travel along the east side of the park's lake and of Loftus Creek as you make your way toward Fullerton Dam.

Look for a new trailhead and entrance to the Natural Area and the sign, "Coyotes Present." The parks department is re-vegetating the area with plantings of native flora. A trail travels around the volleyball and basketball courts. You'll then join a paved walkway on the west side of the lake and improvise a northbound route back.

YORBA REGIONAL PARK

SANTA ANA RIVER TRAIL
From east boundary to west boundary is 2 miles round trip

With a backdrop of the Anaheim Hills to the south and the Chino Hills to the north, 175-acre Yorba Regional Park is located in the mouth of Santa Ana Canyon in the city of Anaheim. Located just up-river from Carbon Canyon Dam, the park extends more than a mile along the Santa Ana River.

This is a kind of kick-back-and-relax park. With its riverside locale, the park has a kind of waterworld theme and boasts four lakes with connecting streams. If ever a park promoted picnicking it's certainly Yorba, which boasts more than 400 picnic tables and 200 barbecue stoves.

The park name is in honor of the Yorba family, who owned Rancho Santiago de Santa Ana, a 62,000-acre Mexican-era land grand on the south side of the river. José Antonio Yorba, a Spanish soldier with the Portolá expedition, was granted the land in 1810 and his son, Bernardo, used his family's holdings by raising animals harvest corn and wheat, planting vineyards and orchards. The area remained agricultural well into the 20th century. Yorba Regional Park opened in 1976.

For the hiker, Yorba's offerings are limited to paths along the Santa Ana River and paved walkways linking the park's lakes and facilities. Bird-watchers say the birding is pretty good along the Santa Ana River, which attracts a variety of waterfowl and shorebirds.

DIRECTIONS TO TRAILHEAD: From the Riverside Freeway (91) in Anaheim Hills, exit on Imperial Highway (I-90) and proceed north 0.25 mile,

River-side, lake-side, all around the park.

crossing the Santa Ana River to La Palma Avenue. At La Palma, turn east and proceed 1.5 miles to the entrance to Yorba Regional Park.

From the Riverside Freeway (91) in Anaheim Hills, exit on Weir Canyon Road. Head North to La Palma Avenue, turn west and proceed to the park entrance.

Parking Lot #10 is a good choice because it's so close to the Santa Ana River Trail.

THE HIKE: Take your pick—the paved bike path along the top of the river bank or the dirt equestrian trail parallel to it. What would be a serene scene—an egret wading at water's edge, for example—isn't due to the high decibel intrusion of the relentless traffic on the Riverside Freeway.

When you reach the sports fields at the western edge of the park, it's time to return unless, of course, you'd rather continue with the Santa Ana River Trail another 20-plus miles to the coast.

For a change in scene, return by way of the lakeshore pathways and take a walk on the shady side. Joining the park's native sycamores are redwoods, as well as trees from faraway lands, including eucalyptus, pepper trees and Canary Island pines.

FEATHERLY REGIONAL PARK

SANTA ANA RIVER TRAIL
From Featherly Regional Park to Yorba Regional Park is 3 miles one way

Those who appreciate a park with a modest number of facilities and amenities and a large amount of acreage left undeveloped will appreciate Featherly Regional Park, located along the Santa Ana River in Anaheim. The park encompasses nearly 800 acres, though fewer than 100 acres are developed.

Like many parcels of land in Orange County before it became parkland, it was originally part of the Yorba family's super-sized rancho before purchase by the Irvine family and used for cattle ranching. For locals, it was long a favorite spot for picnicking and access to the river's swimming holes when it was acquired by the county. Named for a county supervisor, the park was Orange County's third park when it opened in 1970.

Featherly is distinguishable from its near neighbor Yorba Regional Park, also located on the Santa Ana River, five miles west, by its campground. As you might imagine, a campground relatively close to Disneyland is very popular with campers/theme park visitors from around the U.S. and from overseas. Happy campers enjoy evening campfire programs at the park amphitheater.

The green scene includes the Santa Ana River Trail that extends from the Riverside/Orange County line to Huntington Beach. While the 795-acre park is part of the countywide system under the jurisdiction of the Harbors, Beaches & Parks Department, Canyon RV Park, within Featherly Park, is operated by a private concessionaire. At this time, public access to this park is limited to occasional guided nature walks and to campers and by way of the Santa Ana River Trail. (See Yorba Regional Park hike account in this guide.)

DIRECTIONS TO TRAILHEAD: From the Riverside Freeway (91), exit on Gypsum Canyon Road and head north into the park.

CHAPTER THREE

Central County Parks & Preserves

"Quality of living" is often the way proud residents characterize the heart of Orange County. Convenient hiking trails are sometimes recognized as examples of the good life in the same breath as wide streets, good schools and great shopping. Along with a lot of business parks and industrial parks, this part of the county also has many nature parks. The region's parks, whether developed or left in a natural state are very much part of the plans for central OC's communities, particularly the City of Irvine, one of the nation's premiere planned communities. You don't have to go far to find a place to take a hike— always a good thing in my book.

OAK CANYON NATURE CENTER

MAIN ROAD, TRANQUILITY, BLUEBIRD LANE TRAILS
1.5-mile loop with 200-foot elevation gain

Tucked nearly out of sight from a golf course and hillside haciendas, Oak Canyon seems more isolated than it is. And with four miles of hiking trails, the park seems bigger to hikers than it really is.

Credit Oak Canyon Nature Center for getting the maximum use out of 58 acres of parkland with the most minimal of impact. The park hosts many nature-based activities for small children and their parents and for school kids of all ages.

First stop for most visitors is the John J. Collier Interpretive Center, with displays about the local flora and wildlife, including exhibits of birds, insects and mammals. Next is Heritage Trail, a 0.2-mile self-guided interpretive trail that familiarizes visitors with the region's plants and animals.

Younger children get an unusual perspective on nature by "climbing" through a spider web and crawling through a fallen log. Heritage Butterfly Grove is an engaging mixture of art and science, featuring intriguing butterfly sculptures, as well as providing habitat for native butterfly populations.

DIRECTIONS TO TRAILHEAD: From the Riverside Freeway (91) in

Welcome to my web: A kid-sized quandry – how to get through without getting caught.

Anaheim, exit on Imperial Highway and head south. Turn left on Nohl Ranch Road and, after passing Anaheim Hills Golf Course, veer left onto Walnut Canyon Road. Park in the free lot at the end of Walnut Canyon Road close to the entrance of the Oak Canyon Nature Center at 6700 East Walnut Canyon Road.

THE HIKE: Begin on Main Road, which extends 0.7 mile through the length of the canyon. Step off the road to enjoy the 0.3-mile long Tranquility Trail, which ascends from the canyon bottom into the coastal sage scrub and oaks dotting the western canyon wall. Or detour onto 0.3-mile long Stream Trail, which meanders creekside amongst coastal live oak woodland.

Return via (my favorite) Roadrunner Ridge Trail, though due note that particular trail is prone to winter storm damage and subject to closure. Another pleasant return route is via Bluebird Lane and Wren Way trails.

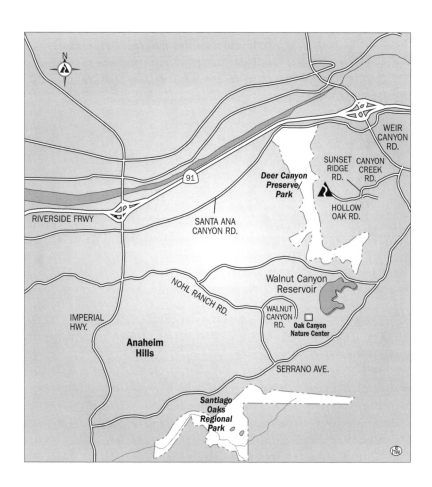

DEER CANYON PARK PRESERVE

DEER CANYON TRAIL
2-mile park walkabout with 300-foot elevation gain

Residents mostly identify themselves as living in "Anaheim Hills," as opposed to Anaheim, though according to postal authorities the name is not accepted for use as an official mailing address.

Nature lovers point with pride at parks and preserves in and around the hills and claim that about thirty percent of the land is protected in park and open space reserves. The consensus by residents and visitors alike is that this breathing room makes the hill country different in appearance and in vibe from other parts of Orange County. These parklands are all the more valuable in contrast to the fast-paced developments in the hills, with new neighborhoods extending toward the Riverside County line.

One of these special parklands, and likely the most obscure, is Deer Canyon Park Preserve, located about a mile-and-a-half as the park's roadrunners run from two freeways, but a world apart. In contrast to long-established, well-known and close-by neighbor, Oak Canyon Nature Center, Deer Canyon isn't yet on most maps and certainly not on the "to do" list of many hikers.

The Anaheim Hills hold scenic wonders, protect wildlife, and attract hikers.

The 130-acre preserve, an Anaheim City park, is bordered by lanes with nature-sounding names such as Canyon Mist, Dove Tree, Rock Garden and Cottontail, and can be accessed by a half-dozen or so streets. The hilly park is habitat for rabbits, squirrels and the deer that gave the canyon its name. Park flora consists of oaks and brush, as well as stray exotics such as bougainvillea that have become established over the years.

The park's trail system consists of a utility company road and some side trails. I suggest bringing a recent map of the Anaheim Hills that shows the neighborhood streets, because you may find yourself exiting the preserve at a different place than you entered.

DIRECTIONS TO TRAILHEAD: From the Riverside Freeway (91) in Anaheim, take the Yorba Linda/Weir Canyon exit and head south 0.75 mile on Weir Canyon Road. At the third stoplight, turn right on Serrano Avenue, then make an immediate right on Canyon Creek Road. Turn left on the Sunset Ridge Road and right onto Hollow Oak Road. Look for the signed Deer Canyon Park Preserve on the left and park on the street near the entrance.

THE HIKE: Head south on the main park road (an Edison service road) toward an unnamed hill (any ideas for a name?), the one crowned by four enormous electrical towers. Step off the road to explore the inviting side trails. Leave the dirt road for a rougher track that bends northwest and climbs first to a bench at a vista point, then to the top of the ridgeline.

Enjoy vistas east and west of the Anaheim Hills, developed and not, as well as plenty of OC cities, including Yorba Linda to the north and Orange to the south. For an optional return, walk down the ridgeline on the footpaths leading back to the Hollow Oak Road trailhead.

SANTIAGO OAKS REGIONAL PARK

WINDES, PACIFICA, WILDERNESS LOOP TRAILS
0.7 mile loop and 2.5-mile loop of the park

Santiago Oaks Regional Park preserves 350 acres of pastoral Orange County, including its splendorous signature oak woodland, groupings of mature ornamental trees and even a grove of Valencia oranges. Such a diversity of environments attracts many species of birds, both common and unusual to the area.

The name of the park, creek and canyon are derived from the old Rancho Santiago de Santa Ana. During the 1930s, Dorment Winde, CFO for Bixby Ranch Company, purchased land along Santiago Creek and planted an orange grove. The ranch house built by the Winde family in 1938 is now the park's nature center.

Stop at the engaging nature center before hitting the trail—lots of park trails, in fact. Sure bets are aptly named Santiago Creek Trail and other footpaths that meander near the creek.

Historic Dam Trail leads to . . . an old dam. With the aid of Chinese laborers, the Serrano and Carpenter Water Company built a clay dam here in 1879. This dam was destroyed by floods, and replaced in 1892 with a more substantial structure of river rock and cement. The dam looks particularly tiny when compared to the huge Villa Park Flood Control dam a short distance upstream.

A view of pastoral OC from days gone by.

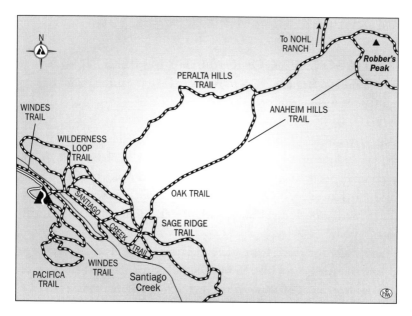

Sample the park's ecosystems with Windes Nature Trail. The 0.75-mile trail and its Pacifica Loop offer clear-day glimpses of the county's coastline. As nature trails go, this one is definitely on the steep side. Reward for following the trail on the ascent up 770-foot Rattlesnake Ridge are good views of the park and beyond.

For a longer (2.5 mile) loop of the park, in a counterclockwise direction, begin with Santiago Creek Trail and follow it to the eastern boundary of the park. Take Sage Ridge Trail and Wilderness LoopTrail westbound back to reconnect with Santiago Creek Trail.

DIRECTIONS TO TRAILHEAD: From the Costa Mesa Freeway (55) in Orange, exit on Katella Avenue and head east. Katella undergoes a name change in a half-mile to Villa Park Road, then a second name change to Santiago Canyon Road. About three miles from the freeway, turn left on Windes Drive and drive 0.75 mile to Santiago Oaks Regional Park.

ROBBERS PEAK

SANTIAGO CREEK, OAK, ANAHEIM HILLS TRAILS
From Santiago Regional Park to Robbers Peak is 3 miles round trip with 700-foot elevation gain

For great views of the Anaheim Hills, Chino Hills and a whole lot of Orange County, take a hike up to the rocky knob known as Robbers Peak. As the story goes, such infamous 19th-century outlaws as Joaquin Murietta and Three-Finger Jack kept watch over rural Orange County. The outlaws would ride down from the hills to rob the Butterfield Stagecoach or ride into the hills to escape the sheriff's posse.

A network of fire roads, footpaths and equestrian trails crisscross the park and extend into the Anaheim Hills. While the hills have hosted their share of suburban development, some of that Wild West feeling still remains. And, at least for now, you can enjoy a ramble up to Robbers Peak and steal a look at what remains of rural Orange County.

Robbers Peak is rather easily accessible from a trail off Serrano Road, which might explain why you might the peak marred by graffiti.

This hike begins amongst the oaks in the regional park, ascends the park's brushy ridges and travels to the 1,152-foot peak via Anaheim Hills Trail.

DIRECTIONS TO TRAILHEAD: From the Costa Mesa Freeway (55) in Orange, exit on Katella Avenue and head east. Katella undergoes a name change in a half-mile to Villa Park Road, then a second name change to Santiago Canyon Road. About three miles from the freeway, turn left on Windes Drive and drive 0.75 mile to Santiago Oaks Regional Park.

THE HIKE: From the parking lot, cross Santiago Creek and follow Santiago Creek Trail amongst the oaks along the north side of the creek. At a signed junction with Oak Trail, and turn left (northeast).

As you ascend, you'll pass a couple of right-forking side trails, pass a junction with Peralta Hills Trail and leave the regional park behind. At a point on the ridge at about 1,000 feet in elevation, you'll get a grand view from suburbia to the Pacific.

Nearing the sandstone peak, Anaheim Hills Trail peels off to the right but you keep following the ridge, curving north then west to the summit. From atop the peak, you can look over the Peralta Hills and trace the path of Santiago Creek. Not so long ago, the view would have taken in hundreds of cattle, orange groves, and barley fields. Nowadays the panorama is considerably less pastoral.

ANAHEIM HILLS

ANAHEIM HILLS TRAIL
From Serrano Avenue, a 3.75-mile loop with 400-foot elevation gain

Housing developments often take the name of the natural features around them, but in one OC locale the naming process is reversed.

Geologists and mapmakers have long referred to the long, low ridge extending west from the Santa Ana Mountains and rising above Santa Ana Canyon as the Peralta Hills, but almost no one uses that name anymore. Today the hills are known as the Anaheim Hills.

The hills honor, or did honor, Juan Pablo Peralta and his family, original owners of the huge Rancho Santiago de Santa Ana. Peralta is an excellent name, historic and euphonious. It recalls the Latin expression per alta, "through the high things." Sounds like a university motto—or a hiker's motto—doesn't it?

Anaheim, which German settlers in 1858 named after the river Santa Ana plus the suffix (home) already names a city, a boulevard, a bay and much more, not to mention the trail system in the hills. I've long urged concerned day hikers and Orange Countians to rally to save the Peralta Hills. And I've been pleased to find Peralta Hills on the Auto Club's Orange County North map and even more pleased that progress has been made in preserving portions of the hills and establishing several segments of the Anaheim Hills Trail System, including a segment that links Santiago Oaks Regional Park with Weir Canyon Regional Park.

On this hike, you'll follow Anaheim Hills Trail over to the western wall of Weir Canyon, and then loop back to the trailhead on suburban streets.

DIRECTIONS TO TRAILHEAD: From the Riverside Freeway (91) in Anaheim, exit on Imperial Highway and head 0.75 mile south to Nohl Ranch Road. Turn left and drive 2.5 miles east to just short of road's end at Serrano Avenue. Find curbside parking on Carnegie Avenue, a block short of Serrano.

THE HIKE: Cross Serrano Avenue and join the dirt fire road passing to the left of Anaheim Hills Elementary School, and ascending a quarter-mile to meet Anaheim Hills Trail. A right turn on the descending trail leads to Santiago Oaks Regional Park (see hike write-up) but you turn left toward Robbers Peak. If you want to summit the peak, take a left-branching rout past a gate.

Anaheim Hills Trail drops toward Weir Canyon and then along a ridge to junction Weir Canyon Trail. Bear left and walk a short distance to the suburban edge where Hidden Canyon Road meets Overlook Terrace. Now you turn into a suburban road warrior and walk a half-mile down Hidden Canyon Road to Serrano Avenue, turn left and walk a mile along Nohl Ranch Road back to the trailhead.

WEIR CANYON WILDERNESS PARK

WEIR CANYON LOOP TRAIL
From Hidden Canyon—a 4-mile loop with 300-foot elevation gain.

From the trail high on the west wall of Weir Canyon, the hiker gets a view of Orange County that's both stereotypical and surprising. The view westward is that of Orange County to the max: houses perched everywhere on the slopes of the Anaheim Hills, several freeways, the city of Anaheim, plus many more cities sprawling toward the coast. In contrast to this 21st-century vista, the view east is minimalist Orange County; that is to say, mostly parkland, a pastoral landscape of hills and canyons that in the right light looks like a plein-air painting made during the late 19th century.

Weir Canyon Wilderness Park (the name wilderness might be stretching the definition a bit, but it's certainly a wilderness compared to the developed areas of the Anaheim Hills) is one of those great so-near-yet-so-faraway places in Orange County to take a hike. It's a pleasure to report it's the park—not nearby subdivisions—that's been extending its boundaries farther into the hills toward the toll road (Highway 241).

Geographers say the Anaheim Hills comprise a long, low ridge extending west from the Santa Ana Mountains and rising above Santa Ana Canyon and the Santa Ana River. Weir Canyon Trail offers a gentle introduction to the considerable pleasures of these hills.

The hills are alive with flowers and their fans—among them, the author.

DIRECTIONS TO TRAILHEAD: From the Riverside Freeway (91) in Anaheim Hills, exit on Weir Canyon Road. Head south 0.7 mile to Serrano Avenue. Turn right (west) and proceed 2 miles to Hidden Canyon Road. Turn left (south) and follow it a half-mile to its end at Overlook Terrace and the signed trailhead. Park along Hidden Canyon Road.

THE HIKE: From the park sign, the trail leads northeast. Ignore a path descending toward the canyon bottom and continue on the main path as it rises and then levels. Enjoy eastward views into Weir Canyon and westward ones of some intriguing sandstone outcroppings.

The path dips into and climbs out of some minor side canyons, skirts some residences at about the 2.5 mile mark, then U-turns and begins heading south. After leading you a mile along the western rim of Weir Canyon, the path drops to the end of Avenida de Santiago. Walk down the steep residential street to Hidden Canyon Road, turn left, and return to the trailhead.

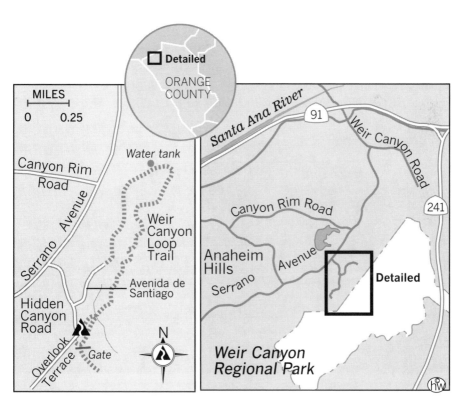

ORANGE HILLS

ORANGE HILLS TRAIL
2.5 mile loop with 300-foot elevation gain

One of Orange County's oldest settlements, incorporated in 1888, the City of Orange now numbers some 140,000 residents. How do all those people fit into the city's 27 square miles? Get an answer to that question by taking a hike to a trio of promontories in the Orange Hills, where summit vistas include most of the city's residences, as well as what remains of the natural environment in the city and county of Orange.

A mile-long ridgetop parkland, which appears as Santiago Oaks Regional Park on most maps and El Modena Open Space on a few, rises above the city and offers the hiker a rigorous hill-climb over slopes blanketed with thick clumps sage and prickly-pear cactus. Considering the highest summit in these hills is but 806 feet in elevation, clear-day vistas are mighty good, particularly to the west across northern Orange County to the LA basin and beyond, and north toward the San Gabriel Mountains.

The trail system can be accessed from several trailheads in the neighborhood off Cannon Street. All the usual warnings about potential hazards are posted at these trailheads but no information about the trails.

DIRECTIONS TO TRAILHEAD: From the Costa Mesa Freeway (55) in the city of Orange, exit on Chapman Avenue and drive two miles east to Cannon Street. Turn left and drive 1.3 miles to Patria Court, where you'll find

Green in spring, brown in autumn – the Orange Hills are delightful to hike all year 'round.

curbside parking close to the northernmost trailhead. (As you motor up Cannon Street, notice a trio of trailheads on your left.)

THE HIKE: The trail parallels Cannon Street, then abruptly turns west and climbs very steeply up to the ridgeline. Up top, the landscape reminded me of a none-too-friendly desert island with red, gray, brown and white volcanic rocks and prickly cholla cactus.

Once you reach the ridgetop the views are good, and they get better as you ascend the first hill and hike highpoint. Look west over the metropolis and give thanks for special places like this open space where you can get away from it all, and look down at it all. "Don't kill our hills!" is the rallying cry of conservationists committed to preserving other parts of these Orange Hills that are threatened by development.

Contemplate hillside preservation as you continue with the southbound path. which dips, climbs a lesser hill, and extends to the top of a third hill. (You'll pass two unsigned connector trails that lead steeply down to Cannon Street, should you wish to shorten your adventure.)

From atop summit #3, it appears as if you've reached the end of the trail, but no, look to the right, north, for an extremely steep footpath that plunges through the brush over rocky slopes. As the path nears a neighborhood and a water tank, it merges with an old dirt road that bends east to meet Cannon Street. Walk the sidewalk or bike path along Cannon Street back to Patria Court.

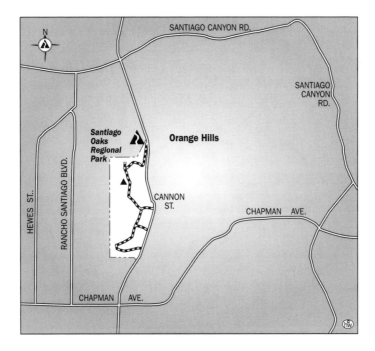

IRVINE REGIONAL PARK

HORSESHOE LOOP TRAIL
Loop around park is 4 miles round trip with 200-foot elevation gain; longer options available

Irvine Park is a classic: stately groves of oak and sycamore, lovely picnic areas and a boat pond ringed with handsome stonework. Add to that heart of the park dating from the 19th century, plenty of ball fields and playgrounds, as well as the Orange County Zoo and the Irvine Park Railroad.

Rolling foothills with accompanying trails border the central part of the park and offer the hiker a chance to get both then and now looks at Orange County.

Irvine Park is a lot of things but one thing it's not: it's not in Irvine! It's located in Santiago Canyon about six miles east of the City of Orange.

Irvine is Orange County's largest (traditional as opposed to wilderness) county park, and now encompasses 477 acres. And Irvine Park is the county's oldest, too. In 1897, James Irvine donated a 160-acre oak grove with the stipulation that the trees should always have the best of care. The grove had long been popular with Orange County residents, particularly with the German immigrants who settled in Anaheim, and was known as the "Picnic Ground" in those days.

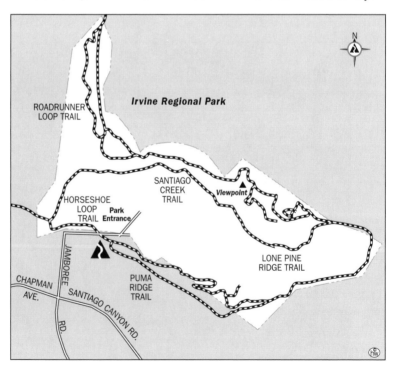

The rugged side of Irvine Park.

Irvine Park is listed on the National Registry of Historic Places. Learn more about the park's colorful history from a well-done exhibit in the interpretive center: how the pond was constructed, the stories of the zoo and miniature railroad, and the park's service to country as an Army post during World War II. The history of the park also offers a window into a century of changing park management policy and philosophy.

Before you head for the hills and the trails that climb them, check out the William Harding Nature Area and a quarter-mile long nature trail by the same name. Even Irvine Park's nature trail is historic; it was created by the Orange County Bird Club in the late 1950s and honors a dedicated club member. Native California flora is the emphasis of the nature area and the path that crosses it.

Horseshoe Trail offers a loop around the historic core of the park. Parallel paths to the north and south of Horseshoe Trail ascend ridges for fine panoramic views. I prefer a counter-clockwise tour of the park and I like to take the ridge route wherever possible. Add the Roadrunner Loop to this hike or put it on your "To Hike" list for the next time you visit Irvine Park and do it as a separate jaunt.

Irvine Park may very well emerge as a kind of Grand Central Hiking Station. Trails lead north into Weir Canyon Wilderness Park and to Irvine Ranch Preserve lands (access at present by guided hike only). The new Mountains to Sea Trail, which extends 22 miles to Newport Beach, begins in the Weir Canyon area of Irvine Park.

DIRECTIONS TO TRAILHEAD: From the Newport Freeway (55), exit on Chapman Avenue (East) and head east 5 miles to Jamboree. Turn left and proceed north a quarter mile to the park entry road and turn right. At a fork you'll need to bear left to pay admission at the park entry station, but note that the right fork (a dead-end road) is where you'll find the start of this hike.

THE HIKE: From the park entry road, join the east-bound Horseshoe Loop Trail. If you continue with this path be sure to explore the short Cactus Canyon Trail.

An (almost immediate) alternative is Puma Ridge Trail, a rather steep, rough and often eroded path that ascends the park's southern ridgeline and travels parallel to Horseshoe Trail. Take in the good views, and descend to rejoin Horseshoe Loop Trail.

The trail makes a horseshoe bend north and west before reaching a junction. Choose between two west-bound paths (the upper or northern trail goes to a viewpoint and connects with Roadrunner Loop Trail. Keep in mind, there aren't many places to cross Santiago Creek, which is can be easily forded at times of low water levels and is a risky venture at times of high water.

The northern trail leads to a developed viewpoint and descends to meet Roadrunner Loop Trail. The eastern leg of the 1.5-mile loop is better defined than the western one, which travels among willows and other riparian growth closer to the creek.

Return to Santiago Creek, cross it, and finish your loop, by trail and park walkway.

Fording Santiago Creek.

MOUNTAINS TO SEA NATIONAL RECREATION TRAIL

MOUNTAINS TO SEA TRAIL
From Irvine Regional Park to Newport Bay is 22 miles one way

Sure it's a multi-use trail which every hiker knows means its more of a bikeway than a hiking trail,

What is a half-day bike ride is a near-marathon day to walk, but Mountains to Sea Trail is also a you-got-to-do-it-once trail, because you experience so much Orange County en route.

Already, Mountains to Sea Trail has gravitas. The trail was designated a "National Recreation Trail" by the National Park Service in 2006. A rigorous application is required before a trail is deemed worthy to be named a National Recreation Trail and only the best nominees make the grade. The designation goes to "exemplary trails of local and regional significance." The last Orange County Trail to earn the honor was the Santa Ana River National Recreation Trail way back in 1976.

As you might imagine, the trailside view is a study in contrasts—the hilly and undeveloped Peters Canyon Park and the residential/commercial developments along Jamboree Road. You walk through a collection of parks and preserves and parts of five cities. Parts of the trail visit Orange County's pastoral past and live up to its billing as "traversing the historic 93,000-acre Irvine Ranch" while in other parts the hiker confronts much too much modernity.

Irvine Co. chairman Donald Bren calls Mountains to Sea Trail the recreational backbone of the Irvine Ranch and also "the recreational heartbeat." Bren, along with some conservationists and trails enthusiasts, see Mountains to Sea Trail as the first of at least three pathways that would cross the county from its hillside communities and parklands to its Pacific shores.

I'm a huge fan of the mountains-to-sea themed trail, though no purist hiker will place Orange County's effort in the same category as, say, the Skyline to the Sea Trail in the Santa Cruz Mountains or the Lemming Trail in the Santa Monica Mountains—hiking trails that stay within the bounds of beautiful parklands.

Orange County's newest National Recreation Trail

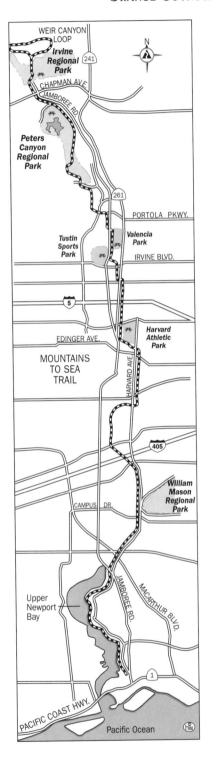

If you're tuning up for one of those long-distance charity hikes, Mountains to Sea Trail is your perfect training path. Hike this path over two cool winter days—or one if it earns you bragging rights.

DIRECTIONS TO TRAIL-HEAD: Mountains to Sea Trail begins in the Weir Canyon area by Irvine Regional Park.

THE HIKE: From Irvine Park, the path crosses Chapman Avenue and tours what might be the most interesting terrain for hikers—Peters Canyon Regional Park. Following this might be the least interesting stretch—the bikeway along Jamboree Road.

You'll pass over, under, or around all the boulevards, parkways and freeways you've come to know and love and hate, but see them from a unique perspective—from a recreational corridor and at a top speed of about three miles an hour.

When you reach the beach on this kind of trail, the tradition (which likely started with the Coast to Coast Path in England) is to kick off your boots and get your feet (or more) wet in the ocean. A celebratory toast with an appropriate beverage—ranging from water to champagne—is also part of the tradition.

PETERS CANYON REGIONAL PARK

LAKE VIEW, LOWER CANYON, EAST RIDGE TRAILS
2 to 6 mile loops

Birds flock to the reservoir at Peters Canyon.

In 1899, "green space," in these parts had an entirely different meaning than it does today. Here in a remote canyon, local sportsmen introduced golf to Orange County.

Santa Ana and Orange duffers leased land from the Irvine Company and laid out a nine-hole course. The "greens" were oil-soaked earthen patches and the fairways were little more than brush-cleared canyon bottom. It must have been hard to make par in Golf Canyon, as it became known.

Today Golf Canyon is the site of Peters Canyon Park, located on the edge of more suburbs-in-the-making on the eastern frontier of the communities of Orange and Tustin. The Irvine Company donated the park land in 1992.

Park highlight is a reservoir, gathering place for many migratory and resident waterfowl. Bring binoculars and watch for herons and egrets along the willow-lined shores. Also watch the skies for the red-tailed and Cooper's hawks circling above the eucalyptus groves located in lower Peters Canyon.

A network of old Irvine Ranch roads and footpaths explore the canyon and its east wall. Most popular is Lake View Trail, a 2-mile path that loops around the reservoir. It's a 6-mile round trip walk to the eucalyptus groves at the park's south end.

DIRECTIONS TO TRAILHEAD: From Highway 55 in Orange, exit on Chapman Avenue and head east 4.5 miles to Jamboree Road. Turn right and proceed a half-mile to Canyon View Avenue, then turn right again. The park is a short distance up the road on your left.

THE HIKE: Join signed Lake View Trail as it meanders along the northern edge of Upper Peters Canyon Reservoir, built in 1931 by the Irvine Company to hold water for its agricultural operations. A lower reservoir was built in 1940, but

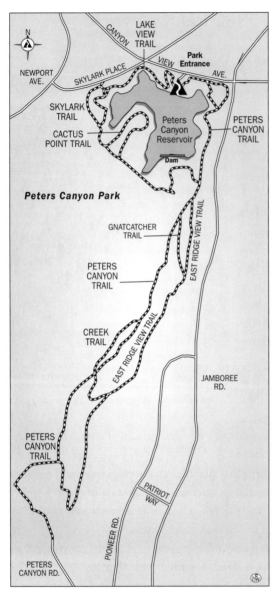

Peters Canyon Park

as you'll see when you visit the lower canyon, it's dry these days, and serves as an emergency flood control basin.

The trail joins a dirt road on the west side of the lake, passes a couple of side trails leading down to the lake, then skirts the dam. Loop back along the east side of the reservoir to the parking area or continue along the canyon bottom on Lower Canyon Trail. As you near the south end of the park, you'll pass a World War II "battlefield." This part of Peters Canyon was used by the U.S. Army during the war to train troops and stage mock battles.

Visit the eucalyptus groves at the park's south end then, if you wish, join East Ridge View Trail for the return back up the canyon. The views promised by this trail's name are of the length of Peters Canyon as well as semi-suburban, semi-pastoral Orange County.

SERRANO CREEK & HERITAGE HILL

SERRANO CREEK TRAIL

From Serrano Creek Park to Heritage Hill Historical Park is 2.5 miles
round trip with 100-foot elevation gain; to Lake Forest Nature Park is 6.5
miles round trip with 300-foot gain

Strictly from a hiker's perspective, Serrano Creek is one of the county's more
intriguing suburban-style linear parks. The creek is no wilderness watercourse,
and you don't really get away from it all, but you do find a measure of quietude en
route to a historical park and a nature park. Future improvements and trail work
could add up to a wonderful hiking experience over the length of Lake Forest all
the way to Limestone-Whiting Ranch Wilderness Park.

The trail begins at Serrano Creek Community Park, where a network of
pathways extend a mile through eucalyptus groves and picnic grounds. When you
reach the park boundary, you can loop back to the trailhead or opt for a longer
jaunt.

Plan a stop at Heritage Hill Historical Park, the county's first historical park,
with four structures on site that help interpret several eras of Saddleback Valley
history. Bennett Ranch House was built in 1908 by the Bennett family, successful
citrus growers. Serrano Adobe, constructed in 1863, is the only surviving adobe
from Don Jose Serrano's Rancho Canada De Los Aliso.

Shade and serenity in Serrano's eucalyptus grove.

St. George's Episcopal Mission, which dates from 1891, was the church for the many English settlers who were attracted to the area because of the land's fruit-farming potential. Kids enjoy visiting the El Toro Grammar School, a one-room schoolhouse used from 1890 to 1914.

Past Trabuco Road, Serrano Creek Trail bends northeast and leads to Lake Forest Nature Park. A nature trail and picnic tables are attractions of this creek-side park.

DIRECTIONS TO TRAILHEAD: From the San Diego Freeway in Irvine, exit on Bake Parkway and head west, then north for 1.5 miles to Toledo Way. Turn right and drive a quarter-mile to Serrano Road. Turn left and look for parking on one of the residential streets on the right (south) side of Serrano Road.

THE HIKE: Choose your paved path and meander among the eucalyptus groves. Dirt trails, including an intermittent one along Serrano Creek offer other options. When you reach the stables and eastern park boundary, cut over to Serrano Road and continue by sidewalk to Heritage Hill Historical Park. Don't be discouraged from visiting when you discover that the park entrance is located behind a supermarket parking lot. I recommend a docent-led tour, if the timing works out for you.

To rejoin Serrano Creek Trail, from the intersection of Serrano Road and Lake Forest Drive, you'll walk east on Lake Forest to Trabuco Road and make a left. Continue to the Trabuco Road bridge over Aliso Creek and look for the trail, a dirt road, on the far side of the bridge.

With rows of homes on the left and the green riparian environment of Aliso Creek on your right, march along the wide dirt track. Expect some hill-climbing and a shortage of shade.

A mile and a half or so from Trabuco Road, the trail approaches some com-mercial buildings, crosses a ravine on a pedestrian bridge, and ducks under Dimension Drive. Stairs lead from the creek back up to street level and to the entrance of Lake Forest Nature Park. Rest, enjoy the park trails and return the way you came.

WILLIAM R. MASON REGIONAL PARK

WETLANDS TRAIL
From Culver Road to Ridgeline Drive is 3.5 miles round trip

Remove about two miles of pavement covering the trails at William R. Mason Regional Park and the hiking experience would go from okay to great. As it is now, the very hard surface, while ideal for cyclists and inline skaters, detracts from the hiking experience and from enjoyment of the natural scene.

As early as 1842, the land was part of José Sepúlveda's Rancho San Joaquin.

Waterside hiking away from the urban scene

In 1876, it was acquired by James Irvine. Originally named University Park for its proximity to UC Irvine, the park was renamed for William R. Mason, a president of the Irvine Company.

The park has two distinct areas. A 9-acre lake is the centerpiece of the developed part of the park, which also boasts plenty of picnic grounds, playgrounds, sand volleyball courts and an amphitheater. The undeveloped side—sometimes referred to as the "Wilderness Area"—consists of 123 acres along Sand Canyon Wash.

While no wilderness, the one-time barley field and now restored wetland is a peaceful place because it's isolated from the sights and sounds of traffic by the canyon's north rim. The trail leads to several distinct natural communities, including grasslands, coastal sage scrub and willows and other riparian growth along the watercourses.

DIRECTIONS TO TRAILHEAD: From the San Diego Freeway (405), exit on Culver Drive. Head south to University Drive. Turn west to the park entrance. Park in one of the easternmost lots—#4, #5, or #7.

THE HIKE: Walk a diagonal one hundred yards or so to the corner of University Drive and Culver Drive. Cross over to the southeast corner and look for the paved pathway just off Culver.

The pathway extends along the south side of the creek and parallels it for much of its length. Two connector trails lead north of University Avenue, while others extend to the neighborhood south of the wetland. Trail's end is Ridgeline Drive.

City of Irvine Open Space Preserve

BOMMER CANYON TRAILS
Guided hikes from 2 to 8 miles round trip

You have to hand it to the city of Irvine for its commitment to parklands. The reaction of many hikers to the words "Wild Irvine" is that it sounds like an oxymoron, but such is not the case. More than one-third of the city is preserved as open space, more than any other Orange County community.

Bommer and Shady canyons are regarded as the centerpieces of the City of Irvine's Open Space Preserve. In turn, this preserve is part of the larger Irvine Ranch Land Reserve.

In 1988, Irvine voters approved what was known as the Open Space Agreement, a landmark in Orange County conservation history that will eventually preserve more than 13,000 acres of wildland throughout the city. This collection of lands, a splendid resource for the dynamic, fast-growing city, is known as the City of Irvine Open Space Preserve.

The city, in partnership with the Irvine Ranch Reserve Trust, offers guided hikes and other nature-oriented activities in Bommer Canyon. The guided hikes (the only way to access the preserve with the exception of one day a month when it's open for independent exploration) lead through oak and sycamore woodlands and past craggy rocky formations. From atop canyon walls, the hiker can survey a fair amount of Orange County and get a glimpse of the Pacific.

Bommer Canyon is a gem and you do get away from it all—thought not that far from it all. The canyon is boxed in-in by a trio of upscale south Irvine communities, including Turtle Rock, Turtle Ridge and Shady Canyon. But the point is, despite the proximity of housing and the toll road, you do get out of audio and visual contact with civilization and enjoy some peace and quiet. Hikers hope park planners will follow-up on the notion of creating a "sage-to-sea" trail system that will cross Irvine and connect to parklands north and south of the city.

Bommer Canyon and Shady Canyon preserve a mixture of ecological communities including coastal sage scrub, native grasslands, and woodlands of oak and sycamore. Wildflower such as Indian paintbrush, buttercups, shooting star, Johnny jump-ups, and Mariposa lily color the canyons with their spring blooms. Biologists point to the canyons' rocky outcroppings, where a variety of rare succulents survive. The outcrops are home and habitat for the western spade-foot toad, coast horned lizard and red diamondback rattlesnake.

The native Juaneño and Gabrieliño were residents of these canyons for many generations. Historians believe the canyon name came from that of a Fransciscan friar from Mission San Juan Capistrano, who worked with the local Native Americans.

From the late 19th century all the way to the early 1970s, Irvine Ranch cowboys used the canyon as a cattle camp. Today Bommer Canyon Cattle Camp, boasting a chuck wagon, picnic table, a covered stage and horseshoe pits. is now a popular "special event" locale for company picnics, weddings, family reunions, group campouts.

The guided hikes offer a variety of experiences, as well as varying distances and amounts of nature interpretation. An easy 2-miler is popular with parents and children and often uses a theme such as "Creepy Crawly Hike" to engage the little ones.

First-time Bommer Canyon hikers will enjoy a mellow 5-miler that has a nice balance of hiking and nature interpretation. If you really want to take a hike, and I mean really hike, sign up for the "Distance Hike" designed for experienced hikers that covers a minimum of 8 miles and as many as 11 miles. Guides vary the route on this one, which always has some vigorous ups and downs.

Then there's a cardio-conditioning fitness hike, in which hikers trek 6 miles (and climb a challenging hill) in just 90 minutes. Quite a workout!

The preserve is open one day a month for self-guided hiking on select trails. Early risers will get the most out of these special days when the reserve is open from 7:30 A.M. to 1 P.M.

To learn more about the hike program or to register for a guided hike in the City of Irvine Open Space Preserve, call the Irvine Ranch Land Trust at (949) 724-6835 or visit www.IrvineOpenSpace.com

DIRECTIONS TO TRAILHEAD: From Culver Drive, turn onto Shady Canyon Road (formerly Bonita Canyon Road) and travel 1.2 miles to an intersection with Bommer Canyon Road. Turn right, proceed 0.8-mile to some buildings, and park on the left away from the picnic area.

HUNTINGTON CENTRAL PARK

SHIPLEY NATURE TRAIL
Loop around Donald D. Shipley Nature Center is 0.5 mile

Former Huntington Beach mayor, the late Donald D. Shipley, was an ardent conservationist who once declared: "We sleepwalk through our environment. Most of us are totally unaware of how little of our natural environment now remains in coastal Southern California. I submit that man may need some natural areas in his human environment much more than does our depleted wildlife."

His namesake nature center, which opened in 1974, is a small enclave within sprawling Huntington Central Park, which extends across Golden West Street between Slater Avenue and Ellis Street, and is the largest city-owned and operated regional park in Orange County. Fenced off from the rest of the park, the 18-acre retreat consists of a variety of native Southern California habitats frequented by a wide variety of birds as well as turtles, opossums, snakes and rabbits. The center serves as an ecological sanctuary for California native plants and wildlife and provides environmental education.

Most visitors to the sprawling 356-acre Huntington Central Park, located in the heart of Huntington Beach, head for Central Park East, which includes Central Library and Cultural Center, the Huntington Beach Playhouse, a sports complex with baseball and soccer fields, walking and jogging trails, and much more. Central Park West is a little more low-key and features Lake Huntington, picnic grounds and playgrounds and the Shipley Nature Center.

The nature center building houses child-friendly nature displays and is a good starting point for the short walk around the

Graceful gates lead to Shipley's natural world.

grounds. Some 30,000 visitors passed through the handsome nature-themed iron gates each year to the center which is owned by the city of Huntington Beach and managed by the nonprofit Friends of Shipley Nature Center. Volunteers are removing such invasive flora as reeds and tamarisk, planting some 50,000 California native plants, and expanding the freshwater wetland habitat.

As you walk the nature trail explore habitats, including oak woodlands, Torrey pines, meadows, and the highlight, Blackbird Pond, a natural freshwater wetland ringed by willows and sycamores.

DIRECTIONS TO TRAILHEAD: From the San Diego Freeway (405) in Huntington Beach, exit on Golden West Street. Drive west four miles or so to the entrance to a parking lot on the right side of the street. Follow the paved pathway down to the nature center.

THE HIKE: From the visitor center and its lovely hummingbird garden and butterfly garden, take the trail to the California flora groupings including coastal sage scrub, oak woodland, chaparral and even a redwood grove. Make your way to Blackbird Pond, named for the red-winged blackbirds that reside among the tules and cattails. After contemplating the pond from an observation deck, loop back to the interpretive building.

For a bit more exercise, leave the nature center and head out on the paved pathways toward Lake Huntington, a man-made lake patrolled by ducks and geese. Circle the lake on dirt and paved trails and improvise a route back to the parking lot near the nature center.

MILE SQUARE REGIONAL PARK

KID'S NATURE TRAIL
0.5-mile walkabout of Natural Area

Park officials describe the City of Fountain Valley's Mile Square Park as "multi-functional," which is certainly the case because it packs a lot of attractions into its 640 acres. A by-the-numbers accounting tallies two golf courses, three soccer fields, two fishing lakes, three playgrounds and four softball fields.

Oh, and one "Urban Nature Area," too.

An old archery range is being radically and creatively transformed into a 20-acre enclave that highlights and interprets the Southland's diverse ecological communities. The Natural Area, as its known, is well worth a stroll on your own. Or take advantage of the occasional ranger-guided nature walk that tours Palm Island, North Lake and the Natural Area.

The Navy acquired the bean field that would one day become Mile Square Park in 1943. Military planners figured that the sparsely populated area was an ideal place for a training base. An air strip was constructed to simulate aircraft carrier-type landings.

After World War II, the fields were used for helicopter pilot training. With the postwar building boom, housing tracts rapidly engulfed the area surrounding Mile Square and it was apparent to all that the land was no longer suitable for flight training. The Department of the Navy leased the land to the county for

Kids' stuff at Mile Square Park.

parkland; in later years it was declared surplus, and in 1973 deeded at no cost to the county for a park.

Decades of park developments have made Mile Square what it is today—a community-oriented park with lots of facilities, miles of jogging and cycling trails, and some 200 acres of grass, trees and picnic areas.

The Natural Area is a fenced-off preserve located in the northwest part of the park. Path meander past a butterfly garden and groupings of chaparral, woodland, marsh and grassland flora. I particularly like the out-of-the-ordinary displays including "Roadside Wildflowers" and "Non-native Natives," the latter a collection of palms, pepper trees and bird-of-paradise—flora so ubiquitous in the Southland that we now imagine that they're native instead of imported from far-away lands.

Ambitious plans are afoot to add more native plant exhibits and construct the Mile Square Youth Camp, designed to offer young children a first camping experience.

DIRECTIONS TO TRAILHEAD: From Brookhurst or Euclid, west and east boundaries respectively of Mile Square Park, get on to Edinger Avenue and enter the park. You can also use the Euclid Avenue park entry.

The main entrance to the Natural Area is from Parking Lot F. A second way into the Natural Area is by way of the Overflow Parking Area.

THE HIKE: This is a wander-at-will walk. A good way to begin is to hike over to the Natural Area's small pond, then pick up the signed Kid's Nature Trail.

CHAPTER FOUR

South County Parks & Preserves

Like other areas of Orange County, South OC boasts modern planned communities, shopping malls and business parks, but there are also more open spaces and places to get away from it all than in other parts of the county. The natural beauty and scenic splendor of South Orange County is preserved in large parklands. Here the hiker will find regional parks with "Wilderness" in their names. The county, as well as such relatively new incorporated cities as Lake Forest have been very proactive in creating and promoting trails.

LIMESTONE CANYON RESERVE

LIMESTONE CANYON TRAILS
To The Sinks is 2.5 miles round trip; to Dripping Springs is 6 miles round trip

For more than a century, Irvine Ranch cowboys were the only ones to roam scenic Limestone Canyon, one of the wildest lands remaining in Orange County. Now, hikers can experience what is now known as Limestone Canyon Reserve by taking a guided hike.

Limestone Canyon, located in southeastern Orange County, borders Cleveland National Forest and Limestone-Whiting Ranch Wilderness Park. The 5,000-acre reserve encompasses coastal sage scrub, chaparral and grassland communities, as well as oak and sycamore woodlands and even fern-surrounded dripping springs.

Limestone Canyon's name came from the cement-making operation of early Santiago Canyon settler Samuel Shrewsbury. Limestone rock was melted, hammered into a powder, then mixed with sand and used as mortar.

Eventually, "cluster developments"—residential communities concentrated in distinct areas to maximize remaining open space, will be constructed off Santiago Canyon Road. In coming years, Limestone Canyon may become accessible to the public and open for self-guided adventures.

Currently, public access includes The Nature Conservancy-led tours oriented to specific user groups, including hikers, cyclists and equestrians, as well as to children, artists, and bird-watchers. Once a month, Limestone Canyon is

Dripping Springs at Limestone Canyon Reserve

Don't fence me in – or out. Take a tour of this amazing land.

open to the public. Call The Nature Conservancy at (714) 832-7478 or check the hike schedule at www.irvineranchlandreserve.org

The hiking in Limestone Canyon ranges in distance from a 2.5 mile out-and-back to an overlook of The Sinks to a 15-mile loop. Depending on the hike, guides offer a range of nature interpretation from a little to a lot.

The 10-mile Limestone Canyon & Loma Ridge hike takes in a lot of the reserve and gets high on the ridgelines for spectacular views of Orange County. The 6-mile round trip jaunt to Dripping Springs is a particularly fine hike as is the 6-mile hike to Bolero Spring via "Hangman's Tree" Canyon.

"The Grand Canyon of Orange County" overstates the case a bit for Limestone Canyon, though The Sinks area of Limestone Canyon, where magnificent sandstone cliffs tower above a ravine, does resemble a mini-Grand Canyon. Hikers get great views of The Sinks, gloriously eroded, multi-layered formations with rugged river rock deposited layers on top and soft ancient marine layers on the bottom.

The Sinks are part of the Sespe Vaqueros Formation, formed 20 to 40 million years ago during a time of lowered sea levels and a more arid climate. The bottom layers (the whitish part) was deposited during humid times. Creeks deposited the top (reddish part) of the Sespe formation; its red color is form the oxidation (rust) of the iron present in the rock.

Another attraction for the hiker is Limestone's lovely and dense oak-sycamore woodlands. The woodlands, along with nearby rock caves, are the favored haunts of several species of bat. Oaks and cliff outcrops offer habitat for a range of raptors: red-tailed hawk, red-shouldered hawk, Coopers hawk, turkey vulture, great horned owl, barn owl and Western screech owl.

Limestone Canyon is a great place for bird-watching. Look for raptors circling over the native grassland (wild eye and purple needle grass) looking for prey. White kites and swallows swoop along the canyon's dramatic walls.

Dripping Springs Grotto is a lovely place with water trickling down rock walls and a kind of hanging garden of flowering plants and the protruding roots of shrubs and trees. Water springs out of fissures in the cliff year-around; its rainwater that's accumulated in a fault. Tangles of wild blackberry, maidenhair fern, scarlet monkeyflower and stream orchid thrive around the grotto.

A hundred years ago ranchers pumped water from Dripping Springs for their cattle to drink. You can see the remains of rusty pipe sticking out of the ground and oriented to the springs.

There aren't any cows around anymore. Or any cowboys. Close your eyes and listen to the dripping springs

DIRECTIONS TO TRAILHEAD: From its intersection with Jamboree Road, head east on Santiago Canyon Road for 5 miles. (If you spot Silverado Canyon Road, you've overshot the turnoff.). Turn right (south) onto Hicks Canyon Haul Road. The hiking begins inside the vehicle gate across the road.

FREMONT CANYON

GUIDED HIKES OF FREMONT CANYON
From Irvine Park to Coal Mine is 5 miles round trip; to Tecate Cypress is 10 miles round trip

Habitat for numerous rare plants and animals, the 475-acre Fremont Canyon Wilderness is one of Orange County's wonders. I'll always count the spring day I hiked Fremont Canyon in the good company of a botanist and field ecologist in the employ of The Nature Conservancy who pointed out to this very amateur naturalist the colorful abundance of flowering plants en route, as one of best days I ever spent on a Southern California trail.

We spotted lots of small animals, as well the tracks and signs of larger ones. Fremont Canyon, which ranges in elevation from 700 to 2,376 feet, is an important wildlife corridor for animals ranging from mule deer to mountain lion.

Currently, public access to Fremont Canyon is limited to The Nature Conservancy-led tours. Call The Nature Conservancy at (714) 832-7478 or check the hike schedule at www.irvineranchlandreserve.org

As the story goes, Fremont Canyon got its name from one Mr. Smith, a mid-19th-century sheepherder who claimed to have traveled with explorer John C. Frémont. Supposedly he talked so much about Frémont, who was California's first governor, that locals began referring to the canyon where he dwelled, and even to Smith himself, as "Fremont."

Contemplate the botanical and geological wonders of Fremont Canyon.

The canyon also appeared on maps as Cañon de la Horca–"Choked Canyon"– because the walls of one fork squeeze or choke close together. Another fork extends to the summit of Sierra Peak prompting another name–Sierra Canyon–that's appeared on some maps.

The guided hikes lead by a huge pile of coal, a mini-mountain of low-grade coal leftover from the canyon's mining days, located about a quarter mile north of the Irvine Dam spillway. From 1864 to 1912, an Irvine Company-owned coal mine was in operation near the mouth of the canyon. Local silver mines and Southern California railroads were key customers for the coal, some of which was transported to Newport's McFadden Pier and loaded on ships bound for San Francisco.

Hikers can visit Fremont Canyon's stands of the rather rare Tecate cypress. The native cypress, which ranges from Orange County south into Baja Mexico, is generally found in chaparral zones of the coastal mountains. The small tree, 20 to 30 feet high, has bright green foliage and an irregular spreading crown.

If you take one of the longer guided hikes–up to the Tecate Cypress or the grand, 15-mile long "Fremont Canyon Loop"–you'll get grand views of downtown Los Angeles, the Palos Verdes Peninsula, Newport Beach, the wide shimmering Pacific and Catalina Island.

While it may be stretching a point to describe Fremont Canyon as "the Yosemite of Orange County," it is true that some of the canyon's rock formations are darn dramatic. And the rocks aren't just a pretty face; they support rare lichens and mosses and the relatively rare speckled rattlesnake. Lizard Rock, one of the few named formations, is a hangout for the granite spiny lizard. Rock caves offer habitat for 11 (!) species of bat.

The north ridgeline of Fremont Canyon hosts Fremont Weather Station. Winds up to 100 mph have been recorded on "Windy Ridge." Want the latest weather report from Fremont Canyon before you take a hike? Go online and get real-time data transmitted from Fremont Canyon: www.wrh.noaa.gov

DIRECTIONS TO TRAILHEAD: At this writing, guided hikes begin at Parking lot #15 at the southeastern boundary of Irvine Park. From the park, you'll be permitted to walk onto–or drive onto–private property via a road that passes under the Toll Road bridge toward Irvine Lake. The hike begins just before a crossing of Santiago Creek.

BAKER CANYON

BAKER CANYON TRAIL
Guided Hike from Baker Canyon Road to Overlook is a 3-mile loop with
400-foot elevation gain

Baker Canyon is an intriguing location for one of The Nature Conservancy's
most family-friendly guided hikes. It's often billed as "A Quiet Walk" which
surely it is, as well as an educational one, with lots of stops for interpretation of
the natural world en route.

You'll begin by following this loop trail by ascending a coastal scrub cloaked
ridge to a vista point and views of the massive sandstone cliffs atop Elephant Peak
and Limestone Canyon. The lower half of the trail travels through chaparral and
riparian communities.

When California was under the Mexican flag, Baker Canyon was known as
Mujer Vieja, "Old Woman." The canyon was later named for Deputy Sheriff
Charles Baker, one of the first lawmen in the region killed in the line of duty after
California achieved statehood.

As the story goes, legendary bandit and convicted horse thief Juan Flores
escaped from San Quentin Prison and hid out in the Santiago Canyon area with a
gang numbering some 50 men. A posse of a half-dozen lawmen led by Sheriff
Barton gave chase and rode into an ambush. The sheriff and three deputies,
including Baker, were shot dead. More posses rode after Flores and he was soon
captured, tried and hung in Los Angeles.

Nature Conservancy crew takes a break on a quiet hike.

Rock formations in Baker Canyon and beyond are striking. Covered first by oceans then by shallow seas, Baker Canyon displays its underwater origins in the form of marine sandstone and seashells. From the Baker Canyon ridgeline, the hiker looks out at the obviously-named Red Rocks across Santiago Creek. These rocks are part of the Sespe Formation, formed 20 to 40 million years ago.

You'll also observe some past and present human uses of Baker Canyon, including a helicopter landing area for the military and for Orange County Fire Authority training. You can't miss the electrical tower that helps carry juice across Orange County from San Onofre to Chino. Last stop on the loop trail is the now-abandoned Axelrod Camp for the Blind.

Currently, public access to Baker Canyon is limited to The Nature Conservancy-led tours. Call The Nature Conservancy at (714) 832-7478 or check the hike schedule at www.irvineranchlandreserve.org

DIRECTIONS TO TRAILHEAD: (Remember, this is a guided hike; the trailhead parking lot is open only for these escorted hikes.) From the Costa Mesa Freeway (55) in Orange, exit on Chapman Avenue and head east. Chapman turns into Santiago Canyon Road which you follow past the Highway 241 toll road and past Irvine Lake to Silverado Canyon Road. Turn left and go only a few hundred feet to Blackstar Road. Turn left and drive 0.4 mile to Baker Canyon Road, the first paved road on the right, and take this road 0.1 mile to the fenced parking area.

LIMESTONE-WHITING RANCH WILDERNESS PARK

BORREGO CANYON, WHITING, VISTA POINT TRAILS
From 4 to 6 miles round trip.

Oak-shaded canyons, grassy hills and handsome, rose-colored sandstone cliffs are some of the attractions of Orange County's Limestone-Whiting Ranch Wilderness Park. The 1,500-acre park, crisscrossed by trails, is a hiker's delight.

First-time visitors are amazed to find a lush oak woodland and rugged hills in such close proximity to suburban developments.

Rancho Canada de los Aliso was the land grant given in 1842 to José Serrano who raised cattle until the great drought of 1864 bankrupted the rancho. Dwight Whiting bought the land in 1885, planting vineyards and olive trees, as well as subdividing it. In 1959, the property was sold to a residential developer and suburbia ensued.

Limestone-Whiting Ranch Wilderness Park, which opened to the public in 1991, is an oasis of green in a fast-growing area of Orange County. While the park is indeed a wild land as its name suggests (a mountain lion killed a mountain biker and attacked another in the park in 2003), the trailhead is anything but. A shopping center is located across Portola Parkway. Near the trailhead is a sculpture entitled "California song," a windmill-topped tower that depicts native birds and wildlife.

Smart hikers travel in pairs at this wild OC park.

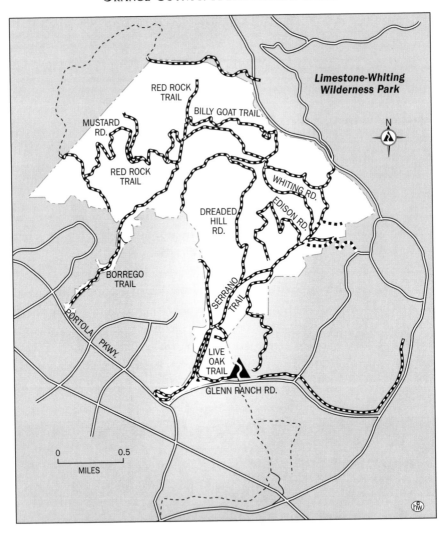

DIRECTIONS TO TRAILHEAD: From Interstate 5 in the El Toro area, exit on Lake Forest Drive and proceed east 4.8 miles to Portola Parkway. Turn left and drive 0.5 mile to the entrance and parking lot of Whiting Ranch Wilderness Park.

THE HIKE: Borrego Trail leads a mile through oak-studded Borrego Canyon, a peninsula of parkland surrounded on three sides by residential and commercial development. The path up Borrego Canyon leads to junctions with other trails that lead to more remote sections of the park.

Three popular hikes (mileage calculated from Portola Parkway trailhead) include: Vista Point Trail (4 miles round trip) leads from Borrego Canyon to a high ridge for excellent views of south Orange County.

Red Rock Trail (4 miles round trip) explores what some rock connoisseurs consider to be one of Orange County's finest formations. It's a 1.5-mile hike to reach Red Rock Trail, a 0.5-mile pathway into the strangely eroded sandstone, and a rare hikers-only path.

The Borrego Trail-Mustard Road-Whiting Road Loop is a grand 6-mile tour of the park. The route climbs through heavily wooded Borrego Canyon, tops out at a junction called Four Corners, then descends Serrano Canyon to Portola Parkway. A mile of walking along the road brings you back to the trailhead.

Borrego Trail, a great way to go, for a hike or a bike.

Dreaded Hill

SERRANO, WHITING, DREADED HILL, SERRANO TRAILS
From Glenn Ranch Road entrance is 5 mile loop with 800-foot elevation gain

According to local hikers, Limestone Canyons and Whiting Ranch Wilderness Park's highest hill had a lot of names, but "Dreaded" was the only one that could be printed on a map and repeated in public. The brutal climb required to reach the top of this hill, which looms to the south of the park's popular Four Corners area, has been known to prompt trail users to describe it with some colorful—and quite off-color—words.

Let's just say that "aerobic torture" is one of the more polite ways to describe the hike. Still, climbing Dreaded Hill has its rewards apart from its test of one's physical fitness. Are the views from the summit worth the climb? Well, only you can answer that question when you reach the 1,624-foot crest. The views from the summit include Orange County near and far, Catalina Island and the wide, blue Pacific.

On a sadder note, atop the hill you'll find a memorial bench with a plaque that reads: "Michael J. Reynolds, 1969-2004. He was doing what he loved." Avid mountain biker Reynolds was killed by a mountain lion in Whiting Park. He was the sixth Californian to be killed by a cougar during the last 100 years and the first ever in Orange County. Following his death, his friends placed the plaque at the summit.

DIRECTIONS TO TRAILHEAD: From the San Diego Freeway (5) on the border between Irvine and Lake Forest, exit on Lake Forest Drive and drive 5 miles north to Portola Parkway. Turn right on Portola Parkway and follow it southwest to Glenn Ranch Road. Turn right, then make a left into the park.

O'Neill Regional Park

After six decades of conservation activity and park-making, O'Neill Park now encompasses more than 3,000 acres of woodland and brushy hills, taking in Trabuco Canyon and neighboring Live Oak Canyon. From the park's ridges, the hiker gets vistas of two scenes typical of rural Orange County: red-tailed hawks circling over classic ranch country in one direction and brand new suburbs—indeed whole communities— in the other. The area around O'Neill has changed almost unbelievably since my Boy Scout days when my troop enjoyed camping here, but the park itself still gives visitors the feeling of getting away from modern life. Park pathways include nature trails, a number of short loops into the hills, and links to lengthy Arroyo Trabuco Trail that extends to Limestone-Whiting Ranch Wilderness Park.

TRABUCO & LIVE OAK CANYONS

LIVE OAK TRAIL
From Trabuco Canyon to Ocean Vista Point is 3 miles round trip with 600-foot elevation gain

The soldier who lost his firearm when marching with Captain Gaspar de Portolá in the 1769 expedition in this hilly region would no doubt be astonished at the number of Orange County placenames inspired by his mistake. *Trabuco*, which means "blunderbuss" in Spanish, now names a canyon, a creek, a plain, a trail, a road and even a ranger district of the Cleveland National Forest.

If the unknown soldier who lost his blunderbuss trekked this way again he would be amazed at the names on the land, and even more amazed at the land itself, so drastically has it changed. Maybe though, he would recognize Trabuco Canyon, at least that part of it saved from suburbanization by O'Neill Regional Park. Here the modern trekker can explore a small slice of the pastoral Southern California of two centuries ago.

This land of grassy meadows, rolling hills and oak woodland was originally part of Rancho Trabuco, two leagues granted to Santiago Arguello in 1841 by

Stately old oaks shade O'Neill's hikers and picnickers.

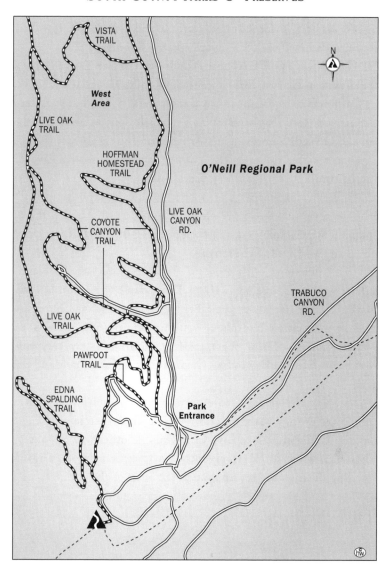

VISTA TRAIL

West Area

LIVE OAK TRAIL

HOFFMAN HOMESTEAD TRAIL

O'Neill Regional Park

LIVE OAK CANYON RD.

COYOTE CANYON TRAIL

LIVE OAK TRAIL

TRABUCO CANYON RD.

PAWFOOT TRAIL

EDNA SPALDING TRAIL

Park Entrance

Mexican Governor Alvarado. The rancho had various lessees and owners until it was purchased by James Flood, a wealthy businessman and his partner Richard O'Neill, a packing house owner. O'Neill built up quite a ranching empire here and elsewhere in California. O'Neill's Orange County property passed to various heirs who, in turn, gave 278 acres of Trabuco Canyon to Orange County for a park in 1948. Today, after various gifts and purchases, the park encompasses 3,000 acres of woodland and brushy hills, taking in Trabuco Canyon and neighboring Live Oak Canyon.

This hike leaves the wooded canyon behind and ascends to Ocean Vista Point. The vistas include nearby peaks, canyons and the promised Pacific.

DIRECTIONS TO TRAILHEAD: From the San Diego Freeway (5) in Lake Forest, exit on El Toro Road and head 7.5 miles east to the junction known as Cook's Corner. Santiago Canyon Road angles left (north) but you veer right on Live Oak Canyon Road (S19) and follow Live Oak Canyon Road east then south 3 miles to the O'Neill Regional Park entrance on the right. Past the park entry station, make a right to reach the parking area and signed Live Oak and Spaulding Nature Trail trailhead in a quarter-mile.

THE HIKE: Continue past the junction with Edna Spaulding Trail on your left and head north. When you reach some hillside water tanks, the trail very briefly joins the water tank road, and then you'll resume with Live Oak Trail on the climb up the west wall of the canyon.

You'll pass junctions with Pawfoot Trail, Homestead Trail and Coyote Canyon Trail as you ascend along a ridge. The views begin before the vista point and what you see are two scenes typical of this side of Orange County: red-tailed hawks circling over classic Southland ranching country and suburbs, as well as suburbs-in-the-making. From the 1,492-foot summit, enjoy clear-day coastal views from Santa Monica Bay to San Clemente, with Catalina Island floating on the horizon.

After enjoying the views, choose between two or more return routes. One way back is by retracing your steps on Live Oak Trail, then joining Coyote Trail to Homestead Trail and back to Live Oak Trail. Another way to go is by way of Valley Vista Trail which drops steeply into Live Oak Canyon. An old park service road paralleling the highway returns you to the heart of the park.

EDNA SPAULDING NATURE TRAIL

SPAULDING NATURE TRAIL
0.8-mile loop through O'Neill Regional Park

Named for the science teacher who was its creative inspiration, Edna Spaulding Nature Trail offers a fine introduction to the oak woodland and coastal sage environments found in O'Neill Regional Park. Pick up a copy of the interpretive brochure for this trail at the park office, and then take a delightful and educational walk.

In addition to lessons about the region's natural history, the trail offers something more: great vistas of Orange County's highest summits, including Santiago Peak and Modjeska Peak, together forming Old Saddleback.

DIRECTIONS TO TRAILHEAD: From the San Diego Freeway (5) in Lake Forest, exit on El Toro Road and head 7.5 miles east to the junction known as Cook's Corner. Santiago Canyon Road angles left (north) but you veer right on Live Oak Canyon Road (S19) and follow Live Oak Canyon Road east then south 3 miles to the O'Neill Regional Park entrance on the right. Past the park entry station, make a right to reach the parking area and signed Live Oak and Spaulding Nature Trail trailhead in a quarter mile.

THE HIKE: As with the Live Oak Trail (see hike write-up), walk the paved road up-canyon one hundred yards or so to a junction. Take the leftward trail a short distance to the beginning of Edna Spaulding Nature Trail.

As you make your clockwise exploration of the nature trail, you'll ascend for fine views of Trabuco Canyon.

After this mild ascent, the path descends to coastal live oak woodlands. The nature trail might just inspire you to take a longer hike in O'Neill Regional Park. (See hike descriptions in this guide.)

ARROYO TRABUCO WILDERNESS

ARROYO TRABUCO TRAIL
From O'Neill Park to Oso Parkway is 6 miles one way with 500-foot elevation loss

One way or another the hike through Arroyo Trabuco Wilderness is an engaging experience. In fact, one-way may be the best way to walk this wildland corridor from O'Neill Park to Oso Parkway across southern Orange County. With the help of a car shuttle, the hiker can enjoy a mostly downhill ramble from a nature center to a mini-mall, a journey from the foothills of the Santa Ana Mountains to trail's end near a Taco Bell.

On a recent down-canyon jaunt, I experienced a collage, indeed collision, of images that included a murmuring creek, grand old oaks and sycamores, a doe and fawn browsing a flower-sprinkled meadow, as well as traffic rushing over my head on the Foothill Transportation Corridor (toll road). In places, all traces of the suburbia that sandwiches Arroyo Trabuco recedes to a respectful distance, and the hiker is left only in the company of chirping crickets, croaking frogs and twittering birds.

Part of this leafy retreat was fashioned by humans, not nature. Road-builders were required to plant a couple thousand native trees—willow, oak, sycamore and

Revel in the autumn splendor on colorful display in Arroyo Trabuco.

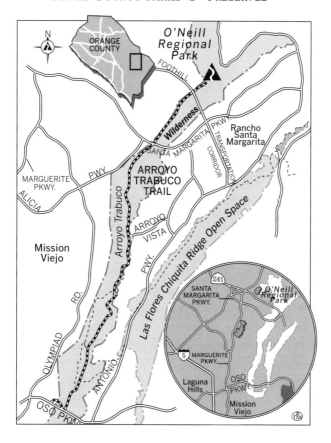

more—in the arroyo in order to offset the environmental effects of the arroyo-crossing parkways

A winter walk can be quite a muddy adventure. A half-dozen knee-high or higher creek crossings can mean a wet and wild journey.

Spring is an excellent time to trek Arroyo Trabuco. Arroyo Trabuco Creek is sprightly, and its banks blossom with monkeyflowers, California poppies and lush green grasses.

By summer, the arroyo is all but dry and the temperature too hot for pleasant hiking. In autumn, the arroyo's numerous sycamores don their fall colors. Cool, coastal breezes (and sometimes hot Santa Ana winds) whisk the yellow-brown leaves from the trees and scatter them along the trail.

DIRECTIONS TO TRAILHEAD: From the San Diego Freeway (5) in El Toro, exit on El Toro Road and drive 7.5 miles to Live Oak Canyon Road (S-19). Turn right and proceed 3 miles to O'Neill Regional Park. There is a vehicle entry fee.

From the entry station, follow the signs west to the far end of the day-use area and the well-marked trailhead.

If you intend to hike Arroyo Trabuco one-way and would like to arrange a car shuttle, you'll want to leave a vehicle or be met at the commercial center located on the southeast corner of Oso Parkway and San Antonio Parkway. Reach this intersection from the San Diego Freeway (5) in Mission Viejo by exiting on Oso Parkway and traveling west a few miles.

The signed southern end of Arroyo Trabuco Trail is actually located 0.3 mile west of San Antonio Parkway on the north side of Oso Parkway; however, there is no parking whatsoever here, so you need to leave your vehicle at or near the mini-mall on the corner of Oso Parkway and San Antonio Parkway. A variety of eateries offer food and refreshment for the hiker.

THE HIKE: Follow the wide path south under towering oaks and sycamores, then under the even more towering spans of the Foothill Transportation Corridor and Santa Margarita Parkway.

About two miles out, the path angles left up toward a canyon wall, topped by houses. A connector trail leads to Arroyo Vista (a street and trailhead for residential access to the Arroyo). After another mile of travel, the trail descends back toward the creek.

You'll alternate travel between wide meadows and the riparian corridor along the creek. After three creek crossings, you'll spot the Oso Parkway bridge over the arroyo. The path crosses under the bridge, then immediately crosses back to intersect a dirt powerline access road that ascends the west wall of the arroyo to trail's end at Oso Parkway. Walk east 0.3 along the sidewalk to reach the shopping center at the corner of Oso Parkway and San Antonio Parkway.

MISSION VIEJO'S OSO CREEK

OSO CREEK TRAIL
2-mile loop with 100-foot elevation gain

The "Oso" bear is long-gone from these parts, but the trail uses a paw print logo on its signage, homage of sorts to the last grizzly bear sighted along Oso Creek. A family-friendly pathway winds along Oso Creek, now a suburbanized stream channel.

Oso Creek is a tributary of one of Orange County's largest waterways, San Juan Creek, which flows from high in the Santa Ana Mountains some 27 miles to the Pacific near Dana Point Harbor. Oso is one of the county's creeks most altered by development: channelization, paving of the flood plain, loss of riparian habitat and biodiversity.

Oso Creek Trail has a collection of natural and cultural attractions along its banks to make it worth the casual hiker's while. En route, you'll encounter a handsome oak grove, a meadow, a butterfly garden and a plant maze. My family's favorite is a peace obelisk, inscribed with the word "peace" in a dozen languages and displaying hundreds of copper relief peace emblems fashioned by community members. Now there's something you don't see very often alongside a trail!

Oso Creek Trail is the chief passageway in Mission Viejo's fledgling trail system. The path links to 2-mile-long Jeronimo Open-Space Trail and connections with Naciente Ridge Trail which, in turn, extends along the ridge by Olympiad Road and eventually descends to Arroyo Trabuco at the city's eastern boundary.

DIRECTIONS TO TRAILHEAD: From the San Diego Freeway (5) in Mission Viejo, exit on La Paz Road and head east a mile to Marguerite Parkway. Turn left and go 0.7 mile to Jeronimo Road. Turn right and park on or near Jeronimo Road where it meets San Fernando Street.

THE HIKE: From the signed trailhead on the Jeronimo Road bridge, switchback down a paved walkway to an oak grove and the creekside portion of the path. Hike downstream on the woodchip-covered trail along a creek bank shaded with sycamores. Stop at the peace monument and, after wishing for world peace, continue to a mini-maze. Kids will espe-

Grizzly—gone but not forgotten.

A monument to peace: give an obelisk a chance.

cially enjoy navigating the low circular hedges to find the center.

Continue down-creek to the butterfly garden and a signed four-way junction. You can cross the bridge here and loop back to the trailhead by following the path on the other side of Oso Creek. For a longer loop, resume your down-stream journey on a paved pathway to La Paz Road.

Return by carefully crossing La Paz at the light and picking up the signed trail at the Thomas R. Potocki Conference Center. You'll saunter past Oso Community Park's sports fields and landscaped mini-gardens. This hike ends back at the Jeronimo Road bridge, but you can continue by traveling under the bridge and joining the dirt pathway that leads through less-developed terrain.

RILEY WILDERNESS PARK

WAGON WHEEL CANYON, MULE DEER, OAK CANYON TRAILS
To Skink Vista Point and beyond is 2 to 3 miles round trip with 300-foot elevation gain

The first time I arrived to hike General Thomas F. Riley Wilderness Park it was after a rainstorm and rangers advised me to step gently along park trails so that my hiking boots would not erode pathways and hillsides. Good advice for all hikers, I thought, as I walked among the ancient oaks of Wagon Wheel Canyon.

However, I soon discovered that the ecological integrity of the park faced a far greater threat than hikers tramping muddy trails. Just 75 yards from the park's Sycamore Loop Trail, two giant earthmovers chewed into the wet earth, molding mountains into building pads for a new subdivision.

Witnessing a disturbing development like the one I saw on this park's southern boundary has a way of horrifying we hikers as well as reminding us of the value of such nature preserves in an ever-more-citified Southland.

The fungus among us –
a mini-forest in a leafy glade.

Riley Wilderness Park may be a wilderness in name only, but its 475 acres offer habitat for deer, raccoons, rabbits, coyotes and a wide variety of bird species. The park preserves a remnant of what the land may have resembled in the 1840s during its days as a rancho: old oak groves and grassy hillsides sprinkled with wildflowers.

Wagon Wheel Park, as it was first known, was acquired by the County of Orange in 1983 and re-dedicated in 1994 as Riley Wilderness Park in honor of a former Orange County supervisor for his considerable conservation efforts in southern Orange County.

About five miles of family-friendly trail weave through the park. Two vista points offer commanding vistas of what's developed and what's not, as well as a panorama of the mile-high peaks of the neighboring Santa Ana Mountains.

A tiny nature center and a drought-resistant landscaping display help visitors learn about the local native plant life. Check out the old wagon parked by the small picnic area and learn how Wagon Wheel Canyon got its name.

DIRECTIONS TO TRAILHEAD: From the San Diego Freeway (405) in Mission Viejo, exit on Oso Parkway and travel a bit more than 6 miles east.

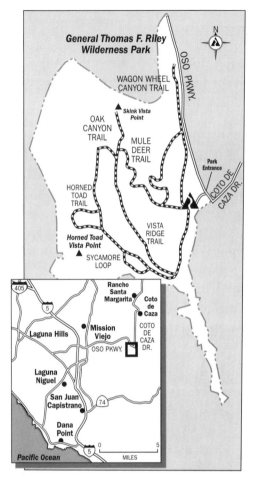

Just before the parkway ends at a junction with Coto de Caza, turn right at the signed entrance for Riley Wilderness Park. Follow the park's gravel access road to a parking area and signed trails.

Park hours are 7 A.M. to sunset daily (closing times vary seasonally, as posted). There is an entry fee.

THE HIKE: For the full (3-mile version) of this walk in the park, join signed Wagon Wheel Trail and head north past some oaks. The path parallels Oso Parkway for a time before it junctions Pheasant Run Trail; join this path which reverses your direction of travel and sends you back south. "Pleasant Run" might be another name for this trail, which is popular with local joggers. After a mellow ascent and descent, the path deposits you on Mule Deer Trail, not far from the trailhead.

Mule Deer Trail winds past antiquarian oaks and cactus patches into the heart of the park. A bit of wooden boardwalk helps hikers over a sometimes soggy meadow. The path climbs gently into a coastal sage scrub community. An interpretive sign explains that less than 5 percent of this community remains in these parts; the other 95 percent has already been lost to development.

At a signed junction, detour north 0.2 mile to ascend the bald ridge capped by Skink Vista Point. Peer through a sighting tube at the crest of the Santa Ana Mountains, including Modjeska Peak (5,496 feet) and Santiago Peak (5,687 feet), as well as suburban developments at the foot of the range.

Return to the junction and descend briefly, but steeply, on Oak Canyon Trail into a coast live oak-lined draw. Seasonal rains fill an old cattle pond that today is a watering hole for numerous birds and animals.

Two short loops off Oak Canyon Trail add to the hiker's perspective. Horned Toad Trail leads to a vista point that overlooks southern Orange County and

Shade and shelter for wildlife and wanderers.

Sycamore Loop Trail tours an old grove of Western sycamore and a subdivision-in-the-making on the park's southern boundary. A final 0.25 mile of northward travel returns the hiker to the trailhead.

Wide-open spaces in Caspers Wilderness Park.

Caspers Wilderness Park

At 7,600 acres, Caspers Wilderness Park is the largest park
in Orange County's regional park system and, to date,
the park most removed from major OC population centers.
With its size, scope wildness and wildlife, the park is
worthy of the "wilderness" in its name. Crisscrossing
Casper are 30 miles of trail, which explore grassy valleys,
chaparral-cloaked ridges and splendid groves of
coastal live oak and sycamore. The best hiking in the park
are through the two major oak-lined canyons—
Bell and San Juan—and along the brushy ridges,
which offer grand clear-day views
from the Santa Ana Mountains to the Pacific.

BELL CANYON

NATURE, OAK, BELL CANYON TRAILS
2 to 4 mile loops

Crisscrossing Caspers Wilderness Park are thirty miles of trail that explore grassy valleys, chaparral cloaked ridges and native groves of coastal live oak and sycamore. Visitors have a good chance of sighting wildlife: Deer, rabbits and coyote, as well as more furtive animals such as foxes and bobcats. Bird watchers will want to consult the park's bird list and test their skill by identifying the many species found in the park.

Centerpiece of the park is oak lined Bell Canyon. Acorns from the oaks were an important food source for the Juaneno Indians who lived in the canyon. As the legend goes, the Indians would strike a large granite boulder with a small rock to make it ring. The sound could be heard for a mile through what is now known as Bell Canyon. "Bell Rock" is now housed in Bowers Museum in Santa Ana.

Bell Canyon, San Juan Canyon, and surrounding ridges were once part of Starr Viejo Ranch, which was purchased by Orange County in the early 1970s. The park honors Ronald W. Caspers, chairman of the Orange County Board of Supervisors, who was instrumental in preserving the old ranch as a park. Reminders of the park's ranching heritage include a windmill and a wooden corral where the branding and loading of cattle took place. The windmill still pumps a

little water, which helps park wildlife make it through the long, hot summers in the Santa Ana Mountains. During summer, the area around the windmill is the park's best bird watching spot.

To learn more about the region's human and natural history, drop by the park's visitor center. Exhibits interpret Native American life, birds, mammals, geology, and much more. The mostly level, Nature Trail Oak Trail Bell Canyon Trail loop described below is only one of many possible day hikes you can fashion from the park's extensive trail network.

DIRECTIONS TO TRAILHEAD: From Interstate 5 in San Juan Capistrano, take the Highway 74 (Ortega Highway) exit. Drive 8 miles inland to the entrance to Caspers Wilderness Park. There is a vehicle entrance fee.

From the entry kiosk, take the park road 1.5 miles to its end at the corral and windmill. There's plenty of parking near the signed trailhead for Nature Trail.

THE HIKE: Nature Trail loops through a handsome grove of antiquarian oak. You might see woodpeckers checking their store of acorns, which the birds have stuffed in hidey-holes in the nearby sycamores. Beneath the oaks are some huge patches of poison oak, but the trail steers clear of them.

You'll pass a junction with a left-branching trail that leads to Gunsight Pass and West Ridge Trail, and soon arrive at a second junction. (If you want a really short hike, keep right at this junction and you'll loop back to the trailhead via Nature Trail.)

Head north on signed Oak Trail, which meanders beneath the oak and sycamore that shade the west wall of Bell Canyon. The trail never strays far from Bell Creek, its streambed, or sandy washes. During drought years, it's difficult to imagine that in the 19th century, black bears used to catch spawning steelhead trout in Bell Creek. Fragrant sages perfume the trail, which is also lined with lemonade berry and prickly pear cactus.

Oak Trail reaches a junction at Post "12." You may take a short connector trail east to Bell Canyon or head north on another short trail, Star Rise, and join Bell Canyon Trail. A wide dirt road, Bell Canyon Trail travels the canyon floor.

Don't miss a visit to the Caspers Wilderness Visitor Center.

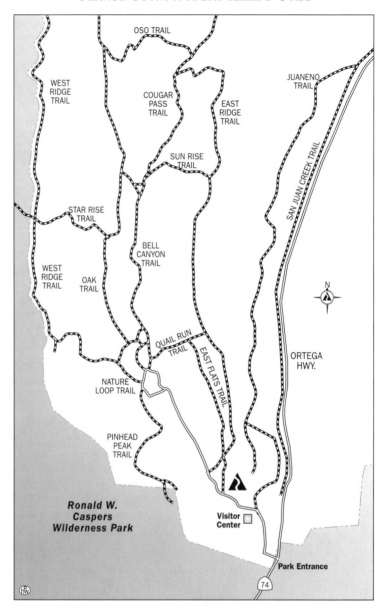

To return to the trailhead, you'll head south on Bell Canyon Trail, which passes through open oak-dotted meadows. Red-tailed hawks roost atop spreading sycamores. The trail returns you to the parking area, within sight of the beginning of Nature Trail, where you began your walk.

PINHEAD PEAK

PINHEAD PEAK TRAIL
From Old Windmill to Pinhead Peak is 1.5 miles round trip with 400-foot elevation gain

Pinhead Peak is short in stature (just 662 feet high), but long on views. The peak and an unnamed neighboring peaklet offer panoramic views of Caspers Wilderness Park which, at 7,600 acres, is a lot of park to view. Beyond the park boundary loom the twin peaks of Old Saddleback—Mt. Modjeska (5,440 feet) and Mt. Santiago (5,860 feet).

If your time is short and you want to get "the lay of the land" the path to Pinhead Peak is a good one to take. Survey the scene from the summit, take a mental snapshot of the cliffs and canyon, and promise yourself that you'll return to the park for a longer hike.

DIRECTIONS TO TRAILHEAD: (See Bell Canyon hike write-up for directions to Caspers Wilderness Park.) Begin at the park's old windmill.

THE HIKE: From the windmill, the path heads south toward the park equestrian area, then curves through a grassy meadow and voila—there you are looking up at Pinhead Peak. Up you go onto the ridgeline that defines the park boundary. Enjoy the view from the top, and from another slightly lower peak 0.1 mile away.

On the way to Pinhead Peak – neither pin-like nor peak-like, but definitely a trail.

EAST RIDGE

EAST FLATS, EAST RIDGE, OSO, BELL CANYON TRAILS
Loop from San Juan Meadows Picnic Area is 7 miles round trip with 500-foot elevation gain

This hike leaves behind (but returns to) the mellow woodlands in the bottom of Bell Canyon and travels the park's high country. This high country isn't all that high—less than 1,000 feet in elevation) but in the case of East Ridge is high enough to offer some fine views of the noted groves of sycamore and coastal live oak along the river terraces below.

True to its name, the trail (2.5 miles one way) traverses Bell Canyon's eastern ridge, a landscape cloaked with chaparral and dotted with prickly pear cactus. The trail links to five more paths that in turn connect to Bell Canyon, so loop opportunities are many and varied. Hike a shorter loop than the one described by descending from East Ridge to the canyon bottom via Quail Run Trail or Sun Rise Trail.

DIRECTIONS TO TRAILHEAD: (See Bell Canyon Trail write-up for directions to Caspers Wilderness Park). This path begins just beyond the San Juan Picnic Area.

THE HIKE: Join East Flats Trail for a brisk quarter-mile ascent to a junction, Bear right on wide East Ridge Trail for a no-nonsense ascent to the ridgeline that it will doggedly follow to its northern terminus.

After passing junctions with steep connectors leading down to Bell Canyon—Quail Run and Sun Rise—East Ridge Trail swings left (west). To the east, a short walk away, is a 900-foot bump on the ridge that offers a grand view of the Santa Ana Mountains.

The trail drops off East Ridge to junction with Cougar Pass Trail which you'll follow a quarter mile to intersect Oso Trail. Head left (west) and cross an ancient river terrace, one of the previous incarnations of Bell Canyon Creek.

After descending to the canyon floor, you'll turn left (south) on Bell Canyon Trail and head down-canyon back to the park road and the trailhead.

SAN JUAN CANYON

OSO, SAN JUAN CREEK, JUANENO TRAILS
Loop from visitor center is 9 miles round trip with 800-foot elevation gain

Dramatic bluffs, oak woodland and grand vistas are all rewards of this long loop over the wall of San Juan Canyon and along the canyon bottom. You could power-through the loop and use it as a conditioning hike for, say, that upcoming High Sierra trek, or you can spend most of a pleasant day touring a less-visited side of the park.

Sometimes the trails in these parts aren't maintained as well as others in the park; you hiking short wearers might just get your legs brush-whacked.

Clear-day views from atop the high canyon walls are superb and take in the summits of the Santa Ana Mountains, the OC-LA lowlands and even the Pacific Ocean.

DIRECTIONS TO TRAILHEAD: From Interstate 5 in San Juan Capistrano, take the Highway 74 (Ortega Highway) exit. Drive eight miles inland to Caspers Wilderness Park.

THE HIKE: From the visitor center, head north up Bell Canyon past the end of the paved road for another mile on the dirt track to a meeting with Cougar Pass Trail. Head right (northeast) a mile to intersect Oso Trail and follow this path on an ascent of the prickly pear-dotted canyon wall to a vista point and a shaded picnic table.

After enjoying the far-reaching views, drop south on Badger Pass Trail to reach San Juan Creek, the Ortega Highway Bridge spanning it, and San Juan Creek Trail. Head down-creek a quarter-mile to a junction with Juaneno Trail.

San Juan Creek Trail extends for several miles alongside (and way too close in The Trailmaster's opinion) Ortega Highway. It's a rather straight trail, too, and popular with mountain bikers. All of this might suggest that the preferred hiker's route is via Juaneno Trail so get to it by heading alongside the west bank of San Juan Creek.

The creekside terrain varies from thick riparian flora to scattered oak with views of the sedimentary cliffs rising high above the trail. Juaneno Trail crests a slope to end at the eastern edge of the San Juan Meadows Group Area.

CHAPTER FIVE

Santa Ana Mountains

Extending the entire length of Orange County's eastern perimeter, the Santa Anas roughly parallel the coast, which has a cooling influence on what is often a very hot range of mountains. Except for the dog days of summer, most days offer pleasant hiking. While some local hikers know and appreciate the range's trails, visitation statistics indicate that in comparison to other Southland ranges, the Santa Ana Mountains may be one of the more overlooked and under-utilized recreation areas in Southern California. If that's the case, get hiking on those great trails that explore the 136,500 acres of mountain range included in the Cleveland National Forest's Trabuco District.

Ortega Highway

When the Ortega Highway, which extends from San Juan Capistrano to Lake Elsinore and crosses the Santa Ana Mountains was completed in 1933, it opened up the mountains to camping and hiking in the same way as the Rim of the World Highway opened up the San Bernardino Mountains and the Angeles Crest opened up the San Gabriel Mountains. During the week it's busy with commuters from southwestern Riverside County commuting to jobs in Orange County and on weekends for recreational drives and motorcycle outings. For the hiker, the road offers great access to trailheads for hiking, both north and south of the highway. The hiking ranges from "leg-stretcher" nature trails to longer explorations through canyons to the tops of the mountains.

EL CARISO

EL CARISO NATURE TRAIL
1.4 mile loop with 100-foot elevation gain

For a family-friendly exploration of the native flora and wildlife of the Santa Ana Mountains, take a hike on El Cariso Nature Trail. The path loops through a variety of flowering shrubs from sage to chamise.

Larger floristic highlights include Coulter pines (so-called "penny pines") planted here, though native to the area. A scattering of oaks and cedar join the pines.

Before you head down the trail, drop into the visitor center at El Cariso Ranger Station. Interpretive exhibits explain the mountain range's ecology and ecology. Pick up a pamphlet (not always available) that points out the highlights of the self-guided trail.

The gentle path contours around a hill above the ranger station and delivers good views of the national forest and the San Mateo Canyon Wilderness. It's not a completely pristine view though; a number of private property inholdings are visible, too.

DIRECTIONS TO TRAILHEAD: From the San Diego Freeway (I-5) in San Juan Capistrano, exit on Ortega Highway (74) and head east 23 miles to El Cariso Ranger Station, located on the right (south) side of the highway. Park in front of the visitor center or in lot across the highway. The nature trail begins just to the right of the visitor center.

THE HIKE: From its beginning on the west (right) side of the visitor cen-

ter, the dirt path ascends briefly through a stand of oak, then heads into the chaparral and coastal sage. The path bends east and, about at half-mile out at nature trail stop #10, note the old mine tunnel.

The trail crosses paved Main Divide Road and winds through a grove of Coulter Pine before bending north and west and crossing Main Divide Road a second time. A last quarter-mile of trail leads across flatland back of a picnic ground and returns you to the trailhead.

Pine cones along the pathway.

SAN JUAN CANYON & FALLS

SAN JUAN LOOP TRAIL
2.1-mile loop with 300-foot elevation gain

Explore San Juan Creek, Canyon and even a seasonal waterfall for this easy-to-access trail just off Ortega Highway. An excellent leg-stretcher for Highway 74 road warriors, this trail offers a fine introduction to the pleasures of the Santa Ana Mountains and Cleveland National Forest.

Spring is a fine time to take this hike. Wildflowers blossom on canyon slopes, the creek bubbles along and the falls cascade at full force. Kids (and adults, too) like to cool off in the creek's pools.

If this hike isn't long enough for you, head up the Chiquito Trail for a few miles.

DIRECTIONS TO TRAILHEAD: Take the Ortega Highway (California 74) turnoff from the San Diego Freeway (5) at San Juan Capistrano. Drive east 20 miles to the paved parking area across the highway from the Ortega Country Cottage Candy Store.

THE HIKE: From the north side of the parking lot, ascend a brushy little hill then drop into the narrow canyon to a perch above San Juan Falls. Detour down to the canyon floor on a short connector trail to a point up-creek from the 15-foot high waterfall.

Continue on the oak-shaded trail through San Juan Canyon to intersect Chiquito trail at about 1.2 mile from the trailhead. Chiquito Trail splits right and turns north, but you bear left and hike south through more lovely oak woodland.

The path parallels the highway. You're separated from the traffic (but not its noise) by a ravine. Skirt—but do not enter—Upper San Juan campground, and stick with the main trail as you pass campground connector trails. The path crosses a mostly shadeless slope, again near the highway, and closes the loop back to the trailhead.

A sweet sight on Ortega Highway: the Candy Store near many trailheads.

LION CANYON

CHIQUITO TRAIL

From Ortega Highway to Chiquito Falls is 10 miles round trip with 1,000-foot elevation gain; from Blue Jay Campground to Ortega Highway is 9 miles one way

"Chiquito," which names a basin, a spring, a waterfall and a trail, is not named after a major brand of banana, but rather the name bestowed upon these features by a forest ranger in 1927 to honor his horse.

The trail crosses hot slopes and travels to, and through lovely, oak and sycamore-shaded Lion Canyon.

Chiquito Trail extends from San Juan Loop Trail to the San Juan Trail that, in turn, connects to Blue Jay Campground. If you can arrange a car shuttle, the way to go is to start from the upper trailhead at Blue Jay and hike down to Ortega Highway.

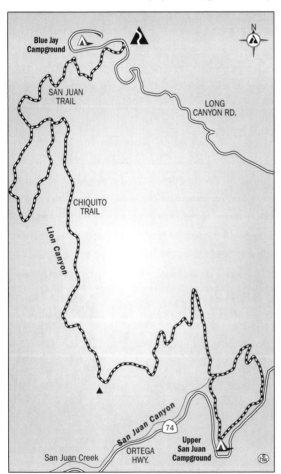

Another fine way to go is an out-and-back from Ortega Highway to seasonal Chiquito Falls, also known as Lion Canyon Falls. The 15-footer is far from a dependable cascade, but the environs around the waterfall is a pleasant picnic ground.

DIRECTIONS TO TRAILHEAD: Take the Ortega Highway (74) turnoff from the San Diego Freeway (5) and drive east 20 miles to the paved parking area across from the Ortega Country Cottage Candy Store. The trailhead is at the east end of the parking area and is signed as the San Juan Loop Trail.

To the upper trailhead:

Shade in Lion Canyon – just when you need it most.

turn off Ortega Highway on Long Canyon Road and drive 2.5 miles to the signed trailhead by the entrance to Blue Jay Campground.

THE HIKE: Embark on the San Juan Loop Trail in a counterclockwise direction. Bear right at the first fork. The loop trail circles the base of a small peak, following a creek much of the way. Soon the trail arrives above San Juan Falls, a pleasant place for the return visit after you've completed this hot hike.

About 1.2 miles from the trailhead, fork right on signed Chiquito Trail, which crosses a tributary creek of San Juan Creek and follows this unnamed creek.

All too soon, the trail leaves this peaceful creek and begins switchbacking up the west side of the canyon. Up, up, up the dry slopes you climb on this trail lined with toyon, buckwheat and chamise. The slopes are alive with lizards and horned toads. In spring, wildflowers abound along the trail. Views are excellent when you emerge in open areas and atop ridges.

After rounding the southern edge of a ridge (and if you're carefully plotting your course on a detailed map, passing from Riverside County into Orange County) Chiquito Trail turns north and heads down along a seasonal creek into Lion Canyon. Five miles from the trailhead, you'll reach Chiquito Trail, located below a bend in the trail.

Now for those of you tramping the trail one-way from Blue Jay Campground, you'll take San Juan Trail, a mellow switchbacking path amidst oaks and across brushy slopes. You'll intersect Old San Juan Trail (a steeper route)

at the 1.25-mile mark and again a half-mile later. Continue another 0.1 mile past this second junction to meet Chiquito Trail. Fork left and drop a quarter-mile into Lion Canyon.

Enjoy the next 2 miles of trail down-canyon past oaks, sycamores and seasonal wildflowers. About four miles of travel from the upper trailhead brings you to Chiquito Falls and its picnic-friendly surroundings. As for hiking much past the falls, well, the picnic is indeed over; a stiff ascent awaits the Chiquito Trail hiker who's Ortega Highway-bound.

UPPER HOT SPRING CANYON

FALCON, HOT SPRING CANYON TRAILS
From Falcon Campground to waterfall is 3 miles round trip with 400-foot elevation gain

Canyons penetrated by roads sometimes hold on to that wild feeling; those crossed only by trail are wilder still. And canyons with neither road nor trail perturbing their tranquility are the wildest canyons of all.

Upper Hot Spring Canyon, lacking roads and (formal) trails, definitely falls into the wildest canyon category, particularly in light of its location—within the boundaries of Orange County. The canyon is one of those places way off hikers' radar because it in no way lives up to the promise of its name (no soothing hot springs are to be found) and has no trail.

At least no developed trail. A faint, but passable use trail will lead those hikers willing to do a bit of rock-hopping, creek crossing and bushwhacking to some pools and a small waterfall.

Take your time on the way down Hot Spring Canyon. It's not difficult hiking, but beware of the loose rock on the canyon walls and the slippery rocks in the canyon bottom.

Hot Spring Canyon may lack name recognition and an established footpath, but it does boast easy access. The upper canyon is located just a few miles from the busy Ortega Highway and near the popular Blue Jay Campground.

(If hiking Upper Hot Spring Canyon is a bit of a challenge, hiking Lower Hot Spring Canyon is truly a blood sport. Those hikers willing to endure 5 trail-less miles of laceration by stinging nettle and thorny brush, slogging through a creek and plunging through innumerable thickets of poison oak will reach a waterfall that's more than 100 feet high. Oh, did I mention the canyon's rattlesnakes?)

Certainly getting off the beaten track increases your chances of a tranquil communion with nature. Last time I hiked there, on a weekend no less, I had Upper Hot Spring Canyon all to myself. Well, almost to myself. A large, handsome coyote trotted in and out of the brush, peering at me a half-dozen times, evidently as curious about me as I was about him.

DIRECTIONS TO TRAILHEAD: From Interstate 15 in Lake Elsinore, exit on Highway 74 (Ortega Highway) and drive 9.5 miles east to Main Divide Road. Turn right (north) and follow the winding road on a 4.5 mile long ascent to Falcon Campground (closed during winter months). You can park in a turnout near the campground entrance. Walk past the vehicle gate and look for Falcon Trail on the left near the top of the campground access road.

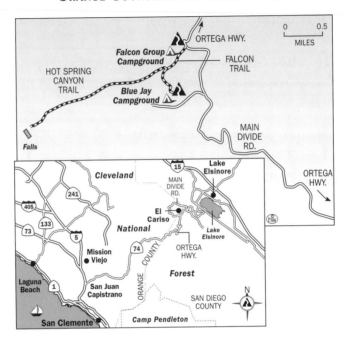

Blue Jay Campground (open all year) is located a short drive farther along Main Divide Road. Signed Falcon Trail begins near campsite #50.

THE HIKE: From Falcon Campground, Falcon Trail descends past some pines, crosses a wooden bridge and splits at an unsigned junction. The main path (Falcon Trail) bears left, while the route to Hot Spring Canyon forks right.

(Those hikers beginning at Blue Jay Campground will follow Falcon Trail for a few minutes toward Falcon Campground. A couple of steep side paths descend to the Hot Spring Canyon route, but it's easier hiking to stick with Falcon Trail a few more minutes until it reaches the unsigned junction mentioned above.)

The path descends with the gully, which soon intersects another at the head of Hot Spring Canyon, which you and the mediocre path continue to follow. What trail there is, picks its way past rock outcroppings and crosses the creek several times; in fact the route actually uses the creekbed as the trail a few times.

Shortly before junctioning a larger (and usually wetter) canyon to the north, you'll emerge atop a rocky perch that overlooks a small waterfall spilling into a grotto. Ferns, mosses and two pools add to the pretty scene.

It's possible to continue down-canyon among the rocks and alders about another 0.5 mile before the canyon bottom all of sudden plays out. Stop. Only the foolhardy will continue over the loose rocks and unstable canyon walls. True, there's another small waterfall and some pools down-creek, but I highly discourage anyone from climbing down-canyon for a closer look.

MORRELL CANYON

BEAR CANYON, MORGAN TRAILS
From Ortega Country Cottage Cand Store to Main Divide Truck Trail is 10 miles round trip with 900-foot elevation gain

This woodsy walk, which crosses the northern edge of the San Mateo Wilderness, is one of the more pleasant outings along the Ortega Highway corridor of the Cleveland National Forest. Coastal live oaks, willows and sycamores shade Morrell Canyon, as well as the seasonal creek that runs through the canyon.

Trail markers point the way in the Cleveland National Forest.

With paved roads accessing both its upper and lower trailheads, Morgan Trail offers the possibility of a one-way hike. Unless you're in a big hurry or require an easy hike instead of a moderate one, I say start at the candy store and do the whole thing, up and back.

DIRECTIONS TO TRAIL-HEAD: From Interstate 5 in San Juan Capistrano, join Highway 74 (Ortega Highway) and drive 20 miles east to Ortega Country Cottage Candy Store. Park in the lot across the highway from the store.

To reach the upper trailhead, continue northeast on Highway 74 a quarter-mile past El Cariso Station to South Main Divide Road (also known as Killen Trail). Turn right (south) and proceed 2.75 miles to the Morgan Trailhead, located on the right (west) side of the road.

THE HIKE: Begin with a mile-long ascent on Bear Canyon Trail to junction Morgan Trail. Join this path, which ascends through an oak woodland, crosses a dirt road in a half mile, and travels along the border of some private lands.

A bit more than halfway along, Morgan Trail bends north and traverses brush- and boulder-dotted slopes. Four miles out, the path crosses the creek over to the west side of Morrell Canyon. The last mile is in many ways the most engaging, as the path stays fairly close to the creek in the bottom of Merrell Canyon, as you hike past oaks and sycamore. A final ascent takes you out over chaparral covered slopes to Main Divide Road and Morgan's upper trailhead.

BEAR CANYON

BEAR CANYON, BEAR RIDGE, SITTON PEAK TRAILS
From Ortega Highway to Pigeon Springs is 5.5 miles round trip with 700-foot elevation gain; return via Bear Ridge Trail is a 6.5-mile loop; to Sitton Peak is 9.5 miles round trip with 1,300-foot gain

Bear Canyon Trail offers a pleasant introduction to the Santa Ana Mountains. The trail climbs through gentle brush and meadow country, visits Pigeon Springs, and arrives at Four Corners, the intersection of several major hiking trails through the southern Santa Anas.

One of these trails takes you to Sitton Peak for splendid, far-reaching views. Along the trail, refreshing Pigeon Springs welcomes hot and dusty hikers to a handsome glen. Bear Ridge Trail offers an alternate return route and a way to make a loop trip out of this jaunt around Bear Canyon.

DIRECTIONS TO TRAILHEAD: Take the Ortega Highway (California 74) turnoff from the San Diego Freeway (Interstate 5) at San Juan Capistrano. Drive

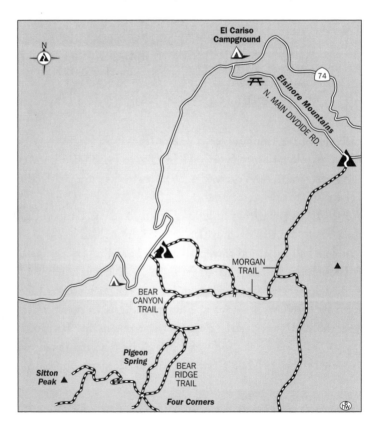

Check your bearings in Bear Canyon.

east 20 miles to the paved parking area across from the Ortega Country Cottage Candy Store. Bear Canyon Trail starts just west of the store on Ortega Highway.

THE HIKE: From the signed trailhead, the broad, well-graded trail climbs slowly up brushy hillsides. The trail crosses a seasonal creek, which runs through a tiny oak woodland.

A half mile from the trailhead, the path enters San Mateo Canyon Wilderness and after a mile, a fork appears on the left (Morgan Trail). Bear Canyon Trail climbs on, skirts the periphery of a meadow and crests a chaparral-covered slope.

Two miles of travel from the trailhead brings you to a signed intersection with Bear Ridge Trail (return route for this hike). Stick with Bear Canyon Trail, formerly known as the Verdugo Truck Trail, and head right (south) 0.75 to Pigeon Springs. The springs, including a horse trough, are located among oaks on the left of the trail.

From the springs, continue another half mile south, and past a gate to Four Corners and a meeting of five trails (fire roads), among them, Tenaja Trail, that descends to San Mateo Creek.

To proceed to Sitton Peak, bear right on Sitton Peak Trail, which begins to climb and contour around the peak. In a mile you'll be at the high point of Sitton Peak Trail, a saddle perched over San Juan Canyon. From this saddle, wend your way on a use trail past rocky outcroppings to the summit. On a clear day, there are superb views of the twin peaks of Old Saddleback (Mt. Modjeska and Mt. Santiago), Mt. San Gorgonio and Mt. San Jacinto, Catalina and the wide Pacific.

Meanwhile, back at Four Corners...head northeast on Bear Ridge Trail for an alternate return to the trailhead. The narrow pathway follows a ridge north, over-looking Bear Canyon. After bending west, the trail meets up again with Bear Canyon Trail.

LUCAS CANYON

BEAR CANYON, VERDUGO, LUCAS CANYON, SITTON PEAK TRAILS

14 miles one-way with 1,300 foot elevation loss

Some regional historians way overstate their case by calling it "The Mother Lode of Orange County," but it is true that gold-seekers did work Lucas Canyon in the late 19th century. The diggins did not pan out like prospectors had hoped, and failed to put Lucas Canyon on the map in any meaningful way.

Lucas Canyon is on the map in a more significant way today, the happy result of the construction of a hiking trail in 1992 that follows the old miners' trail that led through the canyon. This footpath, a long labor of love and the result of count-less hours of volunteer trail-building efforts, was nearly destroyed in the autumn of 1993 when a severe wildfire scorched Lucas Canyon and the surrounding envi-

Ready for some trail work in Lucas Canyon.

rons. But nature—specifically the profligate native vegetation—quickly recovered. In fact, the plant life recovered so quickly that it soon overgrew, in fact threatened to choke off the trail. Volunteers rescued Lucas Canyon Trail once more and it has remained open to the very few hearty souls willing to go the extra mile (or six) to hike it.

At the time of its completion, the trail was noteworthy for being the first trail to offer access from the west side of the mountains to the San Mateo Canyon Wilderness. About 90 percent of the pathway lies within the wilderness.

About half of Lucas Canyon Trail is in Orange County, the other half in Riverside County. The southern trailhead is in Orange County, the northern one in Riverside County.

As longtime readers know, The Trailmaster is not overly fond of hikes requiring car shuttles. Lucas Canyon, however, is an exception. One could fashion an out-and-back round trip of about 15.5 miles round trip by beginning from the lower trailhead at San Juan Fire Station, ascending to Sitton Peak Road, joining and traveling the length of Lucas Canyon Trail to its intersection with Verdugo Trail, and returning the way you came. This is a pretty decent hike, though not as compelling as the one-way route.

With Ortega Country Cottage Candy Store (the upper trailhead) at about 2,000 foot elevation and San Juan Station (the lower trailhead) at 700 feet, you can easily assess which way of this one-way is the easier way. But a heads-up for this hike: It's not downhill all the way; the hiker must ascend to the junction at Four Corners (2,751 feet) descend to the bottom of Lucas Canyon (about 1,000 feet) and back up Sitton Peak Fire Road, before descending back to Highway 74 and the lower trailhead.

To and from Lucas Canyon, the route passes along the southeast ridge of the Santa Ana Mountains across slopes dotted with sage and prickly pear. Native plant aficionados will look for the rare variegated Dudleya, known to grow in Lucas Canyon.

Rewards for the ridge-running portion of the hike are vistas of the San Mateo Canyon Wilderness and the surrounding national forest backcountry. The most challenging parts of this all-day adventure are the switchbacks into and out of Lucas Canyon.

DIRECTIONS TO TRAILHEAD: From Interstate 5 in San Juan Capistrano, take Highway 74 (Ortega Highway) about 12 miles east to San Juan Fire Station, located a quarter-mile east of the Sitton Peak Fire Road trailhead.

To reach the upper trailhead, and the start point for this one-way hike, continue up Highway 74 another 7 miles to the Ortega Country Cottage Candy Store and park in the lot across the highway from the store.

THE HIKE: (See Bear Canyon Trail, page 192). Ascend Bear Canyon Trail 3.2 miles south to Four Corners. From this major hub, head southwest on Verdugo Trail across exposed chaparral-smothered slopes, passing Bluewater Trail and, four miles from Four Corners, intersecting Lucas Canyon Trail.

Now the fun—or at least the downhill—begins. The steep trail and some switchbacks lead down to the bottom of the canyon, that's certainly narrow and precipitous enough to qualify as a gorge. After about 2.5 miles of trail through the canyon, the path angles along the south wall of the canyon, then descends once more to the canyon bottom. The path then bends north and joins a minor tributary canyon in a 2-mile ascent to Sitton Peak Road.

Turn left on the road, and descend two miles and a thousand feet in elevation to meet Highway 74. Walk carefully a quarter-mile east on the highway to San Juan Fire Station, presumably your shuttle point/pickup spot.

From the very beginning, Bear Canyon Trail delights.

Main Divide

The crest of the Santa Ana Mountains is known as the Main
Divide. Extending along the boundaries of Orange and
Riverside Counties, Main Divide Road links Sierra Peak,
Modjeska Peak Santiago Peak (Orange County's highest
summit)and Trabuco Peak with the Ortega Highway (74).
Driving up to the high northern part of the Main Divide is
challenging or downright impossible, while hiking up to it can
be sometimes moderate often strenuous experience. It's great to
hike above the smogline and enjoy terrific views from the Main
Divide itself or from the peaks along it. Mountain bicyclists
often characterize the riding up and down Main Divide as
"epic"; hikers may very well agree.

BLACK STAR CANYON

BLACK STAR CANYON ROAD

From vehicle gate to overlooks is 6 miles round trip with 700-foot elevation gain

Black Star might seem like the title of a sci-fi novel, but the name comes from the Black Star Coal Mining Company that began operations in the canyon in 1878. Known first as Cañon del los Indios (Indian Canyon), the canyon was renamed during the silver/coal exploration days when the Silverado Canyon area hosted extensive mining operations.

Observant hikers will note seams of (rather low-quality as it turns out) coal exposed in the road cuts as they tramp Black Star Canyon Road. The road (closed to public vehicle traffic) passes through both private and public land (Cleveland National Forest) but is open to foot traffic.

Oaks and sycamores, as well as willows and other riparian flora offer shade and greenery en route. Eucalyptus, planed in rows, add to the green scene.

DIRECTIONS TO TRAILHEAD: From the Costa Mesa Freeway (55) in Orange, exit on Chapman Avenue and head east. Chpaman transitions to Santiago Canyon Road and, 11 miles from the freeway, reaches a junction with Silverado Canyon Road. Turn left and travel very briefly (0.1 mile) to Black Star Canyon Road. Make a right and drive a mile to the vehicle gate.

You can also make your way to Santiago Canyon Road via both eastern toll roads and by exiting the San Diego Freeway (5) in Lake Forest on El Toro Road and heaind 7.5 miles to junction Santiago Canyon Road at Cook's Corner.

THE HIKE: Walk around the vehicle gate and follow the usually dry bed of Santiago Creek. A half-mile from the trailhead, the road suddenly swings 90 degrees to enter Black Star Canyon.

The road makes a mellow ascent amidst oaks and sycamores. About 2.5 miles along, the dirt road makes a nearly 180-degree turn to the left and works its way up the brushy canyon wall. As the road snakes upward high above the canyon bottom, you'll get some good views of this end of the Santa Ana Mountains. You can continue another 4-plus miles to Main Divide Road for a 15-mile round trip hike, but most hikers will call it a day and return from the cliffs to the trailhead.

SILVERADO CANYON

SILVERADO TRAIL
From Silverado Canyon Road to Bedford Peak is 7 miles round trip with 2,100-foot elevation gain

When experienced hikers refer to a trek as "a conditioning hike" you know you're in for a workout. The path to Bedford Peak most definitely fits into this category.

From the west (most populated) side of the Santa Ana mountains, Silverado Trail is the shortest and quickest way to Main Divide, the ridgecrest of the range. Of course, short and quick add up to steep as well, which is why this trail offers an aerobic workout.

Reward for the ascent to 3,800-foot high Bedford Peak is a great clear-day panorama of the Santa Ana, San Gabriel and San Bernardino ranges, along with the OC suburbanopolis and the Pacific Ocean.

The name Silverado comes from the high hopes of prospectors who swarmed into the canyon during the late 1870s. A few years later, the silver ore played out, and the boom went bust. These days the canyon is a surprisingly rural enclave of homes, general store and fire station.

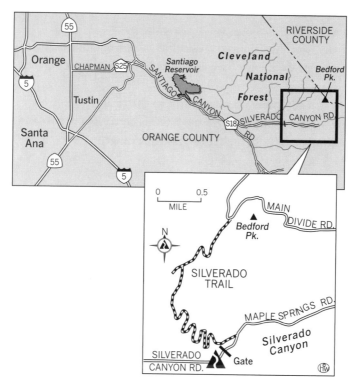

On old maps, and on most new ones as well, Silverado Trail is labeled as Silverado Motorway. Originally constructed for fire patrol and control purposes, the fire road deteriorated over the years and de-evolved (evolved in the opinion of we hikers) into a footpath. Hikers might find it difficult to believe this now-vanished motorway was ever passable by vehicles.

DIRECTIONS TO TRAILHEAD: From the Newport Freeway (55) in Orange, exit on Chapman Avenue and drive east. About 6 miles out, Chapman becomes Santiago Canyon Road and, some 11 miles from the freeway, you'll intersect Silverado Canyon Road. Bear left and continue 5.5 miles to the parking area.

THE HIKE: Walk up the wide, shaded Maple Springs Road (a continuation of Santiago Canyon Road) for 0.1 mile. Just after crossing a seasonal creek, look and turn left (west) on unsigned Silverado Trail. At first it appears the path intends to return you to the trailhead, but it soon turns north and begins a steep, zigzagging ascent of the north wall of the canyon.

The trail is flanked by sage and exposed outcroppings of stratified sedimentary rock known as the Bedford Canyon Formation. Higher and higher you climb on switchbacks that offer ever-grander vistas of Silverado Canyon, until the entire canyon comes into view.

A bit more than 2 miles out, you'll reach a flat spot on the ridge between Silverado and Ladd canyons and a so-so view of the Santa Anas. If you feel sufficiently "conditioned", this is a good turnaround point.

Otherwise, continue along the ridgeline on a steep, but quite inspiring mile of trail to meet Main Divide Road. Turn right and walk 0.3 mile up the road to Bedford Peak.

Bedford is really more of a big bump in the road than a proper peak, but it does provide a modest platform from which to survey peaks near and far, as well as the advancing metropolis on both sides of the range.

MODJESKA CANYON

HARDING TRAIL
From Tucker Wildlife Sanctuary to Goat Shed Overlook is 3 miles round trip with 600-foot elevation gain; to Laurel Spring is 10 miles round trip with 2,300-foot gain

The story of Modjeska Peak and Modjeska Canyon in Orange County began in Warsaw, Poland in the 1870s. Count Karol Bozenta Chlapowski edited a fiercely nationalistic patriotic journal that protested the cultural and political imperialism of Czarist Russia and Germany. He and his wife, acclaimed actress Helena Modrzejewski, and other Polish writers and artists, yearned for the freedom of America and the climate of Southern California.

Helena mastered English, shortened her name to Modjeska, and under the Count's management, began her tremendously popular stage career. Madame Modjeska and the Count bought a ranch in Santiago Canyon and hired professionals to run it. Madame called her ranch "Arden" after the enchanted forest in Shakespeare's *As You Like It*. Infamous New York architect Stanford White was commissioned to design a dream home, which looked out over a little lake, across which glided swans.

For two decades the Chlapowski/Modjeska household was a center of artistic and literary life in Southern California. Today, a state historical marker on Modjeska Canyon Road commemorates their home.

The natural history of Modjeska Canyon is as intriguing as its human history. In 1939, Dorothy May Tucker, a canyon resident, willed her land to the Audubon Society and the Tucker Wildlife Sanctuary was created. California State University Fullerton took over its operation in 1969.

The sanctuary is best known for its hummingbirds, which may be viewed from an observation porch. Because the sanctuary includes a mix

The elegant Madame Modjeska.

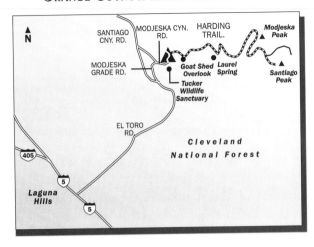

ture of coastal scrub, chaparral and oak woodland environments, it attracts a diver-sity of birdlife. Nearly 200 species have been spotted in the sanctuary.

Two short nature trails wind through the preserve. One trail interprets cha-parral flora, and the other leads along the banks of Santiago Creek.

Tucker Wildlife Sanctuary is the trailhead for Harding Trail, a dirt road that ascends the western slopes of the Santa Ana Mountains. The trail, formerly known as Harding Truck Trail, is used by Cleveland National Forest fire crews and their trucks, but is closed to all other vehicles.

Old Saddleback, comprised of 5,687-foot Santiago Peak and 5,496-foot Modjeska Peak, forms the eastern boundary and highest portion of Orange County. You can reach the peaks via Harding Trail, but this would mean a 20-mile hike. A more reasonable destination, halfway up the mountain, is Laurel Spring, a tranquil rest stop tucked under the boughs of giant bay laurel. En route to the spring, you'll get great views of Madame Modjeska's peak and canyon, as well as much of rural Orange County.

DIRECTIONS TO TRAILHEAD: From the San Diego Freeway (5) in El Toro, exit on El Toro Road (S-18). Drive inland on the road, which after about 7 miles bends north and continues as Santiago Canyon Road. Eight and a half miles from the freeway, veer right onto Modjeska Grade Road, travel a bit more than a mile, then turn right and follow Modjeska Canyon Road a mile to its end at Tucker Wildlife Sanctuary. Park in the gravel lot by a tiny observatory. The trail begins at a locked gate on the north side of the road.

THE HIKE: Harding Trail immediately begins a no-nonsense ascent above Modjeska Canyon which, in all but its lower reaches, is officially known as Harding Canyon. To the northwest is Flores Peak, named for outlaw Juan Flores. As you ascend, notice the lumpy, pudding-like clumps of conglomerate rock

Handsome stone staircase – a reminder of more literary days in Santiago Canyon.

revealed by the road cuts. After a mile, the trail descends a short distance (the only elevation loss on the way to Laurel Spring), rounds the head of a canyon, and ascends to the remains of a funny-looking wood structure that locals call the Goat Shed. Enjoy the view of Modjeska Canyon. If you're feeling a bit leg weary, this is a good turnaround point.

Chaparral-lined Harding Trail continues climbing east along a sharp ridge-line. To your left, far below, is deep and precipitous Harding Canyon, and to your right–Santiago Canyon. Four and a half miles from the trailhead, Harding Trail offers clear-day views of the southern end of the Los Angeles Basin, the San Joaquin Hills and the central Orange County coastal plain, the Pacific and Catalina Island. The view serves notice that you're nearing Laurel Spring. A narrow trail descends 50 yards from the right side of the road to the spring. The spring (unsafe drinking water), waters an oasis of toyon, ferns and wonderfully aromatic bay laurel.

HOLY JIM WATERFALL

HOLY JIM TRAIL
From Holy Jim Creek to Falls is 2.5 miles round trip with 200-foot elevation gain

Holy Jim Trail, creek, waterfall and canyon take their names from "Cussin'" Jim Smith, an early Santa Ana Mountain settler who, when displeased, unleashed a string of unholy epithets. Early 20th-century mapmakers were unwilling to geographically honor such a blasphemer, so they changed his name to "Holy."

The trail is one of the most popular in the Santa Anas, though many hikers go only as far as the falls. Something of a Santa Ana Mountains sampler, the trail offers the hiker a creek, a lush canyon, a waterfall, a hike into history and, with the optional trek to Santiago Peak, a chance to conquer OC's highest summit.

Smith was a beekeeper by profession (perhaps explaining his proclivity toward profanity). His operation and those of neighboring beekeepers were targets of a grizzly bear dubbed "Honey Thief." Believed to be the last grizzly in the Santa Ana Mountains, the bear was shot near the mouth of Trabuco Canyon in 1907.

Evidence of Smith's life in the canyon remain behind in the form of a stone wall from his cabin, which burned in a severe 1908 fire. Fig trees gone wild are descendants from those that once grew in Smith's orchard.

Strictly by the tape measure, Holy Jim Falls at 20 feet high does not wow the hiker with its stature. Ah, but the "wow factor" is the waterfall's setting—a lovely grotto with ferns springing from the rock walls around it.

Some hikers think getting to the trailhead is half the fun. It's definitely a bumpy ride along Trabuco Canyon Road to the trailhead. Passenger cars with good ground clearance can make it over the wash-boarded, pot-holed road. The dirt road is no route for low-slung cars, though the drivers of such vehicles are usually not discouraged from coaxing them to the trailhead.

You'll spot a number of cabins, privately owned but on land leased from the Forest Service, in the Holy Jim-Trabuco Canyon area. During the 1930s, it was Forest Service policy to encourage city dwellers to experience the great outdoors and overnight in a vacation cabin.

DIRECTIONS TO TRAILHEAD: From the San Diego Freeway (5) in Lake Forest, exit on El Toro Road and drive east 7 miles. Turn right on Live Oak Canyon Road and proceed 4.2 miles (a mile past O'Neill Regional Park) to Trabuco Creek Road. Make a left and follow this rough dirt road 4.6 miles to the trailhead parking area just past the volunteer fire station.

A wholly lovely experience on Holy Jim Trail.

THE HIKE: From the trailhead parking lot, hike up the canyon road a half mile to the beginning of the trail. Head up the vine- and oak-filled canyon. The trail stays near Holy Jim Creek, crossing and re-crossing the bubbling waters several times.

You'll spot stone check dams, built in the 1950s by the California Department of Fish and Game in order to create deep pools for fish. A clearing allows a glimpse at Santiago Peak and, while tramping creekside, look for aptly named Picnic Rock.

The trail crosses the creek a final time and comes to a fork. Holy Jim Trail embarks on a climb up Holy Jim Canyon on the way to Santiago Peak, but you take the right fork and head up-creek. A quarter mile of boulder-hopping and creek-crossing brings you face to face with Holy Jim Falls.

HOLY JIM CANYON & SANTIAGO PEAK

HOLY JIM TRAIL

From Trabuco Creek Road to Main Divide Road is 10 miles round trip with 2,200-foot gain; to Santiago Peak is 15 miles round trip with 4,000-foot gain

Looking up at Santiago Peak from various points near the trailhead has a way of prompting hikers to examine their plans: Do we really want to climb way up there?

Well, yes you do. Admit it, Orange County's 5,687-foot landmark peak calls to you. Well, I was referring to a kind of spiritual beckoning to the hiker, but now that we're discussing calling, I should mention that Santiago Peak is topped with transmitting stations and thickets of antennae, so crucial these days to microwave relays and cell phone signals.

The northern Santa Anas were once known as Sierra de Santiago for this dominant peak. Santiago is the higher of the two neighboring summits (Modjeska Peak is the other) comprising Old Saddleback. You can get a 360-degree view from the top of Santiago Peak, but not from any one place, crowded as it is by one of the very densest clusters of telecommunications found on any peak in California. The view includes five counties worth of urban-suburban sprawl, as well as east to Mount San Jacinto and Mount San Gorgonio, south to Mount Palomar, and Catalina Island and San Clemente Island way out in the Pacific Ocean.

Trails and fire roads approach Orange County's highest peak from all

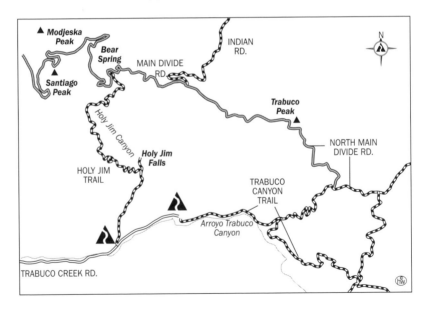

Fine vistas from upper Holy Jim Canyon.

directions, but Holy Jim Trail is the most scenic route to the summit of Santiago. Don't underestimate the challenge of this hike: It's pretty good trail, but the gain is substantial.

DIRECTIONS TO TRAILHEAD: See account of Holy Jim Falls Trail.

THE HIKE: After the last creek crossing, Holy Jim Tail begins a stiff climb up the west side of the canyon. The path presents some hearty switchbacks and begins a lengthy contour along the canyon wall.

About 3.5 miles into the hike, the trail gets less brushy, and there is some flora you can look up to: oaks, sycamores and an occasional big-cone Douglas fir. At the 4.5 mile-mark, the trail meets Main Divide Road by Bear Spring, a tank and water trough built by the Forest Service. The spring was named long ago for the grizzly bears sighted in the high country.

Hit the road for another three miles of hiking on the Main Divide (gaining 1,800 feet) to Santiago Peak. Enjoy the grand vista of most of the Southland's mountain ranges including the Palomars, the San Bernardinos, the San Gabriels and Santa Monicas.

TRABUCO CANYON

TRABUCO CANYON, WEST HORSETHIEF TRAILS

From trailhead to West Horsethief Trail Junction is 3.6 miles round trip with 800-foot elevation gain; loop via Main Divide and West Horsethief Trail is 10 miles round trip with 2,200-foot gain

Trabuco Canyon Trail and Holy Jim Canyon Trail share the same wicked wash-board road approach, and have trailheads only a mile apart, but the latter trail is far better known than the former because of its marquee destination—Holy Jim Falls.

That being said, the path up Trabuco Canyon is not without its rewards. Among the payoffs are the wildflower blooms, said to be among the best in the Santa Anas. Offering fine vistas and a more expansive feeling, Trabuco is a much less traveled trail than Holy Jim.

Trabuco Canyon extends from the Main Divide between Los Piños Peak and Trabuco Peak down the the foothills and flatlands in O'Neill Regional Park (see the hike write-ups in this guide.) The canyon is a tree-lovers delight with grand old oaks, alders, maple, and even some big-cone Douglas fir.

Enjoy a moderate traipse through Trabuco Canyon or opt for a more chal-lenging loop up to Main Divide Road to Horsethief Trail, then a descent back to Trabuco Canyon Trail.

DIRECTIONS TO TRAILHEAD: From the Holy Jim Canyon trail-head, continue another mile to road's end at the Trabuco Canyon trailhead. Park alongside the road.

THE HIKE: The narrow trail (formerly an old road that led to a camp-ground) leads gently up the tree-filled canyon. When the canyon opens up, you get a glimpse up at Trabuco Peak.

At 1.8 miles from the trailhead, you reach the sometimes signed junction with West Horsethief Trail. Picnic down in the canyon bottom and return the way you came or catch your breath and tackle the longer loop.

Take West Horsethief Trail and tackle the steep switchbacks that climb brush-cloaked slopes. After gaining 1,300 feet in just a mile and a half, the trail meets Main Divide Road and some Coulter pines.

Head right on a mellow road-walk, east and then south for 2.5 miles to Los Piños Saddle, some more Coulter pines and the top of Trabuco Canyon Trail. Head down Trabuco Canyon amidst oak and Douglas fir to that junction with West Horsethief Trail, and then retrace your steps back to the trailhead.

LOS PIÑOS PEAK

NORTH MAIN DIVIDE, LOS PIÑOS TRAILS

From Main Divide Road to Los Piños Peak is 4.5 miles round trip with 900-foot elevation gain.

Trail Trivia Question: Name the four highest peaks in Orange County.
1. Santiago Peak (5,687 feet
2. Modjeska Peak (5,496 feet)
3. Trabuco Peak (4,604 feet)
4. Los Piños Peak (4,510 feet)

Experienced hikers—and others with more than a passing interest in the county's geography—may have guessed numbers one and two—the peaks comprising the landmark Old Saddleback. Orange County's number 3 and number 4 peaks are much more obscure.

Los Piños Peak, located about three miles as the hawk flies from the southeast corner of Orange County where it meets both San Diego and Riverside counties, offers terrific clear-day vistas and is well worth the moderate hike. From the summit, the hiker looks down to Lake Elsinore and up at snow-capped Mt. Baldy and the high peaks of the San Gabriel Mountains, as well as over to the San Bernardino Mountains and San Jacinto Mountains. Gaze west over miles of hills and valleys to the great blue Pacific.

The wary trekker might suspect that such a view would come at enormous cost but in the case of Los Piños Peak, only a modest effort is required in order to earn this rewarding panorama.

Another positive aspect of this hike is that the trailhead is accesssible by paved roads. (Veteran travelers of the range's rough dirt roads can tell you what a pain in the axle some of them can be!) The trail itself presents a moderate (but not mountain goat-like) climb.

A great time to scale Los Piños is in the springtime when lupine, bush poppy and ceanothus splash color on the slopes of the mountain. Crisp, clear autumn days are good ones to head for the peak, too. Winter storms sometimes dust the crest of Los Piños with a bit of snow. Stay away from this summit and others in the Santa Anas in summer. It's way too hot for hiking.

DIRECTIONS TO TRAILHEAD: From Interstate 5 in San Juan Capistrano, exit on Highway 74 and follow it 22 miles northeast to Long Canyon Road. Turn left (northwest) and follow this paved road 2.5 miles to Blue Jay Campground, then another mile to a pullout on your left. The gated road is signed "North Main." Park in the pullout.

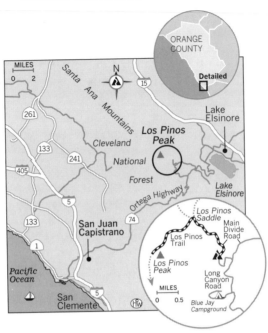

Another way to go: From Interstate 15 in Lake Elsinore, exit on Highway 74 and drive 11 miles southwest to Long Canyon Road, then follow the above directions.

From Highway 74 you can also turn west on Main Divide Road (signed "To Blue Jay Campground") and follow this paved road 4 miles to the trailhead.

THE HIKE: From the gate, follow the wide dirt road, which soon gains elevation and good views. A mile out, look for a particularly good vista of Lake Elsinore and out to high mountain peaks to the north and east.

About 1.25 mile from the start, the road brings you to Los Piños Saddle, where you'll spot guardrails and a convergence of trails. Leave Main Divide Road, which goes right, and step onto signed Trabuco Trail. Almost immediately look left and fork left onto signed Los Piños Trail. The path soon gains the top of the ridge and you quickly learn why Los Piños Trail is often called Los Piños Ridge Trail.

The steep path gains a high point that is only 20 feet lower in elevation than your goal, then dips, climbs again, dips some more, and finally climbs steeply to the top of Los Piños Peak. Savor the great views and retrace your steps back to the trailhead.

San Mateo Canyon Wilderness

Highlight of the Santa Anas is San Mateo Canyon Wilderness, which comprises the southwest corner of the Trabuco Ranger District. More than 60 miles of trail weave through the 40,000-acre wilderness, easily the wildest part of the Santa Ana Mountains. After a good rainfall, Tenaja Falls and San Mateo Canyon Creek are particularly compelling destinations for a hike. The wilderness is habitat for 140 species of birds and even seven kinds of fish, though few people observe them because the remote locale receives little human use. Hikers can begin wilderness explorations from four trailheads—Bear Canyon, Morgan, Tenaja and Tenaja Falls— and join hikers-only footpaths that lead over sage- and chaparral-cloaked slopes and down into deep canyons with creeks and thick oak woodlands.

TENAJA FALLS

TENAJA FALLS TRAIL
1.5 miles round trip with 300-foot elevation gain.

When the Southland is blessed with a rainy, rainy season, Tenaja Falls spills over granite ramparts with great vigor. With five tiers and a drop of some 150 feet, it's a large waterfall, particularly in comparison to other falls in the Santa Ana Mountains.

Tenaja's size is all the more a delightful surprise considering its locale: a rather dry section of the Cleveland National Forest near the boundary of Orange and Riverside counties. Some hikers claim Tenaja Falls is the most intriguing natural highlight of the national forest, and even in that crown jewel of the mountains—the San Mateo Canyon Wilderness.

For Tenaja Falls-bound hikers, there's good news and bad news. Good news: the trail is a wide dirt road, easy enough for the whole family. Bad news: the drive to the trailhead is circuitous to say the least.

For nature photographers, there's one more minor bit of bad news: No viewpoint allows an angle of the whole of Tenaja Falls, that is to say, all five cascades at once.

Count on the many tiers of Tenaja Falls.

Two tiers at a time is the usual view from the trail.

DIRECTIONS TO TRAILHEAD: From I-15 (Temecula Valley Freeway) in Murietta, exit on Clinton Keith Road and drive 5 miles south into Santa Rosa Plateau Ecological Reserve. After a sharp right bend, continue on what is now Tenaja Road for 2 more miles and turn right again to stick with Tenaja Road. Proceed another 4.3 miles to Cleveland Forest Road, turn right and follow this narrow, one-lane pave road to the signed trailhead and parking area on the left.

THE HIKE: Meander over to the fence that bars motorized entry to the San Mateo Canyon Wilderness. Cross the creek on the concrete vehicle ford. If the creek is high, you'll have to wade carefully across, though skilled rock-hoppers can sometimes cross without getting their boots wet. Another creek-crossing option is to walk along the creek until you find a narrower place to cross.

The trail/road ascends northward over brush-clad slopes and before long serves up distant vistas of Tenaja Falls. Just keep walking toward the falls.

The trail leads right to Tenaja's top tier. Exploration of the lower cascades is tricky, and for experienced rock-climbers only. Those granite boulders are darn slippery.

If you're bound and determined to reach the lower falls, a somewhat safer and saner way to go is retrace your steps back down the trail, then bushwhack through the brush to the banks of the creek.

FISHERMAN'S CAMP

FISHERMAN'S CAMP TRAIL
5-mile loop to Fisherman's Camp

For those looking for a longer hike in the area, an adventure awaits: an exploration of the San Mateo Canyon Wilderness. I recommend a 5-mile loop that
begins just 1.5 miles down the road from the Tenaja Falls trailhead.

DIRECTIONS TO THE TRAILHEAD: See San Mateo Canyon hike.

THE HIKE: Walk down an old fire road, now a footpath, often lined with
wildflowers in spring. About 1.5 miles of travel brings you to Fisherman's Camp,
once a drive-in campground and now an oak-and sycamore-shaded trail camp.

From the camp, the path angles north toward San Mateo Canyon and a junction with San Mateo Canyon Trail on the west side of the creek.

To make a loop, hike right, northeast up San Mateo Canyon. You'll cross the
creek a couple of times, traveling along brushy banks dotted with oaks. After two
miles you'll meet Tenaja Falls Trail just below Tenaja Road. Walk 1.5 miles south
on the dirt road back to the trailhead.

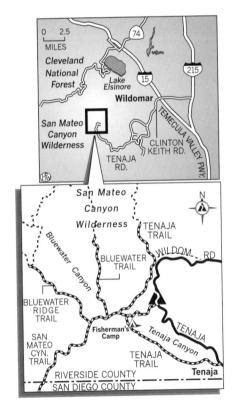

SAN MATEO CANYON WILDERNESS

FISHERMAN'S CAMP, SAN MATEO CANYON TRAILS
From Tenaja Road to Fisherman's Camp is 3 miles round trip with 300-foot loss; loop via Tenaja Road is 5 miles round trip with 400-foot elevation gain; to Lunch Rock is 8 miles round trip with 400-foot loss

Two-hundred-year-old oaks, tangles of ferns, nettles and wild grape, and the quiet pools of San Mateo Creek make the bottom of San Mateo Canyon a wild and delightful place. This section of the Santa Ana Mountains is steep canyon country, sculpted by seasonal, but vigorous streams. San Mateo Creek, a cascading waterway in winter, slows to a gurgle in summer and flows above ground only sporadically in the fall.

San Mateo Canyon Wilderness, set aside by Congress in 1984, protects 40,000 acres of the Cleveland National Forest, including the headwaters and watershed of San Mateo Creek. During the 1930s, anglers were attracted by superb fishing for steelhead and trout. San Mateo Canyon Trail was a favorite route to the fishing holes. Steelhead ran these waters then; current environmental efforts are being made to coax them back.

San Mateo Canyon takes its name from one of the padres' favorite evangelists and holy men. It's the crown jewel of the Santa Ana Mountains, a relatively untouched wilderness of oaks, potreros and cattail-lined ponds. It's a haven for turtles and rabbits. Spring brings prolific wildflower displays. The canyon drops from 3,500 feet to the coastal plain at Camp Pendleton.

This day hike plunges through the southern part of San Mateo Canyon, easily the wildest place in the Santa Ana Mountains. The San Mateo Canyon Trail and other riding and hiking trails in the wilderness have been in use for more than a century. Volunteers work on the trail, but it's often in rough shape. Creek crossings are sometimes difficult to spot.

You can travel almost as far down the canyon as you like in one day. It's nine miles from Fisherman's Camp to the Marine base, with a hundred ideal picnic spots along the way.

DIRECTIONS TO TRAILHEAD: From I-15 (Temecula Valley Freeway) in Murrieta, exit on Clinton Keith Road and drive 5 miles south into Santa Rosa Plateau Ecological Reserve. After a sharp right bend, continue on what is now Tenaja Road for 2 more miles and turn right again to stick wityh Tenaja Road. Proceed another 4.3 miles to Cleveland Forest Road, turn right and follow this narrow, one-lane paved road for a mile to the signed Tenaja Trailhead. Proceed another 2.5 miles to the small parking area on the left side of the road.

Old-time wilderness marker.

THE HIKE: Walk down an old fire road, now a footpath, often lined with wildflowers in spring. About 1.5 miles of travel brings you to Fisherman's Camp, once a drive-in campground and now an oak-and sycamore-shaded trail camp.

From the camp, the path angles north toward San Mateo Canyon and a junction with San Mateo Canyon Trail on the west side of the creek.

Those hikers heading down San Mateo Canyon will follow the trail that climbs among ceanothus to a ridge that offer a view of the canyon. After 0.5 mile, the path switchbacks down to San Mateo Creek and follows it along the heavily vegetated canyon bottom.

Along the creek, the trail may be indistinct; simply continue down-creek. About a mile after reaching the creek, you'll come to a small potrero dotted with oaks and sycamore. Here Bluewater Creek flows into San Mateo Creek and the Bluewater Trail leads off three miles to the Clark Trail and Oak Flat. You can picnic under the oaks near the trail junction and return, or continue down the canyon.

Resume your down-creek passage on the San Mateo Canyon Trail, which follows the right side of the canyon, now and then dropping to wide sandy beaches along bends in the creek. The boulders get bigger, the swimming holes and sunning spots nicer. One flat rock, popular with hikers, has been nicknamed "Lunch Rock." A cluster of massive boulders form pools and cascades in the creek. It's a nice place to linger.

CHAPTER SIX

Chino Hills

Chino Hills State Park, located in Orange, San Bernardino
and Riverside counties, preserves some much-needed
"breathing room" in this fast-growing area.
Considering that three million people live within sight
of the Chino Hills and nine million within a 40-mile radius,
the park's trails offer surprisingly tranquil and
away-from-it-all hiking. Perhaps because reaching
the main trailheads requires driving on a dirt road,
the park is lightly visited. The 13,000-acre park
harbors an admirable biodiversity, including oak woodlands,
stands of native California walnut and extensive grassland.
Stand on the summits of park high points
such as Gilman Peak and San Juan Hill
and you can see parts of four counties
and a glorious amount of room to roam.

CARBON CANYON

CARBON CANYON NATURE TRAIL
2 miles round trip

Carbon Canyon Regional Park offers some much-needed "breathing room" for fast-growing northeastern Orange County. The park has both a natural area with trails that connect to nearby Chino Hills State Park, and a more developed part with wide lawns, tennis courts, ball fields, picnic grounds and a lake.

The park spreads up-canyon behind Carbon Canyon dam. As Orange County grew, so did the need for flood control, and in 1959, a dam was built at the mouth of the canyon. If, as a result of winter storms, the Santa Ana River rises too high, the dam's floodgates will be closed, thus sparing communities downstream of the dam, but flooding the park.

A century ago, the arrival of the Santa Fe Railroad precipitated a minor land boom. Farmers and ranchers rushed to the area. Cattle and sheep were pastured in the canyon now called Carbon.

But it was another boom—an oil boom—that put Carbon Canyon on the map. E.L. Doheny, soon to become one of L.A.'s leading boosters, discovered oil in the area in 1896. His company and several others drilled the foothills of Orange

More than a century ago, it was oil – not scenery – that was the attraction in Carbon Canyon.

County. The name Carbon was applied to the canyon because of the many dried-up oil seeps in evidence.

Santa Fe Railroad tracks were extend-ed to the mouth of Carbon Canyon in order to haul out the oil. At the end of the tracks was the oil town of Olinda, boyhood home of the great baseball pitcher Walter Johnson. "Big Train," as the hurler was known, pitched for the Washington Senators, and led the American League in strikeouts each year from 1912 to 1919. Olinda boomed until the 1940s when the oil fields began to play out.

The undeveloped part of Carbon Canyon Regional Park is a narrow corridor along Carbon Canyon Creek. A one-mile nature trail leads creek-side through an interesting mixture of native and foreign flora. At the park entrance station, ask for

Seedlings establish themselves
in Carbon Canyon.

an interpretive pamphlet, which is keyed to numbered posts along the nature trail, and details points and plants of interest. Rewarding the hiker at trail's end is a small, shady redwood grove.

DIRECTIONS TO TRAILHEAD: From the Orange Freeway (57) in Brea, exit on Lambert Road. Drive 4 miles east on Lambert (which changes to Carbon Canyon Road east of Valencia Avenue) to the park entrance. There's a vehicle entry fee.

THE HIKE: From the parking area, walk back to the entrance station, and you'll spot the signed trail in a stand of pine, just east of the park entrance. On closer inspection, you'll discover that the pines are Monterey pines, native to California, but not to this area. This stand is a holdover from a Christmas tree farm that was operated before the park opened in 1975.

From the pines, the nature trail descends to the Carbon Canyon creekbed. After crossing the creek, the trail forks. (The path to the left leads toward Telegraph Canyon and to a network of hiking trails that crisscross Chino Hills State Park. The 8-mile length of Telegraph Canyon, home of native walnut groves, is well worth exploring.) Carbon Canyon Nature trailheads right with the creekbed. Creek-side vegetation is dominated by mustard, castor bean and hemlock. You'll also find two exotic imports—the California pepper tree, actually

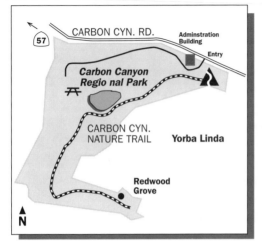

a native of Peru, and some giant reeds, bamboo-like plants that harm the native plant community because they take a great deal of the scarce water supply.

At the trail's mid-point, there's a distinct, but unmarked, side trail that angles across the creekbed to the developed part of the park. If for some reason you want to call it a day, here's your exit point.

As you near trail's end you'll get brush-framed glimpses of Carbon Canyon Dam. The trail ascends out of the creekbed to the park's redwood grove. The redwoods, planted in 1975, have a lot of growing to do before they rival their majestic cousins to the north.

GILMAN PEAK

NORTH RIDGE AND GILMAN PEAK TRAILS
From Carbon Canyon Regional Park to Gilman Peak is 7 miles round trip
with 1,200-foot elevation gain

Gilman Peak, a 1,685-foot Chino Hills promontory, is far from the top of the
world but offers the hiker magnificent vistas—particularly on a clear winter's day.
The San Gabriel Mountains, wearing a mantle of snow, rise to the north above
the San Gabriel Valley. The Santa Ana Mountains border the southeastern vista
while to the southwest the Orange County suburbanopolis spreads to the sea.

To the approaching hiker, Gilman Peak itself does not inspire great expecta-
tions. It appears as little more than just another bump on the ridgetop, a bald
crown scarcely higher than neighboring peaklets. Ah, but the inspirational views
from the summit more than make up for the dull appearance of the peak.

The three reasons for Gilman Peak's success at delivering views are location,
location, and location. The peak is located at the far frontier of three counties: Los
Angeles, Orange and San Bernardino. Parts of a fourth county—Riverside—can be
viewed from the peak also.

Surrounded by all manner of residential, commercial and industrial developments, as well as four freeways, the wilder parts of the Chino Hills are indeed an
island on the land. The range's "island" nature is apparent to the hiker on the
trail to Gilman Peak.

DIRECTIONS TO TRAILHEAD: From the Orange Freeway (57) in
Brea, exit on Lambert Road. Drive 4 miles east on Lambert (which changes to
Carbon Canyon Road east of Valencia Avenue) to the entrance of Carbon Canyon
Regional Park. There's a vehicle entry fee. Limited legal parking (free) also exists
on the south shoulder of Carbon Canyon Road. From wherever you park, join the
dirt road angling southeast just below the road.

THE HIKE: Walk up the dirt road past a citrus orchard to a state park bulletin board and a signed junction. Telegraph Canyon Trail (a dirt road) heads
south, but you join North Ridge Trail (also a dirt road) on a climb past scattered
California walnut.

A bit more than 2 miles from the trailhead, the path gains a sparsely vegetated ridgeline and travels across it. After dipping and rising to a couple "false" summits, you'll reach Gilman Peak. A wide summit trail takes you to the top.

TELEGRAPH CANYON

HILLS-FOR-EVERYONE TRAIL

Along Ranch Road to McDermont Spring is 4 miles round trip with 400-foot gain; to Carbon Canyon Regional Park is 7.5 miles one way with 800-foot loss

Hills-for-Everyone Trail was named for the conservation group that was instru-mental in establishing Chino Hills State Park. The trail follows a creek to the head of Telegraph Canyon. The creek is lined with oak, sycamore and the some-what rare California walnut.

DIRECTIONS TO TRAILHEAD: Chino Hills State Park can be a bit tricky to find. The park is located west of Highway 71 between the Riverside Freeway (91) and the Pomona Freeway (60).

From Highway 71, exit on Soquel Canyon Parkway and travel one mile to a signed left turn at Elinvar Road, which bends sharply left. Look immediately right for a signed dirt road—Bane Canyon Road. Enter the park on this road (which returns to pavement in two miles) and follow signs to the park office and ranger station.

The road forks just before the ranger station. To the right is the ranger sta-tion and visitor center. Bear left one-half mile on the dirt road to a vehicle barrier and trailhead parking. The signed trailhead is located a short distance past the vehicle barrier on the right of the road.

THE HIKE: Hills-for-Everyone Trail descends to a small creek and follows the creek up canyon. Shading the trail—and shielding the hiker from a view of the many electrical transmission lines that cross the park—are oaks, sycamores and walnuts. Of particular interest is the walnut; often the 15- to 30-foot tall tree has

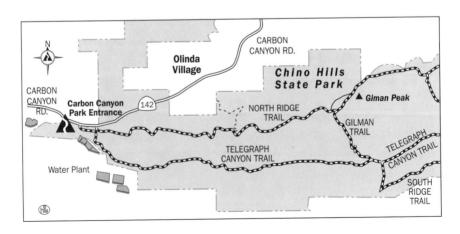

several dark brown trunks, which gives it a brushy appearance.

The trail, which can be quite slippery and muddy after a rain, passes a small (seasonal) waterfall. The slopes above the creekbed are carpeted with lush grasses and miners lettuce.

Wildflowers for everyone on the Chino Hills

Along the trail is found evidence of the park's ranching heritage, including lengths of barbed wire fence and old cattle troughs. For more than a century this land was used exclusively for cattle ranching.

Near its end, the trail ascends out of the creekbed to the head of Telegraph Canyon and intersects a dirt road. McDermont Spring is just down the road. Some of the livestock ponds, constructed during the area's ranching days, still exist, and hold water year-round. McDermont Spring—along with Windmill and Panorama ponds—provides water for wildlife.

To Carbon Canyon Regional Park: Telegraph Canyon Trail (a dirt road closed to public vehicular traffic) stays close to the canyon bottom and its creek. It's a gentle descent under the shade of oak and walnut trees. The walnuts are particularly numerous along the first mile of travel and the hiker not inclined to hike the length of Telegraph Canyon might consider exploring this stretch before returning to the trailhead.

The route passes an old windmill. Farther down the canyon, the walnuts thin out. A lemon grove, owned by the state park but leased to a farmer, is at a point where the dirt road intersects Carbon Canyon Road. Walk along the broad shoulder of the latter road 0.5 mile to Carbon Canyon Regional Park.

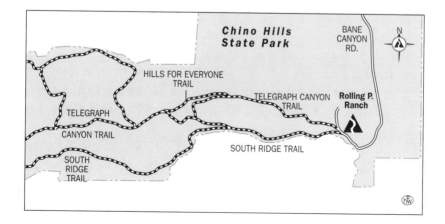

WATER CANYON

WATER CANYON, SOUTH RIDGE, ALISO TRAILS
5 miles round trip with 400-foot elevation gain

Water Canyon may just be the single most compelling locale in the Chino Hills. Grand old oaks and sycamores, along with willows and walnut trees shade this quiet enclave, one of the great natural treasures and pleasures of the Inland Empire.

The steep walls of the canyon add to the hiker's sense of isolation and adventure. Water Canyon is located nearly astride the boundary line between Orange and San Bernardino counties, but seems a hundred miles away from those fast-growing areas.

The canyon is particularly attractive to hikers because it's accessible only by foot. This foot-traffic only designation is something of a rarity in Chino Hills State Park, which has a system of dirt roads that is often heavily used by mountain bikers and horseback riders.

DIRECTIONS TO TRAILHEAD: Chino Hills State Park can be a bit tricky to find. The park is located west of Highway 71 between the Riverside Freeway (91) and the Pomona Freeway (60).

From Highway 71, exit on Soquel Canyon Parkway and travel one mile to a signed left turn at Elinvar Road, which bends sharply left. Look immediately right for a signed dirt road—Bane Canyon Road. Enter the park on this road (which returns to pavement in two miles) and follow signs to the park office and ranger station.

About 0.5 mile before the park office, turn left into the park campground and follow the camp road to its end at a vehicle gate, parking area and signed trailhead.

THE HIKE: Aliso Canyon Trail (a dirt road) heads south across a wide, fairly flat grassland. About 0.5 mile along, the road dips to cross the creek at the bottom of Aliso Canyon. Just before the crossing, note unsigned (upper) Aliso Canyon Trail (your return route on this loop hike) on the right.

Just ahead is a junction with another road. A left on the road leads south to lower Aliso Canyon. Go right about 100 yards. At a hairpin turn, the road bends back south and heads toward Skull Ridge, but you join signed Water Canyon Trail.

The footpath trends west through the lovely, wooded canyon. After a mile, and after passing a towering clump of prickly pear cactus and a sign indicating the end of the trail, the path reaches an open area.

(To continue your exploration of Water Canyon, follow the trail-less canyon

bottom west. After 0.25 mile or so, when you encounter more stinging nettle and poison oak than you can avoid, you might decide discretion is the better part of valor and retreat.)

A more pleasant option might be to follow the path, faint, but passable, which veers northwest away from Water Canyon and climbs rather steeply about 0.4 mile to meet South Ridge Trail, a dirt road. Turn right (east) on the road and enjoy good views to the south and east of the park's rolling hills.

A mile's descent brings you within sight of park headquarters and leads to a junction with the main park road. The signed beginning of Aliso Canyon Trail is also located at this junction. Join this footpath for a 0.75 mile saunter with great views of a windmill (a reminder of this land's pre-park ranching heritage) and some handsome *alisos* (sycamores). The trail meets (Lower) Aliso Canyon Trail, a dirt road. Turn left and retrace your steps back to the trailhead.

SAN JUAN HILL

SOUTH RIDGE TRAIL
To the top of San Juan Hill is 6 miles round trip with 1,200-foot elevation gain

When the land for Chino Hills State Park was purchased in the mid 1980s, there was a lot of grumbling about the high cost—from the public, from politicians, and even from some conservationists who figured purchasing a redwood grove or two was a better use of hard-to-come-by funds.

Nowadays the large park seems like a bargain. And nowhere is this more apparent than on the trail to the park's high point, San Juan Hill.

The first glimpse of the park's great value is obvious when hiking the half mile of South Ridge Trail and looking at what you're leaving behind: all manner of brand-new suburbia pushing right up to the park's southern boundary. Without a park, every buildable slope would likely be smothered in subdivisions.

Farther up the trail, most traces of civilization vanish, and the hiker enters a wonderfully pastoral landscape of rolling grassland and drifts of oak. It would be difficult to place a dollar value on this wonderful experience.

Deer gambol through the high grasses, hawks circle overhead and a refreshing breeze (often) keeps the temperature down. Atop San Juan's slopes, hikers are often joined by kite-flyers, who take advantage of the robust gusts.

While that famed San Juan Hill in Cuba was a difficult charge for Theodore Roosevelt and his Rough Riders to make in an 1898 battle of the Spanish-American War, you should have a rather mellow time conquering the San Juan Hill perched on the border of Orange and San Bernardino counties. The trail to 1,781-foot San Juan Hill is a well-graded fire road.

DIRECTIONS TO TRAILHEAD: From the Orange Freeway (57) in Brea, exit on Imperial Highway (90) and head southeast 4.5 miles to Yorba Linda Boulevard. Turn left (east) and drive 1.3 miles to Fairmont Boulevard. Turn left (east) and drive 1.5 miles to Rim Crest Drive. Turn left and proceed 0.3 mile to the signed trailhead on the right. Park alongside Rim Crest Drive. Heed the curbside parking signs because public parking is permitted only on some lengths of Rim Crest Drive; some parking is for residents (by permit) only.

THE HIKE: Walk 40 yards up the fire lane to the park information bulletin board and the signed beginning of South Ridge Trail. Begin your journey eastward with an ascent that soon removes you from virtually all of the sights and sounds of civilization.

The moderate climb leads over hills covered with wild oats, rye, mustard and wild radish. Trees are few and far between atop these hills, which means both little shade and unobstructed views of the surrounding countryside. Only the high-voltage powerlines bisecting the hills detract from the near-pastoral landscape.

Nearly three miles out, you'll reach a junction with the signed path to San Juan Hill. Walk 50 yards up a fire road toward a powerline tower, then join the narrow, unsigned footpath on the right leading 0.1 mile to the summit of San Juan Hill.

Crowning the hilltop is a concrete, hexagon-shaped column that reads: SAN JUAN 1896. Puzzle over this number as you enjoy the billowing grass and the usually breezy summit, as well as commanding vistas of the Chino Hills.

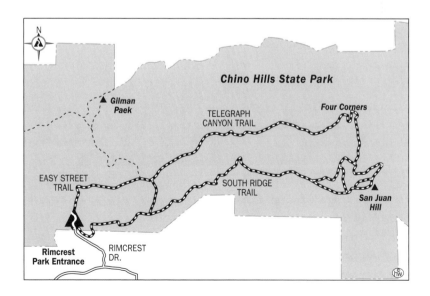

COAL CANYON

SANTA ANA RIVER, COAL CANYON TRAILS
From Green River Road into Coal Canyon is 5 miles round trip

For many years, the Coal Canyon interchange off the Riverside Freeway was the exit to nowhere. Developers intended to construct 1,500 homes and an industrial park in the canyon, but their plans were thwarted by the Hills for Everyone, the conservation group that spearheaded an epic two-decade long preservation effort.

Activists worked so diligently to preserve the canyon because it was considered one of the most environmentally valuable, yet unprotected, open spaces in Southern California. Additionally, the canyon is a critical wildlife corridor between the Chino Hills and Santa Ana Mountains.

Surely it was a Southern California conservation milestone when a key 650-acre portion of the canyon was added to Chino Hills State Park. Caltrans later closed the Coal Canyon freeway off-ramps and on-ramps in 2003. Surely it was the first freeway interchange relinquished for conservation purposes in California history.

The freeway underpass is being restored and re-vegetated for the passage of both wildlife and park visitors. Such corridors are particularly crucial to species that roam far and wide, such as the bobcat and mountain lion, badger and black-tailed jack rabbit.

It's unlikely many of the drivers and passengers in the quarter-million cars and trucks that hurtle over the wildlife corridor every day have any idea that Coal Canyon gives creatures great and small safe passage under the freeway.

Q: What do you call a freeway interchange that is ripped out to make a wildlife crossing?

A: A good start!

Who says conservationists don't have a sense of humor?

Right now you'll have the feeling of hiking a park-in-the making. In years to come, Coal Canyon might be a gem of a preserve to visit, but at present it's best to approach the canyon with a spirit of adventure and realize that you're one of its first visitors. the trail system (dirt roads), such as it is, lends itself to improvisation by the hiker. In contrast to the other side of Chino Hills State Park, don't look for a terrific signed trail system and the usual park amenities (picnic grounds, restrooms) any time soon.

Don't be tempted to drive down the closed Coal Canyon freeway exit. For one thing it's dangerous and for another, you can't get into Coal Canyon from the underpass anyway, because the wildlife corridor is bounded by a very high fence.

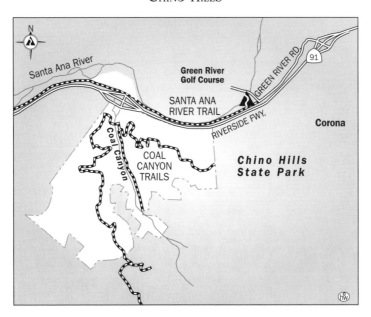

In fact, Coal Canyon isn't all that convenient for humans to reach. You can't get to the trailhead, even if there was a trailhead, by car. You can pedal along a bikeway to the Coal Canyon underpass but bicycles are forbidden in this part of the state park. The sole option for hikers is to walk the bike path alongside the freeway for a mile to the entry to the canyon.

But let's not kvetch about the challenges of getting into Coal Canyon and instead take a philosophic approach: Just think how difficult it was for animals to get across the freeway without becoming road-kill.

DIRECTIONS TO TRAILHEAD: From the Riverside Freeway (91), a few miles west of Highway 71 in Corona, exit on Green River Road. Head west a mile and park just before the road bends north and enters Green River Golf Course and near the signed beginning of the Santa Ana River Trail (a bike path).

THE HIKE: Walk alongside Green River Road, parallel to the freeway, and join signed Santa Ana River Trail. Follow the bike path on a noisy mile walk to the freeway overpasses spanning Coal Canyon. Head south along the underpass on "the wildlife corridor" and, after passing under the freeway, reach the signed boundary of Chino Hills State Park.

You'll see a couple dirt fire roads climbing eastward and westward but for the first-time Coal Canyon explorer, I suggest continuing up-canyon from the broad mouth of the canyon on the rough dirt road heading south on the east side of the canyon. After a mile's ascent, the road peters out, though you can continue up-canyon alongside the seasonal creek, where you might just discover, after generous winter rains, a small waterfall.

CHAPTER SEVEN

Riverside County Parks & Preserves

In addition to huge well-known desert recreation areas such as Joshua Tree National Park and Palm Springs in the eastern portion of the county, Riverside County also entices the hiker with parks and preserves close to population centers. In recent decades, the county has witnessed phenomenal Inland Empire-style growth; that is to say, the construction of many highways and suburbs, so creating more parks and trails is crucial to residents and visitors alike.

Hike to the top of Mt. Rubidoux, located on the west side of Riverside, for a 360-degree panorama of the county—one very different from the view of a century ago.

Put Santa Rosa Plateau on your "To Hike" list; it's the one place that looks much as it did 100 years ago.

MT. RUBIDOUX

MT. RUBIDOUX TRAIL
3 mile loop with 500-foot elevation gain

The isolated, 1,337-foot high granite hill towering above the Riverside's western edge has long been a landmark to travelers and residents alike, ever since the 1880s when Riverside emerged as the quintessential Southern California citrus town. The mountain was named for one of its 19th-century owners, wealthy ranchero Louis Robidoux.

Frank Miller, owner of the lavish, pride-of-Riverside Mission Inn, purchased the mountain in 1906 with the intention of using the mountain as an attraction to sell residential lots at its base. Mt. Rubidoux was landscaped and a road constructed to the summit, where a cross was planted. Some historians believe America's first Easter sunrise service took place atop Rubidoux in 1909 and inspired similar observances around the continent.

Credit the developers for going all out on the road; they hired the engineer who designed Yellowstone National Park's road system. While the developers originally viewed Rubidoux strictly as a way to boost lot sales, their vision (particularly Miller's) soon expanded dramatically.

The road to Rubidoux was designed to be more than a mere recreational walk or drive; it was a pilgrimage to a cross and to monuments of famous men of the time. This "trail of shrines" ascended to a long white cross honoring missionary

The Old Bell, Rubidoux Mt., Riverside, Cal.

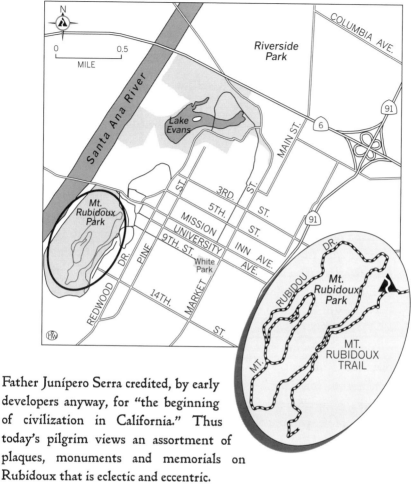

Father Junípero Serra credited, by early developers anyway, for "the beginning of civilization in California." Thus today's pilgrim views an assortment of plaques, monuments and memorials on Rubidoux that is eclectic and eccentric.

Rubidoux's most significant sights-to-see are the Peace Tower and Friendship Bridge. Frank Miller was a lifelong advocate for world peace and his friends con-structed the distinct tower to honor him in 1925.

For many, many years, Mt. Rubidoux was a drive, not a hike. Arrows painted on rocks indicated an "up" route and "down" route for autos. The mountain has been closed to vehicles since 1992.

Autumn sunsets, when nearby mountains glow red, purple and blue, are par-ticularly memorable. Winter brings vistas of snow-capped summits.

Locals access the mountain from several trailheads, but the best route for first-time Rubidoux ramblers is by way of the Ninth Street gate, an inspired beginning for what can be an inspiring jaunt.

DIRECTIONS TO TRAILHEAD: From the Pomona Freeway (60) in Riverside, exit on Market Street and proceed east into downtown. Turn west (right) on Mission Inn Avenue and drive 7 blocks to Redwood Drive. Turn left and head 2 blocks to Ninth Street, turn right and continue 2 more blocks to the distinct trailhead (gated Mt. Rubidoux Drive) on the left. Park safely and courte- ously on adjacent residential streets.

From the Riverside Freeway (91) in Riverside, exit on University Avenue and head west through downtown to Redwood Drive. Turn left, travel one block, then turn right on Ninth Street. Proceed two more blocks to this hike's start on the left.

THE HIKE: Pass through the entry gate and walk along and landscaped lane past pepper trees, eucalyptus and huge beaver tail cactus. After 0.3 mile of south- bound travel, the road makes a very tight hairpin turn north and nearly–but not quite–intersects the downward leg of Mt. Rubidoux Road, which makes a similar hairpin turn from north to south. Note this junction because on your return jour- ney you'll need to cross from one leg of the road to the other to close the loop.

The road ascends rather bare slopes, dotted with brittle bush, mustard and century plant. Lupine and California poppies brighten the way in spring.

After passing a memorial to Henry E. Huntington, "man of affairs, large in his bounty, yet wise," the road bends west, then south. City views are exchanged for more rural ones, including the Santa Ana River that gave Riverside its name.

The main Mt. Rubidoux road junctions a circular summit road, which you'll join to see the sights–the Peace Tower, Friendship Bridge and plenty of plaques. From the Father Junipero Serra Cross at the summit or from one of the peak's other fine vista points, partake of the 360-degree panorama of great mountains and metro-Riverside.

Return to the main Mt. Rubidoux Road for a short (0.75 mile) descent that loops south, east, then back north. Just as this downward leg bends sharply south, leave the road and step over to the other road leg that you used to ascend the mountain. Retrace your steps a final 0.3 mile back to Ninth Street.

BOX SPRINGS MOUNTAIN

SKYLINE TRAIL
4' to 6-mile loop with 500-foot elevation gain

Far too steep for suburban housing developments, the Box Springs Mountains in Riverside County remain a place to get away from it all. "It" in this instance is the hustle and bustle of the Inland Empire which surrounds this little-known mountain range.

Little-known the mountains may be, but remote they are not. Four free-ways—the San Bernardino, Riverside, Pomona and Escondido—surround the Box Springs Mountains. Their location might remind football fans of a quarterback barking signals: "10-91-60-215-Hike!"

The peaks of the range rise sharply from the floor of the Moreno Valley to 3,000 feet and offer commanding clear-day views of the city of Riverside, the San Bernardino and San Jacinto Mountains, as well as a great portion of the Inland Empire.

The mountain's namesake peak, as well as 2,389 acres of native Southern California coastal sage terrain is preserved in Box Springs Mountain Park under the jurisdiction of Riverside County. The park is a natural island amidst one of the fastest growing urban and suburban areas in California.

Vegetation includes members of the coastal sage scrub community: chamise, lemonade berry, brittlebush, white sage, black sage and buckwheat. More than 30 types of wildflowers brighten the park's slopes in the spring.

Wildlife—coyotes, jackrabbits, skunks and kangaroo rats—is attracted by the tiny springs that trickle from the mountain. Wildlife biologists call Box Springs

Commanding views of the wild side of the Inland Empire.

235

Mountain a "habitat island" because it provides a home for animals while being surrounded by development.

The mountains, along with "The Badlands" to the east of the range, were shaped in part by the San Jacinto Fault, a major branch of the San Andreas system. Some geologists believe that the granites of Box Springs were once attached to the granites of the San Jacinto Mountains but were moved to their present location, some 20 miles, by lateral displacement along the fault.

Perhaps the most eccentric resident of Box Springs Mountain was Helene Troy Arlington, who moved to the mountain in 1945. The self-styled hermit secluded herself in a mountain retreat she called Noli Me Tangere, a Latin phrase meaning "Do Not Touch Me."

Arlington was devoted to dogs, particularly Dalmatians, and kept many of them in her home. She wrote canine poems and magazine articles under the pen name "Dear Dog Lady." On a plot of land next to her home she established "Arlington Cemetery," a final resting place for her four-legged friends.

Dogs, in fact, were her only friends. She sold her land to the Riverside County Parks Department in 1974 and moved to Arlington, Virginia to be near the grave of her long-dead husband Masefield. She wrote the parks department: "There was no reason to remain there any longer, as I still do not have one friend in California."

Park trails include 3-mile long Pigeon Pass Trail, which offers great views, and 1.5 mile long Ridge Trail which travels over Box Spring Mountain. (Avoid Two Trees Trail, which climbs from Two Trees Road in Riverside to meet Box Springs Mountain Road inside the park. Trailhead access is poor, as is the trail itself.)

The park's premiere path is Skyline Trail, which loops around Box Springs Mountain. If Riverside can be said to have a skyline, this is it; not tall office buildings but skyscraping granite and a top-of-the-world view.

DIRECTIONS TO TRAILHEAD: From the Pomona Freeway (60) in Moreno Valley, exit on Pigeon Pass Road. Proceed some 4.5 miles north, then a short distance west. Pigeon Pass Road turns north again, but you continue west, joining a dirt road and following the signs into Box Springs Mountain Park. Signed Skyline Trail is on your right.

THE HIKE: From Box Springs Mountain Road, Skyline Trail heads west, soon serving up views of the city of Riverside. Next the trail contours north, passing rock outcroppings that are geologically and aesthetically similar to those found atop Mt. Rubidoux, Riverside landmark and site of a long-popular Easter service.

The path comes to an unsigned junction. Skyline Trail angles east and begins contouring around a hill back to the trailhead. Hardier hikers will join an extension of the trail known as "Second Loop" and make an even larger circle back to the trailhead.

LAKE PERRIS

TERRI PEAK TRAIL
From Campfire Center to Terri Peak is 3.5 miles round trip with 800-foot elevation gain; to Indian Museum, return via lakeshore, is 6 miles round trip

Perris in the Spring. No need to battle the hordes of tourists flocking to that other similar-sounding place of romance across the Atlantic. No need to travel 6,000 miles and spend lots of money to have a good time.

For just a few euros you can visit a manmade wonder, *Lac de Paris*, otherwise known as Lake Perris State Recreation Area. So pack *du pain et du vin* and head for the most romantic Pomona Freeway offramp in all of Southern California.

Few nature-lovers—or lovers of any kind—have discovered the romance of Perris. True, a million and a half visitors come to the lake each year, but the only nature most are interested in is that found wriggling on the end of a hook.

While the parc is oriented to *les autos et les bateaux*, there is a network of trails for those visitors who wish to explore Perris à pied. Perris pace-setters will enjoy the trek to Terri Peak, easily the most romantic spot in all of the Bernasconi Hills.

Springtime colors the hills with a host of wild fleurs, including goldfields, California poppy, fiddleneck, baby blue eyes and blue dicks. The view from Terri Peak on smog-free days is très fantastique.

DIRECTIONS TO TRAILHEAD: From the Pomona Freeway (60), a few miles east of its intersection with I-215, exit on Moreno Beach Drive and proceed 4 miles to the park. Immediately after paying your state park day use fee at the entry kiosk, turn right on Lake Perris Drive. Look sharply right for the strange-looking international symbol indicating a campfire and an amphitheater. Park in the campfire/interpretive center lot. The unsigned trail begins to the left of the campfire area.

THE HIKE: The trail ascends gradually west and occasionally intersects a horse trail. The unsigned path is tentative at first but an occasional wooden post helps keep you on the trail, which climbs boulder-strewn slopes.

The coastal scrub community—sage, buckwheat, chamise and toyon predominates. Also much in evidence are weedy-looking non-native species, as well as mustard, prickly pear cactus, morning glory and Russian thistle.

The trail climbs to a small flat meadow then turns southwest and climbs more earnestly to the peak. From atop Terri Peak, enjoy clear-day views of the San Bernardino Mountains to the northeast and the Santa Ana Mountains to the southwest. Below is fast-growing Moreno Valley, checkerboarded alternately with

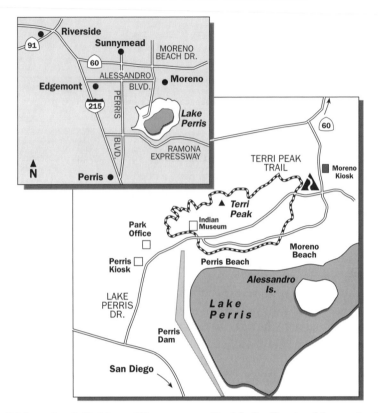

green fields and subdivisions. You can see all of Lake Perris, Alessandro Island, and hundreds of boaters, anglers and swimmers.

The trail from Terri Peak down to the Indian Museum is sometimes in poor condition. You may lose the trail a couple of times; however you won't get lost because it's easy to stay oriented with the lakeshore on your left and the Indian Museum ahead.

After a steep descent, the trail bends sharply east and deposits you at the Indian Museum's parking lot. The museum includes exhibits interpreting the Cahuilla, Chemehuevi, Serrano and other desert tribes and how they adapted to life in the Mojave Desert region.

From the museum, you follow the asphalt road down to Lake Perris Drive, cross this main park road and continue down to Perris Beach. Here, and at Moreno Beach one mile to the west, you may cool off with a swim.

Improvise a route along the lakeshore using the sidewalk and bicycle trail until you spot the main campground entrance on your left. Enter the camp- ground, pass the kiosk, then pick up the intermittent footpath that winds through the campground. This path and some improvisation will bring you to Lake Perris Drive and back to the trailhead.

Santa Rosa Plateau Ecological Reserve

Ancient and rare Engelmann oaks, as well as vernal pools and
thousands of acres of rolling grassland are preserved in
Santa Rosa Plateau Ecological Reserve, located at the southern
end of the Santa Ana Mountains in Riverside County.
An excellent trail network explores the plateau,
which is pastoral Southern California at its finest;
that is to say, the least changed since the days of
the caballeros and gracious haciendas.
Atop the plateau, time seems to have stopped at 1840.
The reserve is more than a park or some
much-needed breathing room in this
fast-developing part of the Inland Empire;
it's an ecological treasure, recognized by
UNESCO as a biosphere reserve.

TENAJA OVERLOOK

GRANITE LOOP TRAIL
Loop from the Visitor Center to Tenaja Overlook is 1.6 miles

Hard-riding Spanish vaqueros called the deep holes in the creekbed, *tenajas*. The holes held water year-around and provided crucial summer water sources for both cows and cowboys. Today the tenajas (Spanish for "tanks") offer habitat for many plants and animals, some uniquely adapted to life with these basins-in-the-bedrock.

Granite Loop Trail offers a good look at the tenajas as well as something of a microcosm of the reserve. For many visitors, hikers or not, the pathway is the primary—and often only—experience of the plateau.

Dedicated botanist Tom Chester reports that every shrub and tree found along Granite Loop Trail is native flora. He lists more than 160 annual and perennial herbs on his web site.

The 1.2 mile loop, along with an additional 0.4 mile out-and-back for a good look at the tenajas, makes a great family-friendly introduction to the reserve. The hike begins at the visitor center, open on the weekends. Ask reserve staff or volunteers about longer loops you can do from this trailhead including Vista Grande Trail, a trail that lives up to the promise of its name.

DIRECTIONS TO TRAILHEAD: Most Orange County and L.A. County residents bound for the reserve will opt for the Riverside Freeway and take it eastbound to the I-15 south. In the Widomar area, between Lake Elsinore and Murietta, exit I-15 on Clinton Keith Road. Drive 4 miles southwest to the Santa Rosa Plateau Ecological Reserve Visitor Center.

THE HIKE: Join northbound Granite Loop Trail from the west side of the parking lot.(Don't head out on Wiashal Trail, that other northbound trail that parallels Clinton Keith Road.) A brief descent brings you to an oak-shaded picnic area perched above a creekbed. The path descends along the creekbed then ascends a boulder-strewn slope.

A half-mile or so from the trailhead, Granite Loop Trail intersects Vista Grande Trail, which you'll join for the short walk to Tenaja Overlook. With enough rainfall, some good-sized pools form along Cole Creek.

Return to Granite Loop, soon crossing Waterline Road and meandering among the ancient oaks. Contemplate the inspirational scene by taking a seat on one of the strategically placed benches under the old oaks. Leave the oaks behind and close the loop with a mild ascent back to the trailhead.

ENGLEMANN OAKS EXPLORATION

COYOTE, OAK TREE TRAIL
From Hidden Valley Trailhead to Oaks is 2.2 miles round trip.

A family-friendly interpretive trail probes the unique world of the Englemann oak and offers a good look at other reserve highlights as well, including native grasses and the unique tenajas. Learn about the rarity of this oak species and how few of them are protected.

Engelmann oaks were once widespread throughout the western U.S., but now range only between San Diego and Santa Barbara. The oaks were named for German-born physician/botanist Dr. George Engelmann, who explored and collected specimens in this country during the last century.

Engelmann oaks are gnarled fellows, with a kind of checkered trunk and grayish leaves. Engelmanns are noticeably different from their more common cousins, the coast live oaks. Coast live oaks are fuller, with smoother bark and leaves that are shiny green. Coast live oaks grow in lower, wetter locales, while the Engelmanns take higher and drier ground.

Oak Tree Trail travels by Cole Creek, lined by oak and sycamore. Look for the tenajas, small pools in the creekbed, home to turtles and frogs.

You'll also observe purple needle grass along the nature trail. Field ecologists credit Vail family ranchers, who purchased the plateau in 1904 and operated a cattle ranch for 60 years, for its wise grazing practices that resulted in the protection of what is considered to be the best remaining California bunchgrass prairie. Mule deer and even the occasional badger can be spotted in the grasslands.

DIRECTIONS TO TRAILHEAD: Most Orange County and L.A. County residents bound for the reserve will opt for the Riverside Freeway and take it eastbound to the I-15 south. In the Wildomar area, between Lake Elsinore and Murietta, exit I-15 on Clinton Keith Road. Drive 4 miles southwest to the Santa Rosa Plateau Ecological Reserve Visitor Center, then continue 1.5 miles to the Hidden Valley Trailhead.

THE HIKE: Join Coyote Trail and angle southeast a half-mile, crossing oak-dotted grasslands to intersect Trans Preserve Trail. Stay left and descend to Oak Tree Trail.

Begin the loop on either leg and tour the famed oaks, the path's former trailhead near the intersection of Clinton Keith Road and Tenaja Road, and the environs of Cole Creek. Once you've looped the loop, return to the trailhead the way you came.

TRANS RESERVE

COYOTE, TRANS PRESERVE, VERNAL POOL TRAILS
From Hidden Valley Trailhead to Vernal Pools is 6 miles round trip

Use your imagination and step back a century and a half in time to an era when Santa Rosa Plateau was part of the 47,000-acre Rancho Santa Rosa granted to cattle rancher Juan Moreno by Governor Pío Pico. The adobes dating from 1845 that you'll visit on this hike will certainly help you imagine mid-19th century California.

Fortunately for those of us who would like a glimpse into that bygone era, the landowners following Juan Moreno did little to this early California landscape of oak woodlands, rolling grasslands and vernal pools but use it for grazing cattle. The relatively gentle use of the land is in part responsible for the remarkable bio-diversity flourishing on the Santa Rosa Plateau today. By some estimates, the plateau hosts about half of all the species of plants and animals considered to be rare in the Inland Empire.

Good thing a sizeable portion of Old SoCal was preserved because off the plateau it's very much the 21st century; that is to say, huge housing developments have pushed up Clinton Keith Road and left today's ecological reserve something of an island on the land.

Citizen activists, attempting to thwart a developers plans to construct 4,000

Take a hike on Trans Preserve Trail through Santa Rosa Plateau Preserve,
now Santa Rosa Plateau Ecological Reserve.

homes on the plateau, worked in concern with national, state and county govern-ment, as well as The Nature Conservancy, to come up with the money to pur-chase the property and make it a preserve, which now totals 8,300 acres. The Nature Conservancy handles resources management while Riverside County Regional Parks and Open Space District provides for visitors.

Trans Preserve and a supporting cast of trails offer a grand tour of the reserve. Depending on your time, inclination and energy level, you can hike for two hours, four hours or an entire day on the reserve's 18 named trails. The extensive trail network in the reserve's southeast section allows for plenty of options and seems to encourage a hiker's spontaneous decision-making.

This hike takes you to the vernal pools atop Mesa de Colorado and to the ver-nal pools. The mesa is capped with basalt, meaning it's an ideal rainwater collec-tor. Depressions in the rock collect water into seasonal ponds. One pool measures nearly 40 acres and is considered one of the largest in California.

The vernal pools offer habitat to the unusual fairy shrimp and some rare plants that ring the waterline. In winter, seasonal pools attract waterfowl, includ-ing grebes, Canada geese and green-winged teal. The pools are a colorful sight in spring when goldfields and other wildflowers surround them.

DIRECTIONS TO TRAILHEAD: Most Orange County and L.A. County residents bound for the reserve will opt for the Riverside Freeway and take it eastbound to the I-15 south. In the Wildomar area, between Lake Elsinore and Murrietta, exit I-15 on Clinton Keith Road. Drive 5 miles southwest to the Santa Rosa Plateau Ecological Reserve Visitor Center. Continue another mile as the road turns abruptly right (west) and assumes a new name—Tenaja Road. Proceed another half mile farther to Hidden Valley Trailhead, where you'll find parking on both side of the road and the trailhead on the south side.

THE HIKE: Begin on Coyote Trail, named for one of the many animals that roam the reserve, though birders tend to watch for white-tailed kites when hiking along this path. A half-mile's travel brings you to a junction, where you gear right (south) on Trans Preserve Trail.

Across the reserve you go, hiking over the rolling hills and viewing both woodlands and native grasslands. Trail junctions for paths leading east and west may tempt you, but stick with Trans Preserve Trail all the way up to the top of Mesa de Colorado and a junction with Vernal Pool Trail.

Hike east and check out the vernal pools, then descend from the mesa to the historic adobes, located a bit more than three miles from the trailhead. After tak-ing a break and inspecting the oldest structures in Riverside County, head north on Lomas Trail.

Bear right on Monument Road, and follow it only for a brief time, because

Lomas Trail soon resumes and you'll follow it northbound. When you reach Tenaja Truck Trail, cross it to reach Oak Tree Trail (see Englemann Oaks Exploration in this guide). Take the left fork of this looping nature trail and hike in close company with the rare Englemann oaks to Trans Preserve Trail, which you follow southwest to the Coyote Trail.

Okay, after all those turns, trails and junctions, you know what to do now: retrace your steps a half-mile on Coyote Trail back to the trailhead.

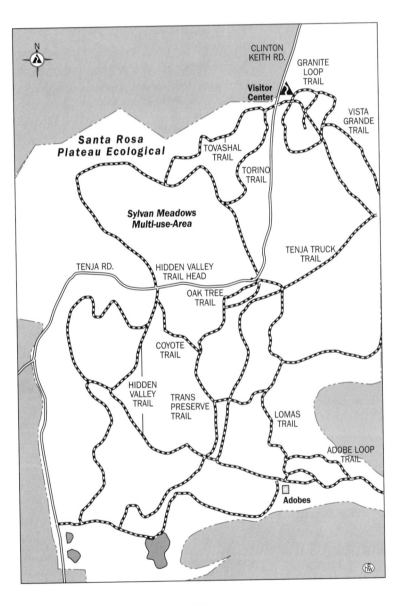

SYLVAN MEADOWS

TOVASHAL, SYLVAN MEADOWS & TORINO TRAILS
Loop from Visitor Center through Sylvan Meadows Multi-Use Area is 2.2 miles with 100-foot elevation gain

As a result of a purchase of a 1,000-acre ranch located to the west of the plateau in 1996, Santa Rosa Ecological Reserve now has an adjoining area less sensitive to human visitors. Sylvan Meadows Multi-Use Area can host such activities as mountain biking and picnicking without grave concerns about the effects of human use on rare and fragile flora.

The land is also something of a buffer between the heart of the reserve and approaching civilization. Half-million dollar estate lots are for sale "overlooking and adjacent to Sylvan Meadows" and "providing a forever view of snow-capped mountains, city lights and the Pacific Ocean."

This short loop hike offers a meander through meadows that are indeed sylvan—a portion of the reserve's renowned bunchgrass prairie. If you'd like to extend this hike by 3.5 miles or so, consider hiking out-and-back to Stevenson Canyon, where you'll find a memorable oak woodland.

Keep an eye out and an ear cocked for mountain bikers; riders can zoom right up on you along Sylvan Meadows trails.

DIRECTIONS TO TRAILHEAD: Most Orange County and L.A. County residents bound for the reserve will opt for the Riverside Freeway and take it eastbound to the I-15 south. In the Wildomar area, between Lake Elsinore and Murietta, exit I-15 on Clinton Keith Road. Drive 4 miles southwest to the Santa Rosa Plateau Ecological Reserve Visitor Center.

THE HIKE: Cross Clinton Keith Road to the west side and hike 0.1 mile through oak woodland and over a bridge to a trail junction. Head right on Tovashal Trail (the left fork is Torino Trail, the loop's return leg.) Offering a sampling of woodlands and grasslands, the trail extends a short mile to meet Sylvan Meadows Road at the northern edge of a an impressive meadow graced by statuesque old oaks.

Turn left on the dirt road and hike 0.4 mile to a signed junction with Torino Trail. Take this path across brushy and oak-dotted slopes back to the bridge and then return to the visitor center and parking lot.

CALIFORNIA CITRUS STATE HISTORIC PARK

CITRUS INTERPRETIVE TRAIL
From Gazebo to Gage Canal is 1.25 miles round trip

Park visitors are greeted by a replica of an orange juice stand, located on the corner of Van Buren Boulevard and Dufferin Avenue. In the days before interstate high-ways and reliable auto air conditioners, stands offering fresh squeezed orange juice and lemonade were a common sight and popular with thirsty motorists.

The brightly colored stand is an appropriate welcome to California Citrus State Historic Park, which tells the story of how "Citriculture" influenced the landscape—and culture—of Southern California, as well as how it helped shape public perception of the region.

Navel oranges, Valencia oranges, lemons and grapefruit are grown in the park, which boasts some 186 acres under cultivation by a nonprofit corporation. Check out the park visitor center, which resembles a packing house, and features exhibits that tell the story of California's citrus industry. Docents sometimes give talks and conduct walks.

Arts and Crafts aficionados will love the Sunkist Center and what's often referred to as "the park within the park". Visitors have the opportunity to walk through an old-fashioned park, created in the Craftsman/California bungalow motif of the first two decades of the 20th century. Landscape architects of the era designed parks to provide gentle paths for strolling, areas (without equipment) for children to play, and plenty of picnic grounds. The idea was to offer park-goers

a quiet place to relax and restore their spirits.

The park has an intriguing interpretive path, as well as other trails leading past the citrus groves. A palm lined gravel path leads to groves and past grove memorabilia to a knoll, which offers grand clear-day views of the San Gabriel Mountains and San Bernardino Mountains.

DIRECTIONS TO TRAIL-HEAD: From Highway 91 (the Riverside Freeway), in the Arlington Heights area of Riverside, exit on Arlington Blvd. and travel 2 miles southeast to Dufferin Avenue. Turn left then make a right into the park and a left into the first parking lot. The inter-

pretive path begins at the gazebo by the Sunkist Center. If available, pick up an interpretive pamphlet at the gazebo.

THE HIKE: The five-stop tour includes a historical overview of the intro-duction of the orange to Southern California and a visit to the park's Varietal Collection, which numbers more than 100 kinds of citrus trees, including California's commercial species and exotics from around the world.

Other gentle lessons along the way help hikers learn about the three essentials for successful citrus production: good soil, suit-able climate (different species thrive best in specific microclimates), and water. In rain-challenged Southern California, irrigation is truly the lifeblood of citrus production so it's fitting that the interpretive path offers a

good look at the Gage Canal, a 20-mile waterway that tapped the Santa Ana River in San Bernardino and brought water to the groves now part of the state park. The canal, built by Matthew Gage between 1885 and 1889 is still used by area citrus farmers.

UCR BOTANIC GARDENS

GARDEN TRAILS
Loops around the garden of 0.5 mile or 1 mile or more with up to 300-foot elevation gain

Located on the eastern edge of the University of California, Riverside campus, this 40-acre botanic reserve contains an eclectic collection of more than 3,500 species. The garden offers an array of hikes over hilly terrain through several different landscapes. Four miles of footpaths and a flat, paved wheelchair-accessible trail explore the garden.

The Garden is divided into three major sections:
• The Horticultural Collections, featuring flower, herb, cactus gardens and a subtropical fruit orchard
• The Geographical Collections, featuring native plants of South Africa, Southwest Deserts, Sierra Foothills, Baja California, and Australia
• The Unplanted Riverside Coastal Sage Scrub Community and grassland

Pick up a copy of the free garden map, which will allow you to follow the many paths to your chosen destination. Entrance is free, although a modest donation is requested for each visitor. Open daily from 8 A.M. to 5 P.M.; closed New Year's Day, July 4th, Thanksgiving and Christmas Day.

Take your time and enjoy exploring this oasis where pond creatures, birds, botanical wonders and happy hikers coexist quite happily.

DIRECTIONS TO TRAILHEAD: From Interstate 215/State Highway 60, exit Martin Luther King Boulevard, and turn right. Turn right again at Canyon Crest Venue to enter the UCR campus, and go right again on West Canyon Drive, which winds around to become South Campus, then East Campus Road. Look for

A tranquil place in busy Riverside.

the Botanic Gardens signs intermittently spaced on signposts along the way. You will pass Parking Lot 10 and then reach the more secluded, tree-lined approach to the Botanic Garden. Parking requires an inexpensive hourly permit (25 cents at this writing) which is available just beyond the Garden gates. Note: Massive amounts of freeway construction nearby may lead to changes due to road closures or detours.

SAN TIMOTEO CANYON STATE PARK

Not yet open for hiking: contact park for more information

When San Timoteo Canyon State Park opens, it will bring some much-needed "breathing room" to the fast-growing Inland Empire. Park highlights include trails for hiking and horseback riding, a relatively untouched canyon and some important historical resources, including the San Timoteo Schoolhouse. One of San Timoteo's most famous residents was the teenaged Wyatt Earp, whose family lived in the canyon from 1864 to 1868.

Conservation groups have worked with the California Department of Parks and Recreation since 1999 to establish a state park in scenic San Timoteo Canyon. Movie producer Gale Ann Hurd donated her ranch land to the Riverside Land Conservancy, which purchased other property in the canyon. A good-sized park of some 10,000 acres is the goal.

San Timoteo Canyon extends from the mountain headwaters of San Timoteo Creek to its confluence with the Santa Ana River. The 14-mile long canyon, ranges from one-quarter to one half mile wide, and slopes downward from 2,400 feet in elevation at its eastern end to 1,200 feet at its western end. The south side of the canyon is flanked by severely eroded hills known as the badlands.

During prehistoric times, San Timoteo Canyon served as a kind of border between the native Serrano to the north and the Cahuilla to the south. The canyon was later used by a number of Hispanic and Anglo ranchers. In 1873 a watering station was established at El Casco, where the first transcontinental railroad line passed through the canyon.

A seasonal creek flows through the canyon, which is lined with willows and cottonwoods. The canyon's north slopes are blanketed with chaparral, including chamise, ceanothus and scrub oak. California buckwheat and various sages predominate on the dry, south-facing slopes.

San Timoteo Canyon's natural attractions are many. Spring blooms include California poppy, lupine, popcorn flower and elderberry. Mule deer, coyote, black-tailed jack rabbit, deer mice and raccoons are among the mammalian occupants of the canyon.

Contact the park for information about access to the park and hiking possibilities.

OC Park Contacts

Aliso and Wood Canyons
Wilderness Park
28373 Alicia Parkway
Laguna Niguel, CA 92677
(949) 923-2200

Aliso Beach
31131 Pacific Coast Hwy.
Laguna Beach, CA 92652
(949) 923-2280

Arroyo Trabuco
30892 Trabuco Cyn. Rd.
Trabuco Canyon, CA 92678
(949) 923-2260 or (949) 923-2256

California Citrus State
Historical Park.
1879 Jackson Street
Riverside, California 92504
(909) 780-6222.

Capistrano Beach
35005 Beach Road
Capo Beach, CA 92675
(949) 923-2280

Carbon Canyon Regional Park
4442 Carbon Canyon Road
Brea, CA 92823
(714) 973-3160 or (714) 973-3162

Caspers Wilderness Park
33401 Ortega Hwy.
San Juan Capistrano, CA 92675
(949) 923-2210

Clark Regional Park
8800 Rosecrans Ave.
Buena Park, CA 90621
(714) 973-3170

County Of Orange RDMD/
Harbors Beaches & Parks
1 Irvine Park Road
Orange, CA 92869
(714) 973-6865 or (866) OCPARKS

Cleveland National Forest
Trabuco Ranger District
1147 East Sixth Street
Corona, CA 92879
(951) 736-1811

Craig Regional Park
3300 State College Blvd.
Fullerton, CA 92835
(714) 973-3180

Doheny State Beach
25300 Dana Point Harbor Dr
Dana Point, CA 92629
(949) 496-6171

Featherly Regional Park
24001 Santa Ana Canyon Road
Anaheim, CA 92808
(714) 771-6731 or (714) 637-0210

Heritage Hill Historical Park
25151 Serrano Road
Lake Forest, CA 92630-2534
(949) 923-2230

Huntington Central Park
P.O. Box 190
Huntington Beach, CA 92648
(714) 536-5486

Irvine Regional Park
1 Irvine Park Road
Orange, CA 92862
(714) 973-6835 or (714) 973-3173

Laguna Coast Wilderness Park
20101 Laguna Canyon Road
Laguna Beach, CA 92651
(949) 923-2235

Laguna Niguel Regional Park
28241 La Paz Road
Laguna Niguel, CA 92677
(949) 923-2240 or (949) 923-2243

Limestone/Whiting Ranch Parks
P.O. Box 156
Trabuco Canyon, CA 92678
(949) 923-2245

Mason Regional Park
18712 University Drive
Irvine, CA 92612-2601
(949) 923-2220 or (949) 923-2223

Mile Square Regional Park
16801 Euclid
Fountain Valley, CA 92708
(714) 973-6600

Niguel Botanical Gardem
29751 Crown Valley Parkway
Laguna Niguel, CA 92677
(949) 425-5126

Oak Canyon Nature Center
6700 E. Walnut Canyon Road
Anaheim, CA 92807
(714) 998-8380

Orange County Ocean Institute
24200 Dana Point Harbor Dr.
Dana Point, CA 92629
(949) 496-2274

O'Neill Regional Park
30892 Trabuco Canyon Road
Trabuco Canyon, CA 92678
(949) 923-2260 or (949) 923-2256

Peters Canyon Regional Park
8548 E. Canyon View Ave.
Orange, CA 92869
(714) 973-6611 or (714) 973-6612

Riverside County Regional Parks &
Open Space District
4600 Crestmore Road
Riverside, CA 92509
(951) 955-4310

Salt Creek Beach
33333 S. Pacific Coast Hwy.
Dana Point, CA 92629
(949) 923-2280

San Clemente State Beach
225 Avenida Califia
San Clemente, CA 92672
(949) 492-3156

San Joaquin Wildlife Sanctuary
c/o Sea & Sage Audubon Society
P.O. Box 5447, Irvine CA 92616
(949) 261-7963

Santa Rosa Plateau Ecological
Reserve
39400 Clinton Keith Road
Murrieta, CA 92562
(951) 677-6951

Talbert Nature Preserve
P.o. Box 4048
Santa Ana, CA 92702
(949) 923-2250 or (866) 627-2757

Thomas F. Riley Wilderness Park
30952 Oso Parkway
Coto De Caza, CA 92679
(949) 923-2265 or (949) 923-2266

UCR Botanic Gardens
University of California
Riverside, CA 92521-0124
(951) 784-6962

Upper Newport Bay
2301 University Drive
Newport Beach, CA 92660
(949) 923-2290

Yorba Park
7600 E. La Palma
Anaheim, CA 92807
(714) 973-6615 or (714) 973-6838

BEST HIKES WITH KIDS . . .

How long ago was it that you conquered snowy summits, explored remote canyons and partied hearty with the Sierra Club Singles after a fifteen-mile hike with the 20s and 30s Sierra Club Singles? Seems like a century ago, huh? When you have children, it can seem like the simplest hike is more difficult to organize than a Himalayan expedition.

But parents, don't hang up your hiking boots. Tell your children to take a hike—with you, of course. Children learn first-hand about nature and get valuable lessons in sharing and cooperation.

If you could use a little motivation to get on the trail, join a family outings group. I highly recommend the Sierra Club's Little Hikers, which welcomes families with children (newborn to pre-teen). Four- to ten-year-olds most enjoy the hikes, chosen for their level terrain as much as for their natural beauty.

A few tips:

• Keep your children in sight at all times. That may seem obvious, but you'd be surprised how fast kids can get off the trail.

• Repeat and repeat again all instructions ranging from snack breaks to porta-potty locations.

• Choose a hike with fairly modest elevation gains. Children prefer intimate settings, such as a little creek or a clump of boulders to those vast scenic panoramas favored by adults.

• When children travel in groups, the kids motivate each other to go farther and faster. And there's lots less whining.

• If young spirits sag, try two games to regain good humor and maintain that all-important forward progress up the trail. With younger children, "play dog;" that is to say, throw an imaginary stick to the next tree en route and have them fetch it. "One-two-three-jump" is another popular game. With a parent holding each hand the child hikes along one-two-three steps, then jumps as parents raise arms and swing the hopefully-no-longer reluctant little hiker into the air.

• It's lots better for everyone to stop frequently and travel slowly than to try to make the kids go faster and then have to carry them. If parents know what kids can and can't do, everyone has a great time on the trail.

Hiking with Dogs

Many dogs love to take a hike and love the "quality time" with their owners. Hiking with a dog on a trail beats walking the dog around the block any day. For many hikers, a dog is man's best trail friend—particularly for those who hike solo.

A dog is an energetic hiking companion and, with a superior sense of smell and relatively low proximity to the ground, may notice things about the natural world that would otherwise escape your attention.

Take sufficient time to prepare canine companion and you'll discover that a well-equipped owner and well-trained dog will be the best of trail buddies, each enhancing the other's experience.

First, make a candid assessment of your dog's energy level and condition. Not every good dog is a good hiker. Many dogs love to hike, though, and, with some conditioning outings, will improve over time. If you have any doubts, ask the vet if your dog is sufficiently physically fit for hiking.

WHERE YOU CAN HIKE WITH A DOG

NATIONAL FOREST In most cases, dogs are permitted on trails. Exceptions are certain posted areas, such as wilderness, sensitive habitat or special wildlife areas that are off-limits to dogs.

STATE PARKS No dogs are permitted on trails in California State Parks.

CITY, COUNTY, REGIONAL PARKS All bets are off when it comes to local parklands and their respective dog policies. Call before you go and ask whether dogs are allowed on the trail.

- Make sure your dog has up-to-date vaccinations and current identification tags.
- Only hike where dogs are allowed.
- Help you dog out with some flea and tick repellant.
- Bring water and a collapsible bowl. Dogs can get dehydrated and overheated, just like humans.
- Heed leash laws
- Don't allow your dog to chase squirrels, deer or other wildlife.
- Clean up after your dog. If your dog brings it into the park, you need to hike it out. Use zippered plastic bags for disposal of waste. If you are far from the trailhead, bury dog poop in a "cathole," well off the trail.
- You and your dog must yield to all other trail users including cyclists and equestrians. Leash up and allow other trail users to pass.
- After the hike, check your dog for ticks and foxtails.

TRAIL NOTES

A PARK IN THE MAKING: ORANGE COUNTY GREAT PARK

Think Central Park in New York, Golden Gate Park in San Francisco and Griffith Park in Los Angeles—and now, Orange County Great Park.

The closure of the El Toro Marine Corps Air Station, in the heart of Orange County, has provided Orange County community leaders and visionaries with an opportunity virtually unheard-of in this day and age. Thanks to an innovative partnership between the City of Irvine, the County of Orange and the Department of the Navy, almost six square miles of the former air station have been set aside for open space, as well as recreational and educational purposes. Expect the park to take some five years for completion—a project well-worth the wait. www.ocgp.org.

SANCTUARY IN THE CITY

One of the most recognizable of Orange County's landmarks is located in the middle of suburbia, but it offers a respite on foot like no other. Rev. Robert Schuller founded his ministry now known as the Crystal Cathedral more than fifty years ago. The magnificent cathedral was designed by architect Philip Johnson, seats nearly 3,000 and serves a congregation 10,000 members strong.

But I prefer to walk the lovely grounds of the park-like campus, to admire the stunning architecture, and the statuary, and especially to contemplate the inspirational quotations inscribed on the pathways—many of which mention walking. It's a contemplative meander through a special place.

Guided tours of the grounds are offered Monday through Saturday from 9:30 A.M. to 3:30 P.M.; the Crystal Cathedral is located at 12141 Lewis Street, Garden Grove; call the Visitor Center at (714) 971-4013

NATURE TODAY MAGAZINE

This publication is subtitled "in Southern California and Beyond," but it is published in Brea and focuses primarily on Orange County's natural world. The bi-monthly promotes and advocates for the outdoors, and it includes feature stories as well as an extensive calendar of events, listing organized hikes, special events and children's activities at Orange County parks. It's available free of charge at many park outlets, or contact the publication at www.naturetoday.net.

WORKING TO PRESERVE
ORANGE COUNTY'S OPEN SPACE

ORANGE COUNTY WILD

The Mission Statement begins, "...to proactively develop and implement a cohesive strategy to preserve, protect, and enhance our wildland forest, park reserve resources, from the mountains to the Pacific." It's a coalition of managers of wilderness areas, parks, and conservancy organizations that are dedicated to educating the public, acquiring open space supporting ongoing programs and service. www.orangecountywild.com.

FRIENDS OF THE FOOTHILLS

An organization dedicated to protecting South Orange County's remaining open space and maintaining clean water in the creeks and surf. It is currently involved in the issue of protecting San Onofre State Beach from the proposed Foothill-South Toll Road. (949) 361-7534

RANCHO MISSION VIEJO OPEN SPACE

In 2001, the proposed development of the new residential area of 14,000 homes known as Rancho Mission Viejo spurred the building of a coalition of several environmental groups who helped shape and modify the project. Several years of negotiation culminated in the reduction in the acreage of the project and the protection of the San Mateo Creek Watershed with its population of southern steelhead trout, along with the habitat of the endangered arroyo toad and the California Gnatcatcher.

The preservation of this open space at Rancho Mission Viejo stands out as a true environmental action success story involving the tireless efforts of uncounted experts and volunteers. www.ranchomissionviejo.com/openspace.

DONNA O'NEILL LAND CONSERVANCY

This 1,200-acre wilderness reserve provides recreational access to the public, as well as the opportunity for outreach education and biological research for this sensitive natural resource. The organization sponsors a full calendar of events, including lectures, nature walks and astronomy nights to allow the public to enjoy the many wonders of this special land. www.theconservancy.org.

THE TEN ESSENTIALS

By now, I've forgotten each and every one of the Ten Essentials on one hike or another. And always regretted it. I've left the trail map in the car and grabbed a bag of hamster food instead of a bag of trail mix off the kitchen counter. When airport security confiscated my trusty Swiss Army knife out of my day pack, I assured myself I could do without a pocket knife for a week of hiking. (Naturally, I needed it several times . . .)

How many essential are there in the Ten Essentials?

No, this isn't a whimsical question like "Who's buried in Grant's tomb?"

Some hiking experts count ten or even fourteen essentials. And what about the day pack, essential to carry those essentials, shouldn't that count as an essential? New hikers argue that a cell phone should be the eleventh essential while veterans insist is should be "common sense."

1. Map
2. Compass
3. Water
4. Extra Food
5. Extra Clothing
6. First-Aid Kit
7. Pocket Knife
8. Sun protection
9. Flashlight
10. Matches and Firestarter

Discover The Trailmaster Way to Hike

Available at bookstores or from
www.TheTrailmaster.com

HAPPY TRAILS
N
E
W
S
The JOY of Hiking
Hiking The Trailmaster Way
JOHN MCKINNEY, THE TRAILMASTER
America's Hiking Expert
MAP
TRAIL
WILDERNESS PRESS

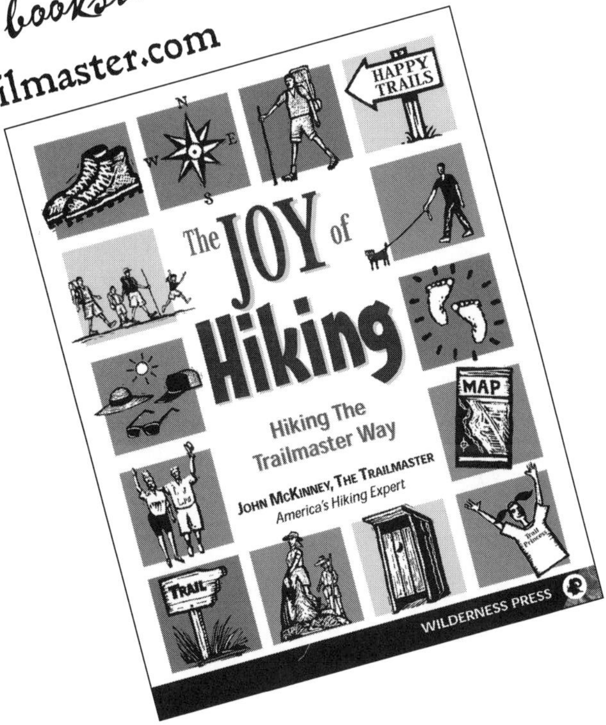

HIKING FOR BODY AND SOUL
Get fit and uplift your spirit

WHAT TO TAKE
Food, gear, apparel, accessories: What you need and what you don't

TRAILS AND TERRAIN
Hiking in all seasons and in all weather conditions

COMPANIONS ON THE TRAIL
Bring the kids, friends, and dogs – or hike on your own

TRAILS NEAR AND FAR
America's best trails, Europe's famed footpaths

Index

Cartographer Hélène Webb is an artist and cartographer for maps and illustrated marine charts. A USCG Captain, Hélène shares her expertise and love for the Santa Barbara Channel with charter sail trips and sailing lessons. Contact her at www.aquarelle.com

Editor Cheri Rae has a long background in lifestyle sports and served on the editorial staff of *Runner's World, Bicycle Sport,* and many other magazines. As a book editor, she's particularly fond of projects with California themes and subjects.

Book designer Jim Cook is a master typography with more 30 years of experience in designing fine books. A native with a deep appreciation for California and the natural world, he decided to evoke the Great Hiking Era in books designed for The Trailmaster.

Artist Timothy A. Genet is a landscape artist born and raised in Southern California. His Early California painting style captures the essences and beauty of his native state. The cover painting, Laguna Canyon, was inspired by the golden orange vegetation of the local area; it comprises sketches in ink and colored pencil.

Long-time Los Angeles Times hiking columnist John McKinney is the author of a dozen books about walking, hiking, and nature. McKinney writes articles and commentaries about walking for national publications, promotes hiking and conservation on radio and TV, and serves as a consultant for hiking tours and hiking-related businesses. Contact him at www.thetrailmaster.com